The Autism
Encyclopedia

The Autism Encyclopedia

edited by

John T. Neisworth, Ph.D.
Professor Emeritus

and

Pamela S. Wolfe, Ph.D.
Associate Professor

The Pennsylvania State University
University Park

·P A U L·H·
BROOKES
PUBLISHING Cº®

Baltimore • London • Sydney

Paul H. Brookes Publishing Co.
Post Office Box 10624
Baltimore, Maryland 21285-0624

www.brookespublishing.com

Typeset by Auburn Associates, Inc., Baltimore, Maryland.
Manufactured in the United States of America by
The Maple Press Co., York, Pennsylvania.

The following entries were adapted by permission from material appearing on the
Behavior Analyst Certification Board web site (http://www.bacb.com): *applied behavior
analysis (ABA)* (p. 12), *Behavior Analyst Certification Board®* (*BACB®*) (p. 24), *Board
Certified Associate Behavior Analyst^{TM}* (*BCABA®*) (p. 28), *Board Certified Behavior
Analyst^{TM}* (*BCBA®*). Copyright © 1998–2004 BACB®. All rights reserved.

The information provided in this book is in no way meant to substitute for a medical or
mental health practitioner's advice or expert opinion. Readers should consult a health or
mental health professional if they are interested in more information. This book is sold
without warranties of any kind, express or implied, and the publisher and authors disclaim any liability, loss, or damage caused by the contents of this book.

A portion of the royalties from the sales of this book is being donated to autism-related
organizations.

Library of Congress Cataloging-in-Publication Data
The autism encyclopedia / edited by John T. Neisworth and Pamela S. Wolfe.
　　p.　　cm.
Includes bibliographical references.
ISBN 1-55766-671-7 (layflat pbk.) — ISBN 1-55766-795-0
1. Autism—Encyclopedias.　2. Developmental disabilities—Encyclopedias.
I. Neisworth, John T.　II. Wolfe, Pamela S.

RC553.A88A847 2005
616.85′882′003—dc22　　　　　　　　　　　　　　　　2004017030

Contents

About the Editors

John T. Neisworth, Ph.D., Professor Emeritus of Special Education; Academic Director, Applied Behavior Analysis Program, The Pennsylvania State University (PSU), 227 CEDAR Building, University Park, PA 16802

John T. Neisworth is Professor Emeritus of Special Education at PSU, where he is also Academic Director of the Applied Behavior Analysis Program and an instructor in the Autism Outreach Program. He is on the Planning Committee of the National Autism Conference and Pennsylvania Autism Institute, which received the University Continuing Education Association Exemplary Program Award in 2001. Dr. Neisworth has authored or co-authored numerous research articles and texts in special education, early intervention, and behavior analysis, including *Childmate: A Manual for Early Childhood Providers,* co-authored with Angela Capone and Tom Oren (Delmar Learning, 2004); *Temperament and Atypical Behavior Scale (TABS): Early Childhood Indicators of Developmental Dysfunction,* co-authored with Stephen J. Bagnato, John J. Salvia, and Frances M. Hunt (Paul H. Brookes Publishing Co., 1999); and *LINKing Assessment and Early Intervention: An Authentic, Curriculum-Based Approach,* co-authored with Stephen J. Bagnato and Susan M. Munson (Paul H. Brookes Publishing Co., 1997). He is co-founding editor of *Topics in Early Childhood Special Education* and currently an editorial board member of that journal as well as the *Journal of Early Intervention, Child and Family Behavior Therapy,* and *Infants & Young Children.* He co-edited a 1999 special issue on autism for *Infants & Young Children.* He was co-recipient of the 1995 Award for Best Article from the American Psychological Association (Division 16). He is past chair and current co-chair (with Stephen J. Bagnato) of the Recommended Practices in Assessment for the Division for Early Childhood of the Council for Exceptional Children. In 2002, Dr. Neisworth received the Lifetime Achievement Award from the Pennsylvania Association for Applied Behavior Analysis.

Pamela S. Wolfe, Ph.D., Associate Professor of Special Education, The Pennsylvania State University (PSU), 212A CEDAR Building, University Park, PA 16802

Pamela S. Wolfe is Associate Professor of Special Education at PSU. She is Academic Director of the PSU Professional Certificate in Autism and a lead instructor in the PSU Applied Behavior Analysis Program. Dr. Wolfe has written numerous articles in international and national journals as well as book chapters on transition, advocacy, and functional academics. She serves on several editorial boards, including those for *Exceptionality, Journal for Vocational Special Needs Education,* and *Research and Practice for Persons with Severe Disabilities.* Dr. Wolfe has directed a number of federally funded research and training grants. She is co-director of the PSU Autism Specialist Program, which trains students in autism, applied behavior analysis (ABA), and communication disorders.

Drs. Neisworth and Wolfe have collaborated on a variety of projects. Along with other PSU faculty, both were recipients of the 2003 University Continuing Education Association Excellence Award for Outreach (ABA). Drs. Neisworth and Wolfe have served as co-editors of a special autism issue of the journal *Exceptionality* and are members of the Pennsylvania Autism Focus Group. They currently are collaborating on the development of a national outreach series on autism education for PSU.

Contributors

Lynn Adams, Ph.D.
Associate Professor
Radford University
Box 6961
Radford, VA 24142

Britta Alin Åkerman
Psychologist and Psychotherapist
Professor
Stockholm Institute of Education
Stockholm, Sweden
SE 116 20

Keith Allen, Ph.D.
Professor of Pediatrics and Psychology
Munroe-Meyer Institute
985450 Nebraska Medical Center
Omaha, NE 68198

Laura Arnstein, Ph.D., BCBA
Postdoctoral Fellow
Medical University of South Carolina
Department of Developmental Pediatrics
135 Rutledge Avenue
Post Office Box 250567
Charleston, SC 29414

Lynn Atanasoff, Ph.D.
Psychological Assistant
Cen-Clear Child Services, Inc.
1633 Philipsburg-Bigler Highway
Philipsburg, PA 16866

Teresa Babula, B.A.
Graduate Student, School Psychology
The Pennsylvania State University
111 CEDAR Building
University Park, PA 16802

Devender R. Banda, Ph.D., BCBA
Assistant Professor
Department of Special Education
Kean University
1000 Morris Avenue
Union, NJ 07083

Jamie Capri Barbarich, M.S., BCBA
Anne Arundel County Public Schools
160 Funke Road
Glen Burnie, MD 21061

Simon Baron-Cohen, Ph.D.
Professor and Director
Autism Research Centre
Cambridge University
Douglas House
18 B Trumpington Road
Cambridge, United Kingdom CB2 2AH

Catherine Barthélémy, M.D., Ph.D.
Professor of Physiology, Child Psychiatrist
University Hospital, Child Psychiatry
    Center
2 boulevard Tonnellé
Tours 37044 CEDEX
France

Janice H. Belgredan, M.Ed.
Consultant
Tuscarora Intermediate Unit 11
2527 US Highway 522 South
McVeytown, PA 17051

Scott Bellini, Ph.D.
Assistant Director
Indiana Resource Center for Autism
Indiana Institute on Disability and
    Community
Indiana University, Bloomington
2853 East 10th Street
Bloomington, IN 47408

Raphael Bernier, M.S.
Graduate Research Assistant
University of Washington
CHDD Building
Columbia Road
Seattle, WA 98195

Ellen R. Borsuk, M.S.
Doctoral Candidate, School Psychology
The Pennsylvania State University

Natalie Brunnhuber, B.S., M.Ed.
Special Education Teacher
Stafford County School District
31 Stafford Avenue
Stafford, VA 22554

Leah Bucknavage, B.A.
Doctoral Candidate, School Psychology
The Pennsylvania State University
224 CEDAR Building
University Park, PA 16801

Janis Chadsey, Ph.D.
Professor
University of Illinois at Urbana-
    Champaign
1310 South 6th Street
Champaign, IL 61820

Judith H. Chan, Ed.M., B.S.
Doctoral Candidate, School Psychology
The Pennsylvania State University
125 CEDAR Building
University Park, PA 16802

Kristin V. Christodulu, Ph.D.
Director
Center for Autism and Related Disabilities
1400 Washington Avenue
Social Science 251
Albany, NY 12222

Richard J. Cowan, Ph.D.
Assistant Professor
School Psychology
Kent State University
405 White Hall
Kent, OH 44242

Kathryn Craig, B.A., M.Ed., BCBA
Behavior Analyst

Krista Dalbec-Mraz, B.A.
Doctoral Candidate
University of Connecticut

Robert A. Da Prato, M.D.
Chief Medical Officer
Department of Defense
Military Entrance Processing Station
7545 Northeast Ambassador Place
Portland, OR 97220

Lynn A. Weeks Dell, M.S., CCC-SLP
Educational Administrator
Capital Area Intermediate Unit
55 Miller Street
Summerdale, PA 17093

Curtis K. Deutsch, Ph.D.
Research Scientist
Eunice Kennedy Shriver Center
Harvard Medical School
200 Trapelo Road
Waltham, MA 02452

Winnie Dunn, Ph.D., OTR, FAOTA
Professor and Chair
Department of Occupational Therapy
    Education
University of Kansas Medical Center
3901 Rainbow Boulevard
3033 Robinson Hall
Mailstop 2003
Kansas City, KS 66160

V. Mark Durand, Ph.D.
Dean, College of Arts & Sciences
University of South Florida St. Petersburg
140 Seventh Avenue South
St. Petersburg, FL 33701

Deborah Fein, Ph.D.
Board of Trustees Distinguished Professor
   of Psychology
University of Connecticut
406 Babbidge Road, Unit 1020
Storrs, CT 06268

Emily Fenichel
Editor, *Zero To Three* Journal
Editor-in-Chief, ZERO TO THREE
   PRESS
2000 M Street, NW, Suite 200
Washington, DC 20036

Julie L. FitzGerald
The Pennsylvania State University
224 CEDAR Building
University Park, PA 16802

Richard M. Foxx, Ph.D., BCBA
Professor of Psychology
The Pennsylvania State University,
   Harrisburg
777 West Harrisburg Pike
Middletown, PA 17057

Theresa A. Gibbons, B.S., M.A.
Doctoral Candidate, School Psychology
The Pennsylvania State University
111 CEDAR Building
University Park, PA 16802

Jennifer M. Gillis, M.A., BCBA
State University of New York at
   Binghamton
Department of Psychology
Post Office Box 6000
Binghamton, NY 13902

Carol Gray
Director, The Gray Center for Social
   Learning and Understanding
2020 Raybrook SE, Suite 302
Grand Rapids, MI 49546

Mark T. Harvey, Ph.D., BCBA
Research Assistant Professor
Vanderbilt University
Box 40, Peabody College
Nashville, TN 37203

Marilyn Hoyson, Ph.D.
Chief Operating Officer
The Watson Institute
301 Camp Meeting Road
Sewickley, PA 15143

Charles A. Hughes, Ph.D.
Professor of Special Education
The Pennsylvania State University
227 CEDAR Building
University Park, PA 16802

Daniel E. Hursh, Ph.D., BCBA
Professor of Educational Psychology
Department of Advanced Educational
   Studies
West Virginia University
Morgantown, WV 26506

Lisa A. Husar, M.S., M.Ed.
Behavior Specialist
The Watson Institute
301 Camp Meeting Road
Sewickley, PA 15143

Lisa A. Jamnback, M.D.
Child and Adolescent Psychiatrist
Allegheny General Hospital
4 Allegheny Center, 8th Floor
Pittsburgh, PA 15212

Christopher Jones, B.A., M.S.
Doctoral Candidate
Department of Psychology
University of Washington
Box 351525
Seattle, WA 98195

Garland Jones, B.A.
Graduate Student
University of Connecticut
101 South Street
Vernon, CT 06066

Elizabeth A. Kelley, M.A.
Doctoral Candidate
Department of Psychology
University of Connecticut
406 Babbidge Road, Unit 1020
Storrs, CT 06269

Craig H. Kennedy, Ph.D., BCBA
Professor of Special Education and
  Pediatrics
Vanderbilt University
Box 328, Peabody College
2201 West End Avenue
Nashville, TN 37203

Thomas P. Kitchen
Curriculum/Behavior Specialist
Dr. Gertrude A. Barber National Institute
Elizabeth Lee Black School
100 Barber Place
Erie, PA 16507

Jamie M. Kleinman, B.S.
Graduate Student
University of Connecticut
406 Babbidge Road, Unit 1020
Storrs, CT 06269

Nancy Kneff, M.S., CCC-SLP
Senior Speech-Language Therapist
The Watson Institute
301 Camp Meeting Road
Sewickley, PA 15143

Kasey Marie Kotz, B.A.
Doctoral Candidate, School Psychology
The Pennsylvania State University

Steve Kroupa, Ph.D.
Clinical Director, Division TEACCH
Assistant Professor, Department of
  Psychiatry
University of North Carolina at Chapel
  Hill
Chapel Hill, NC 28303

Sue H. Krul, M.Ed.
Lead Teacher
The Education Center
The Watson Institute
301 Camp Meeting Road
Sewickley, PA 15143

Richard M. Kubina, Jr., Ph.D., BCBA
Assistant Professor
The Pennsylvania State University
209 CEDAR Building
University Park, PA 16802

E. (Rocky) Landers, B.S., M.A.,
  Post-bachelor's Certificate in
  Occupational Therapy
Occupational Therapist
CIU/SASD
State College, PA 16801

Johanna F. Lantz, M.S.
Doctoral Candidate
Indiana University
201 North Rose Avenue, #40215
Bloomington, IN 47404

Marcia K. Laus, M.Ed.
Educational Consultant
The Watson Institute
301 Camp Meeting Road
Sewickley, PA 15143

David L. Lee, Ph.D.
Assistant Professor
Special Education
The Pennsylvania State University
227 CEDAR Building
University Park, PA 16802

RinaMarie Leon-Guerrero
Doctoral Candidate and Graduate Assistant
University of Washington
Box 357925
Seattle, WA 98195

Fan-Yu Lin, Ph.D., BCBA
Assistant Professor of Special Education
Advanced Studies in Education
California State University, Stanislaus
801 West Monte Vista Boulevard
Turlock, CA 95382

Rachel L. Loftin, M.A.
Doctoral Candidate, School Psychology
Indiana Resource Center for Autism
Indiana University
2853 East 10th Street
Bloomington, IN 47404

Catherine Lord, Ph.D.
Professor and Director
University of Michigan Autism &
  Communication Disorders Center
  (UMACC)
1111 East Catherine Street, Room 18
Ann Arbor, MI 48109

Jessica Lord, B.A.
Doctoral Candidate, Clinical Psychology
University of Connecticut
406 Babbidge Road, Unit 1020
Storrs, CT 06269

James K. Luiselli, Ed.D., ABPP, BCBA
Senior Vice President
Applied Research, Clinical Training, and
  Peer Review
The May Institute
1 Commerce Way
Norwood, MA 02062

Monica D. Manning, B.L.A., M.S., BCBA
Speech-Language Pathologist
State College Area School District
154 West Nittany Avenue
State College, PA 16801

Catherine M. Marcell, M.S.
School Psychologist
Special Education District of Lake County
18160 Gages Lake Road
Gages Lake, IL 60030

Janelle Matesic, M.S.
Certified School Psychologist
The Pennsylvania State University
University Park, PA 16802

Michael E. May, M.S., BCBA
Doctoral Candidate
Vanderbilt University
328 Peabody Station, MRL
Nashville, TN 37013

James K. McAfee, Ph.D.
Associate Professor of Special Education
The Pennsylvania State University
208 CEDAR Building
University Park, PA 16802

James McPartland, M.S.
University of Washington
Center on Human Development and
  Disability
Box 357920
Seattle, WA 98195

Catherine R. Meier, B.A.
Graduate Student
The Pennsylvania State University
111 CEDAR Building
University Park, PA 16802

Donna Meloy, M.Ed.
Early Intervention School Psychologist
Berks County Intermediate Unit #14
1111 Commons Boulevard
Post Office Box 16050
Reading, PA 19612

Donald J. Meyer, M.Ed.
Sibling Support Project of The Arc of the
  United States
6512 23rd Avenue, Northwest, Suite 213
Seattle, WA 98117

Jack Michael, Ph.D.
Professor Emeritus
Western Michigan University
1000 Berkshire Drive
Kalamazoo, MI 49006

Linda Crane Mitchell, Ph.D.
Assistant Professor
Early Childhood Intervention Specialist
Ashland University
College Avenue
325 Bixler Hall
Ashland, OH 44805

Brenda Smith Myles, Ph.D.
Associate Professor
Special Education
University of Kansas
1122 West Campus Road
Lawrence, KS 66045

Samuel L. Odom, Ph.D.
Otting Professor of Special Education
Department of Curriculum and Instruction
School of Education
Indiana University
3234 W.W. Wright Education Building
201 North Rose Avenue
Bloomington, IN 47405

Maryjo M. Oster, B.A.
Doctoral Candidate, Education Theory and
    Policy
The Pennsylvania State University
311B Information Sciences and Technology
    Building
University Park, PA 16802

Phil Parette, Ed.D.
Kara Peters Endowed Chair
Illinois State University
Campus Box 5910
Normal, IL 61790

Susan Wuchenich Parker, M.Ed.
Developmental Therapist
Graduate Student
University of Pittsburgh
427 Meridian Drive
Pittsburgh, PA 15228

James W. Partington, Ph.D., BCBA
Director, Behavior Analysts, Inc.
1941 Oak Park Boulevard, Suite 30
Pleasant Hill, CA 94523

Grace E. Peters, B.A., M.C.S.W.
Licensed Clinical Social Worker
The Watson Institute
301 Camp Meeting Road
Sewickley, PA 15143

J. Michael Pickle, M.Ed., Ph.D.
Assistant Professor
St. Cloud State University
A259 Education Building
720 Fourth Avenue, South
St. Cloud, MN 56301

Valerie J. Postal, M.S.Ed., BCBA
Doctoral Candidate, School Psychology
The Pennsylvania State University
137A CEDAR Building
University Park, PA 16801

Jeanette C. Ramer, M.D.
Associate Professor of Pediatrics
Penn State Children's Hospital
Penn State Milton S. Hershey Medical
    Center
500 University Drive
Hershey, PA 17033

Nancy P. Rapp, M.Ed.
Program Coordinator
LEAP Preschool
The Watson Institute
200 Linden Street
Pittsburgh, PA 15215

A. Celeste Roberts, M.Ed.
Doctoral Candidate
Vanderbilt University
Post Office Box 128374
Nashville, TN 37212

Diana L. Robins, Ph.D.
Assistant Professor of Psychology
Georgia State University
33 Gilmer Street, Southeast
Unit 2
Atlanta, GA 30303

Lise Roll-Pettersson, Ph.D.
Assistant Professor of Education
Stockholm Institute of Education
Trekantsragerv 3
Stockholm, Sweden 10074

Raymond G. Romanczyk, Ph.D., BCBA
Professor
State University of New York at
    Binghamton
Institute for Child Development
Binghamton, NY 13902

Lisa A. Ruble, M.S., Ph.D.
Assistant Professor of Pediatrics
University of Louisville
571 South Floyd Street, Suite 100
Louisville, KY 40202

Kathy Ruhl, Ph.D.
Professor of Special Education
The Pennsylvania State University
Department of Educational and School
   Psychology and Special Education
212 CEDAR Building
University Park, PA 16802

Britta Saltonstall, M.Ed., BCBA
Graduate Student & Consultant
Special Education Department
University of Washington
102 Miller Hall, Box 353600
Seattle, WA 98195

John Salvia, D.Ed.
Professor Emeritus
The Pennsylvania State University

Celine A. Saulnier, Ph.D.
National Alliance for Autism Research
   (NAAR) Fellow in Child Psychology
Yale Child Study Center
230 South Frontage Road
Post Office Box 207900
New Haven, CT 06520

Marcia L. Schatz, M.Ed.
Special Education Teacher
The Watson Institute
301 Camp Meeting Road
Sewickley, PA 15143

Hannah Schertz, Ed.S., M.S.
Doctoral Candidate
Indiana University
201 North Rose Avenue
Bloomington, IN 47405

Denise Lynn Schilling, Ph.D., PT
Assistant Professor
SUNY Upstate Medical University
Room 2227 Silverman Hall
750 Adams Street
Syracuse, NY 13214

Eric Schopler, Ph.D.
Professor and Founder
Division TEACCH
University of North Carolina at Chapel
   Hill
Campus Box #7180
100 Renee Lynne Court
Chapel Hill, NC 27510

Kimberly A. Schreck, Ph.D., BCBA
Assistant Professor
The Pennsylvania State University,
   Harrisburg
777 West Harrisburg Pike
Middletown, PA 17057

Joseph R. Scotti, Ph.D.
Professor of Psychology and Eberly Family
   Professor of Outstanding Public Service
West Virginia University
Box 6040
Morgantown, WV 26506

Gerald L. Shook, Ph.D., BCBA
Executive Director
Behavior Analyst Certification Board, Inc.
1705 Metropolitan Boulevard, Suite 102
Tallahassee, FL 32312

Jane Singletary, OTR/L, BCP
Senior Therapist
The Education Center
The Watson Institute
301 Camp Meeting Road
Sewickley, PA 15143

J. David Smith, Ed.D.
Professor of Education and Psychology
The University of Virginia's College at
   Wise
One College Avenue
Wise, VA 24293

Latha V. Soorya, Ph.D., BCBA
Psychology Fellow
Mount Sinai School of Medicine
One Gustave Levy Place, Box 1230
New York, NY 10029

Dana J. Stevens, M.Ed., BCBA
Graduate Student and Practicum
  Supervisor
University of Washington
102 Miller Box 353600
Seattle, WA 98195

Wendy L. Stone, Ph.D.
Professor of Pediatrics
Vanderbilt Children's Hospital
426 Medical Center South
2100 Pierce Avenue
Nashville, TN 37232

Anne Sullivan, M.Ed.
Executive Director
Magnolia Speech School
733 Flag Chapel Road
Jackson, MS 39209

Jennifer Harris Tepe, M.Ed.
Developmental Specialist
Doctoral Candidate, Early Intervention
University of Pittsburgh

Karen Toth
Doctoral Candidate
University of Washington
Autism Center
CHDD Box 357920
Seattle, WA 98195

Michele M. Trettel, M.Ed.
Program Director
The Education Center
The Watson Institute
301 Camp Meeting Road
Sewickley, PA 15143

Vicci Tucci, M.A., BCBA
Tucci Learning Solutions, Inc.
1730A Day Valley Road
Aptos, CA 95003

Maria G. Valdovinos, M.S., M.A., Ph.D.,
  BCBA
Postdoctoral Fellow
Vanderbilt University
Box 74, Peabody College
Nashville, TN 37203

Ljiljana Vuletic
Doctoral Candidate
University of Toronto
252 Bloor Street West
Toronto, Ontario M5S 1V6
Canada

Gregory L. Wallace, M.A.
Research Fellow
Child Psychiatry Branch, National
  Institute of Mental Health
Building 10, Room 4C110
10 Center Drive, MSC 1367
Bethesda, MD 20892

Marley W. Watkins, Ph.D.
Professor of Education (School Psychology)
The Pennsylvania State University
125 CEDAR Building
University Park, PA 16802

Paul Wehman, Ph.D.
Professor of Physical Medicine and
  Rehabilitation
Director
Rehabilitation Research & Training Center
  on Workplace Supports
Virginia Commonwealth University
Post Office Box 842011
Richmond, VA 23284

Barbara Yingling Wert, Ph.D.
Assistant Professor
Bloomsburg University
200 North 4th Street
Bloomsburg, PA 17815

Amy M. Wetherby, Ph.D.
Laurel Schendel Professor of
  Communication Disorders
Department of Communication Disorders
Florida State University
Tallahassee, FL 32306

Holly Williams, M.Ed.
The Pennsylvania State University
Special Education

Sharise Wilson, B.A.
Graduate Student
The Pennsylvania State University
Department of Educational and School
  Psychology and Special Education
227 CEDAR Building
University Park, PA 16802

Julie M. Wolf, M.A.
Graduate Student
Department of Psychology
University of Connecticut
406 Babbidge Road, Unit 1020
Storrs, CT 06269

Pamela J. Wolfberg, Ph.D.
Assistant Professor
Department of Special Education
San Francisco State University
1600 Holloway Avenue
San Francisco, CA 94132

Jean M. Wood, B.A.
Graduate Student, School Psychology
The Pennsylvania State University
University Park, PA 16802

Robert H. Zabel, M.Ed., Ph.D.
Professor of Special Education
Kansas State University
301 Bluemont Hall
Manhattan, KS 66506

Melissa L. Zona, B.A.
Doctoral Candidate, Clinical Psychology
University at Albany
State University of New York
1400 Washington Avenue
Social Sciences 251
Albany, NY 12222

Preface

From A to Z, this encyclopedia offers definitions and descriptions of the array of terms related to the study and treatment of autism and other pervasive developmental disorders (PDDs). From Leo Kanner's pivotal paper in 1943 to the present, autism research and practice have expanded to encompass multiple disciplines and professions. The multiplicity of specialties makes for an ever-expanding and often confusing assortment of terms that makes even veteran professionals go to texts and web sites for clarification. Our initial enthusiasm for the project soon turned to an uneasy realization that we might be facing a gargantuan task. Indeed, professionals as well as parents may be overwhelmed by the welter of jargon related to autism and other PDDs. The complex nature of these disorders and the multidisciplinary requirements for research, assessment, and treatment generate a profusion of specialized terms that are not easily or clearly comprehended even by professionals outside specific disciplines.

We knew that we could not take on this task alone. As editors, we certainly admit our unfamiliarity with jargon from specialties outside of ours (special education and applied behavior analysis). We initially recruited contributors by asking colleagues at several universities whom we knew could offer authoritative entries. Next, we contacted editorial board members of autism-related journals as well as authors of texts and chapters on autism and other PDDs. And, we certainly contacted many respected practitioners and researchers referred to us by those already participating. We are, indeed, thankful for the enthusiastic participation of the wide range of professionals upon whom we called for their expertise and their ability to explain themselves concisely and clearly.

IDENTIFYING AND SELECTING TERMS FOR INCLUSION

An initial concern in the development of the encyclopedia was to decide which terms to include and exclude. We decided on a formative procedure.

First, we listed terms included in autism courses offered at Penn State as well as terms included in what we regarded as recommended autism textbooks; this produced an initial list of about 275 terms. Next, we asked a focus group composed of an expert from medicine, from speech-language pathology, and from physical/occupational therapy. As a result of the expert consultations, we then had a list of about 380 terms. The third phase in building the list was to ask contributors of definitions to also suggest any additional terms they thought desirable; this resulted in a compilation of more than 500 terms. In the final phase, we were faced with the dilemma about what terms *not* to include.

Most people at all familiar with the field of autism know that there are innumerable reports, speculations, recommendations, and proposed treatments that have their basis in evidence that is less than acceptable to the scientific community. Anecdotal reports, testimonials, correlations, coincidence reports, and poorly designed studies abound; this state of affairs often confounds or diverts quality service delivery and drains valuable time and resources. Administrators in state departments of child health and special education must make decisions concerning what assessments and interventions to promote, support, and fund; these decisions are not easy, clearcut, or without political, professional, and parental pressures. We relied on guidelines from the New York State Department of Health, Early Intervention Program (1999), as well as our literature search and, admittedly, our biases, to make exclusionary decisions.

We decided to err on the side of including a number of terms that do not have a substantial evidence base but do have appreciable interest or advocacy and possible promise. Our apologies to those professionals who contributed terms based on scientifically validated approaches and treatments. These professionals may not appreciate being in the company of the "less than rigorous." On the other hand, we may be criticized by those professionals who either do not find in this encyclopedia certain terms related to materials or treatments they advocate or do not concur with the characterization of terms or what constitutes appropriate evidence. In brief, we included terms sometimes related to emerging approaches that do not yet have convincing evidence. Furthermore, we also included some terms related to methods that have been subjected to rigorous study and shown to be unfounded; these are included because they may still be of interest to some seeking more information (we note the lack of research support where appropriate).

Editing the material provided by the contributing authors included two sometimes-difficult tasks. First, because of page constraints, we found it necessary to abbreviate many definitions. Often, excellent discussions and elaborations had to be abridged or deleted; of course, we struggled to retain the core content and intent of each contributor. We tried also to keep a balanced selection of terms from multiple disciplines. Contributors, however, reviewed the edited versions of their contributions for final approval.

We say thank you again to all who made this project possible and hope that this resource will be of great value to the professionals and parents who work together to help individuals who face the challenge of autism.

REFERENCES

Kanner, L. (1943). Autistic disturbances of affective contact. *The Nervous Child, 2,* 217–250.

New York State Department of Health, Early Intervention Program. (1999). *Clinical practice guideline: The guideline technical report. Autism/pervasive developmental disorders: Assessment and intervention for young children (age 0–3 years)* (Publication No. 4217). Albany: Author.

Using This Encyclopedia

Following are sample entries to highlight the various features of this encyclopedia. Many of these features are elaborated on the pages that follow.

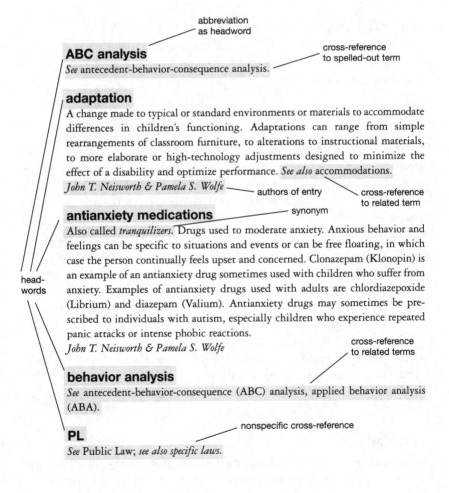

abbreviation
as headword

cross-reference
to spelled-out term

ABC analysis

See antecedent-behavior-consequence analysis.

adaptation

A change made to typical or standard environments or materials to accommodate differences in children's functioning. Adaptations can range from simple rearrangements of classroom furniture, to alterations to instructional materials, to more elaborate or high-technology adjustments designed to minimize the effect of a disability and optimize performance. *See also* accommodations.

John T. Neisworth & Pamela S. Wolfe

authors of entry

cross-reference
to related term

antianxiety medications

synonym

Also called *tranquilizers.* Drugs used to moderate anxiety. Anxious behavior and feelings can be specific to situations and events or can be free floating, in which case the person continually feels upset and concerned. Clonazepam (Klonopin) is an example of an antianxiety drug sometimes used with children who suffer from anxiety. Examples of antianxiety drugs used with adults are chlordiazepoxide (Librium) and diazepam (Valium). Antianxiety drugs may sometimes be prescribed to individuals with autism, especially children who experience repeated panic attacks or intense phobic reactions.

John T. Neisworth & Pamela S. Wolfe

head-
words

cross-reference
to related terms

behavior analysis

See antecedent-behavior-consequence (ABC) analysis, applied behavior analysis (ABA).

nonspecific cross-reference

PL

See Public Law; *see also specific laws.*

ALPHABETICAL ORDER

Entries are arranged alphabetically, word for word, including spaces but ignoring hyphens:

    control condition

    co-occurring

    core deficits

    developmental surveillance

    developmentally appropriate practice (DAP)

    hand regard

    hand-over-hand assistance

AUTHORSHIP

The authors of each entry are listed in italics following the entry, except as noted in Appendix B, which was written primarily by John T. Neisworth and Pamela S. Wolfe.

CROSS-REFERENCES

Cross-references for abbreviations appear throughout the encyclopedia. In these cases, the cross-reference points the reader to the spelled-out term (e.g., ABA . . . *see* applied behavior analysis) or to the full name of a public law (e.g., IDEA . . . *see* Individuals with Disabilities Education Act). Likewise, cross-references for informal or synonymous terms send the reader to more comprehensive or different technical terms (e.g., brain imaging . . . *see* neuroimaging; self-stimulatory behavior . . . *see* stereotypic behavior).

In most cases, one or more related terms of interest are listed at the end of the entry, after the words *see also*. These related terms lead the reader to other entries that expand or further explain the topic of interest. In some cases, the related terms may present a contrasting view from that presented in the principal term (e.g., pseudoscience . . . *see also* best practice guidelines, empiricism, experimental design).

APPENDICES

Selected screening, assessment, and instructional materials are listed separately in Appendix A. Governmental, professional, and advocacy organizations are listed in Appendix B. Grouping these materials in the appendices, rather than scattering them throughout the encyclopedia, provides single listings for ease of perusal. (These materials are not cross-listed with entries in the body of the encyclopedia due to the redundancies associated with doing so.) The entries in Appendix A consist of selected materials, not a comprehensive listing; we did not list materials that were still in development or not readily available or that, in our judgment based on research, did not as yet have sufficient validation or field use.

Acknowledgments

We could detail the many people who helped make this encyclopedia possible, but that would take many pages to do. We certainly acknowledge the many contributors to this effort. We especially want to thank Glenda Carelas, whose administrative/secretarial assistance was crucial to the organization and logistics needed to get the project off to a great start and to manage the plethora of emails and correspondence during the process of completion. Glenda was central to the collaborative effort. Devender R. Banda, while a doctoral student at Penn State, provided great assistance by contributing a number of terms and assisting us in detailing the evidence base for a number of entries. Finally, we would be remiss if we did not praise Mika Sam Smith, Editorial Supervisor at Paul H. Brookes Publishing Co. Her meticulous attention to detail and consistency added greatly to the strength of this resource. It is difficult to fully express our gratitude.

To my father, H. Glenn Wolfe

—PSW

To Mike, a wonderful father to my grandchildren Samantha and Rachel

To Bob Smith, my mentor for life

—JTN

AAC

See augmentative and alternative communication. *See also* alternative communication.

ABA

See applied behavior analysis.

ABC analysis

See antecedent-behavior-consequence analysis.

accommodations

A term used in the Individuals with Disabilities Education Act (IDEA), its amendments, and its regulations (Assistance to States, 2003) to refer to environmental changes related to the education of an individual with disabilities, especially with regard to assessment of learning. *See also* adaptation, Individuals with Disabilities Education Act (IDEA).
John T. Neisworth & Pamela S. Wolfe

ACTH

Adrenocorticotropic hormone; *see* hormone therapy.

activities of daily living (ADLs)

Self-care tasks such as grooming, bathing, eating, bowel and bladder management, toilet hygiene, functional mobility, and device care. These basic life functions are used as benchmarks for independence. More complex life functions are clustered into *instrumental activities of daily living,* including care of others, community mobility, financial management, home management, shopping, and emergency and safety procedures. *See also* functional limitations, functional outcomes, self-help skills.
Winnie Dunn

activity-based instruction

Also called *activity-based intervention*. *See* embedded skills, naturalistic interventions.

acuity

Degree of clarity of sensory stimuli; physical ability of the sensory organs to receive input. The term *acuity* is used with reference to hearing and vision. Visual acuity is the accuracy of the eyes to see both close and distant objects (normal visual acuity is 20/20). Auditory acuity is the ability to hear with measured decibels. Normal auditory acuity (in which there is no negative impact on communication) is 0–15 decibels. Acuity can be corrected with glasses (for vision) and hearing aids (for hearing).
Winnie Dunn

ADA

See Americans with Disabilities Act of 1990 (PL 101-336).

adaptation

A change made to typical or standard environments or materials to accommodate differences in children's functioning. Adaptations can range from simple rearrangements of classroom furniture, to alterations to instructional materials, to more elaborate or high-technology adjustments designed to minimize the effect of a disability and optimize performance. *See also* accommodations.
John T. Neisworth & Pamela S. Wolfe

adaptive behavior

Typical performance on daily tasks and activities related to personal and social sufficiency. As individuals age, the types of adaptive behaviors they exhibit typically increase in complexity. Examples in young children include self-care (e.g., dressing), communication (e.g., verbal expression and reception), and socialization (e.g., relating to peers). Examples of adult adaptive behaviors include self-care (e.g., holding a job, managing money), communication (e.g., advanced reading and writing), and socialization (e.g., acting responsibly toward others) (Sparrow, Balla, & Cicchetti, 1984b). *See also* activities of daily living (ADLs), adaptive skills, daily living skills, self-help skills.
Krista Dalbec-Mraz & Julie Wolf

adaptive skills

Conceptual, practical, and social skills that permit a person to function in everyday life and to deal with, and change in response to, everyday environmental demands. Individuals with autism show a unique pattern of adaptive skills as compared with normative groups (Schatz & Hamdan-Allen, 1995). Such individuals typically have strong daily living skills but only intermediate communication skills and significantly low scores in socialization skills. Adaptive skills can be assessed using one of many standardized measures of adaptive behavior such as the Vineland Adaptive Behavior Scales (VABS; Sparrow, Balla, & Cicchetti, 1984a, 1984b) that have been normed for individuals with autism (Carter et al., 1998). Adaptive skills must be assessed to diagnose mental retardation, a disorder commonly found in individuals with autism (American Association on Mental Retardation, 2002). *See also* adaptive behavior, daily living skills, self-help skills.
Leah Bucknavage

ADHD

See attention-deficit/hyperactivity disorder.

ADLs

See activities of daily living.

advocate

Person who speaks, writes, or acts in support of or in defense of a person or cause. Individuals with disabilities and their families may act as their own advocates or appoint others to secure appropriate services and programs. *See also* Americans with Disabilities Act (ADA) of 1990 (PL 101-336), self-advocacy.
John T. Neisworth & Pamela S. Wolfe

age appropriate

Matching of activities, materials, and environments to a child's age. Depending on the child's development (delayed or typical), either chronological or developmental age (DA) may be used to guide decisions regarding appropriateness. *See also* developmental age (DA).
John T. Neisworth & Pamela S. Wolfe

AIT
See auditory integration therapy.

allergy
A term coined in 1906 by Austrian pediatrician Clemens Von Pirquet that originally referred to a maladaptive persistent altered reactivity to substances (allergens) that did not similarly affect most people. Although there are many mechanisms for persistent altered reactivity (e.g., congenital and acquired enzyme deficiencies, operant and respondent conditioning), current medical convention restricts the term *allergy* to altered reactivity of cellular and antibody (immunoglobulin) components of the immune system. Unfortunately, there is minimal research in the area of immunologic allergy, particularly food allergy, as a cause of autism (Lucarelli et al., 1995). There is robust evidence, however, that elimination diets may substantially improve the behaviors associated with autism. In this area of food-induced illness, current popular as well as older medical literature frequently use *allergy* in its original connotation, incorporating both immune (food allergy) and nonimmune (food intolerance) mechanisms. Although the underlying biobehavioral cause of altered reactivity to dietary constituents may remain undiscovered, long-term treatment for either immune or nonimmune adverse food reactions involves primarily the reduction or elimination of offending foods from the diet. *See also* diet therapy, food intolerance, immunoglobulin.
Robert A. Da Prato

alternate assessment
Methods and materials for gathering information regarding a child's status that can supplement, complement, or replace traditional assessment that is based on normative and criterion referencing. Alternate assessment includes surveys of a child's environment (ecological assessment), how a child accomplishes or attempts activities (qualitative measures), appraisals of parent stress and family needs, informed clinical opinion, and authentic procedures (measures of child skills in natural, ongoing routines and situations rather than "tabletop testing").
John T. Neisworth & Pamela S. Wolfe

alternative communication
See augmentative and alternative communication (AAC).

American Sign Language (ASL)
A standardized manual communication system often used by individuals with learning impairments. ASL has its own structure, meaning, and grammar and is not simply a manual code for English. The system can be used to convey subtle and abstract meaning as well as concrete information. In addition to hand signs, nonmanual components such as facial expression, posture, and eye contact increase the utility and effectiveness of ASL. ASL is the preferred language of individuals in the United States and Canada who are deaf. ASL can also be useful for children with autism who do not use spoken language. Individuals may be taught sign language as a temporary or sustained method of communication, although the use of pictures and symbols has increasingly replaced sign language in autism instruction. *See also* augmentative and alternative communication (AAC).
John T. Neisworth & Pamela S. Wolfe

Americans with Disabilities Act (ADA) of 1990 (PL 101-336)
U.S. civil rights law that forbids discrimination against individuals with disabilities with regard to access to public services, employment, transit, and certain businesses. The ADA broadly defines disability as a physical or mental impairment that substantially limits one or more major activity. The ADA has generated controversy, particularly in who is considered to have a disability. *See also* advocate, disability.
John T. Neisworth & Pamela S. Wolfe

amino acids
Commonly referred to as the building blocks of proteins. Proteins are a structurally and functionally diverse family of very large organic molecules formed from only 20 different amino acids chemically linked in various combinations and lengths. As proteins are digested and metabolized, they are sequentially split into smaller units: proteins → peptides → amino acids → smaller metabolic end products. The relevance of proteins and their metabolic products to autism is based primarily on three observations:
1. Proteins (e.g., in phenylketonuria; Lowe, Tanaka, Seashore, Young, & Cohen, 1980), peptides (e.g., opioid peptides from wheat and milk; Shattock, Kennedy, Roswell, & Berney, 1990), and amino acids (e.g., glutamate, tryptophan; Moreno-Fuenmayor, Borjas, Arrieta, Valera, & Socorro-Candanoza, 1996, and McDougle et al., 1996, respectively) have well-described adverse behavioral effects.

2. Quantitative and qualitative changes in neuroactive proteins, peptides, and amino acids (Visconti et al., 1994) are very frequent in individuals with autism as compared with controls without autism (Israngkun, Newman, Patel, Duruibe, & Abou-Issa, 1986), although the pattern of these changes is highly individualized.

3. Therapy assumed to reduce the effects of or exposure to neurotoxic proteins, peptides and amino acids by diet (elimination diet; Knivsberg, Reichelt, Hoien, & Nodland, 2002), nutritional and digestive enzyme supplementation (e.g., vitamin B_6 and magnesium), and pharmacotherapy can be dramatically beneficial for specific individuals. The heterogeneity of behavioral, metabolic, and physiologic abnormalities found in the wide spectrum of autism makes it unlikely that one underlying cause and one universal remedy exist. Proteins and their metabolic and digestive end products are just one aspect of a comprehensive approach to the diagnosis and treatment of autism, an approach that because of the heterogeneous nature of autism should be both individual and biobehavioral. *See also* diet therapy, vitamin B_6 and magnesium therapy.

Robert A. Da Prato

amygdala

A structure located under the cortex (the ½"-thick layer covering the cerebrum) in the temporal lobe. It is part of the limbic system and known to play an important role in the processing of emotions and other social information. Amygdala damage leads to impairments in emotional perception, decision making about emotional stimuli (e.g., whether a person is trustworthy), emotional arousal, face processing, and emotional learning (i.e., associating certain stimuli with positive reward and others with negative reward). There is a growing literature examining both structural and functional abnormalities of the amygdala in autism and other pervasive developmental disorders (PDDs). Postmortem research suggests that neurons in the amygdala are smaller and more densely packed in individuals with autism. In addition, animal models of autism are found in primates with very early bilateral amygdala damage. Studies of functional impairment of the amygdala find hypoactivation of the amygdala in response to fearful stimuli and social judgments (Aggleton, 2000). *See also* social cognition, social impairment.

Diana L. Robins

analog condition functional analysis

A functional behavior assessment method that involves systematic control and manipulation of variables surrounding a target behavior to identify the potential function of the behavior (Iwata, Kahng, Wallace, & Lindberg, 2000). Analog conditions resemble the contexts in which behavior might occur. During these conditions, various potential factors (attention, demands, access to tangible items and reinforcing activities, access to self-stimulation) are isolated and delivered systematically contingent on target behaviors. For example, if anecdotal sources of information suggest that teacher attention might be supporting a child's disruptive behavior, analog conditions can be arranged wherein attention might be experimentally varied to assess its effects. See also applied behavior analysis (ABA), functional behavior assessment (FBA), functions of behavior.
Thomas P. Kitchen

analysis of verbal behavior (AVB)

AVB is not a distinct and separate methodology or science; it is an applied behavior analysis (ABA) approach that is used to teach communication. AVB employs the many effective procedures based on ABA (e.g., reinforcement, prompting, fading, task analysis). A major feature is the use of Skinner's (1957) analysis of the functions of language (e.g., to request, to name things, to refer to things not immediately present), which departs from a developmentally based language approach. The functional analysis of language is a major approach for teaching communication skills to children with autism (see Appendix A for curricula). See also applied behavior analysis (ABA), verbal behavior (VB).
John T. Neisworth & Pamela S. Wolfe

anecdotal observation

See antecedent-behavior-consequence (ABC) analysis.

anecdotal report

A report that uses words to qualitatively document an event or behavior. Anecdotal reports are sometimes referred to as *incident reports.* Reports should be as descriptive and factual as possible. See also informal assessment.
Dana J. Stevens

Angelman syndrome

A severe genetic disorder and developmental delay characterized by lack of or minimal speech with relatively higher communication skills; movement or balance disorder; and atypical verbal behavior such as frequent laughter, excitability, hand flapping movements, hyperactivity, and short attention span. Anatomic markers typically include delayed or disproportionate growth in head circumference, seizures, tongue thrusting, feeding problems during infancy, frequent drooling, excessive chewing, increased sensitivity to heat, and sleep disturbance. Individuals with Angelman syndrome have sometimes been misdiagnosed as having autism, cerebral palsy, or other developmental disorders.
John T. Neisworth & Pamela S. Wolfe

annual goal

A broad written expectation of what a child with disabilities will attempt to accomplish within a given period, usually 1 school year, such as "This year Nicholas will improve his communication skills." The written goals describe the child's current needs as indicated by present educational levels documented on the evaluation report. A child's annual goals are a required part of the individualized education program (IEP). *See also* individualized education program (IEP), individualized family service plan (IFSP).
Susan Wuchenich Parker

antecedent

A stimulus or event that immediately precedes a behavior. For example, a person drives her car down the road and stops at the light. She hears a horn beep and looks behind her to see her neighbor, who waves at her. In this situation, the horn beep serves as an antecedent to the person's behavior of looking at the car behind her. Antecedents form the first part of the *three-term contingency* of antecedent-behavior-consequence (ABC). *See also* antecedent-behavior-consequence (ABC) analysis, establishing operation (EO).
Richard M. Kubina, Jr.

antecedent-behavior-consequence (ABC) analysis

First described by Bijou, Peterson, and Ault (1968) as *anecdotal observation,* an ABC analysis identifies conditions that precede and follow problem behavior. These conditions may then be changed to modify the behavior (experimental analysis of behavior). ABC analyses are a central feature of

applied behavior analysis (ABA) and may take a number of different forms, often involving study of behavior using direct observation and by people (e.g., parents, teachers) who are knowledgeable about the behavior. Validity and reliability are sometimes questionable if direct observation is used over an extended period of time. *See also* applied behavior analysis (ABA), functional behavior assessment (FBA).
Robert H. Zabel

antianxiety medications

Also called *tranquilizers.* Drugs used to moderate anxiety. Anxious behavior and feelings can be specific to situations and events or can be free floating, in which case the person continually feels upset and concerned. Clonazepam (Klonopin) is an example of an antianxiety drug sometimes used with children who suffer from anxiety. Examples of antianxiety drugs used with adults are chlordiazepoxide (Librium) and diazepam (Valium). Antianxiety drugs may sometimes be prescribed to individuals with autism, especially children who experience repeated panic attacks or intense phobic reactions.
John T. Neisworth & Pamela S. Wolfe

antibiotics

See antiyeast therapy, *Clostridium tetani,* dysbiosis.

antidepressant medications

Medications that treat symptoms of depression, generally by increasing the amount of neurotransmitter serotonin in selected brain pathways by blocking the reuptake of these chemicals into the neuron. Recently developed selective serotonin reuptake inhibitors (SSRIs, e.g., fluoxetine [Prozac], sertraline [Zoloft], paroxetine [Paxil], citalopram [Celexa]) have provided medication alternatives for anxiety, obsessive behavior, and depression that have fewer side effects than older medications used for these purposes. Other classes of medication, including tricyclic antidepressants (imipramine [Janimine, Tofranil]) and serotonin receptor agonists (buspirone [BuSpar]), are also useful in treating these symptoms. Children with autism frequently develop anxieties and obsessive traits for which antidepressants are useful. Few studies have examined the response of children and adolescents with autism to antidepressant medications, but there is a great deal of clinical experience that suggests significant benefit. Buspirone has been evaluated in two studies examining the response in individuals with autism. Both stud-

ies showed a 50%–60% positive response rate, with greatest improvements in anxiety and some change in irritability (Buitelaar, van der Gaag, & van der Hoeven, 1998). Fluoxetine has been evaluated more frequently. The largest study documented an excellent response in 17%, a good response in 52%, and a fair or poor response in 31% of the 129 children evaluated. Side effects are usually quite tolerable, except some children become more fidgety or agitated and need to stop taking this medication. The most responsive symptoms to fluoxetine included anxiety, irritability, stereotypic movements, and speech impairment. Of interest is the observation that the individuals with the best response had a family history of bipolar disorder or significant depression (DeLong, Teague, & Kamran, 1998). *See also* bipolar disorder, depression, psychoactive medications, psychopharmacology.
Jeanette C. Ramer

antigluten therapy

An experimental approach for reducing the behaviors associated with autism based on tenets of the opioid excess theory. (Opioids are chemicals in the brain that affect interactions among neurons.) In the 1990s, it was speculated that the origin of autism is influenced by excessively high levels of unmetabolized peptides that affect the opioid receptors in the brain. When the natural processes of the system are disrupted, a variety of consequences result. For example, Panskepp (1979) noted similarities between autism and extended exposure to morphine (which is opioid based), including a reduced sensitivity to pain, decreased social interaction, a desire for constancy or ritual, and a slower pattern of cognitive development (Shattock & Whiteley, 2002). Certain proteins are more likely to form opiate-like peptides; two of these proteins, gluten and casein, are present in common foods. Gluten is found in wheat, oats, barley, rye, and their derivatives; casein is found in cow's milk. If excessively high levels of opiate-like peptides are producing the behaviors associated with autism, changes in diet should produce a decrease. Proponents point to instances of lowered levels of behavior associated with autism and improvements in language related to antigluten therapy. Critics of the approach note the correlational, rather than experimental, evidence. Critics also attribute the changes in behavior to reactive effects. Rather than resulting from changes in the diet, the differences in the behaviors are viewed as a function of the expectations of the participants of the study. *See also* casein, diet therapy, gluten free, leaky gut syndromes, peptide, secretin.
J. Michael Pickle

antipsychotic medications

Medications used to treat the disorganized thinking and poor awareness of reality noted in adults with schizophrenia. Early antipsychotic medications were associated with a significant number of side effects, including sedation, withdrawn affect (reduced socioemotional expressiveness), and development of unusual movements of the head and body. Some individuals with autism were noted to improve when treated with haloperidol (Haldol), an atypical antipsychotic medication, but not when given the traditional antipsychotic medications (e.g., chlorpromazine [Thorazine], thioridazine [Mellaril]). In the 1990s, newer atypical antipsychotic medications were developed. Of these, risperidone [Risperdal], appears to be the most effective for individuals with autism spectrum disorders (Masi, Cosenza, Mucci, & De Vito, 2001). There are now 10–15 studies published that show positive effects of this medication on symptoms such as hyperactivity, fidgetiness, stereotypic movements, anger control, and changeability of mood (Zuddas, Di Martino, Muglia, & Cianchetti, 2000). For some children, there was also improvement in functional skills including language and socialization. *See also* psychoactive medications, psychopharmacology.
Jeanette C. Ramer

antiyeast therapy

A treatment for autism spectrum disorders (ASDs) based on the premise that increased yeast overgrowth (e.g., resulting from antibiotic treatment) leads to the development of autism symptoms (Rimland, 1994). Specifically, yeast may overgrow, cause irritation to the intestinal wall, and allow food proteins to cross into the bloodstream. It has been theorized that either these food proteins (e.g., casein, gluten) or the by-products of yeast metabolism elicit antibody response or directly attack selected brain pathways. Therapy includes use of *probiotics* (bacteria that normally inhabit the gastrointestinal tract and compete with yeast), a diet that eliminates yeast-containing foods, and medications that suppress yeast growth. This treatment approach, while evidently safe, remains in the category of unproven therapies and has not been subjected to sufficient scientific study (New York State Department of Health, Early Intervention Program, 1999a). *See also* antigluten therapy, casein, diet therapy, dysbiosis, leaky gut syndromes.
Jeanette C. Ramer

anxiety

Tension or nervousness felt prior to the occurrence of a real or imagined event. Certain physiological symptoms may be present, such as sweating, heart palpitations, change in breathing, and stomach uneasiness. Anxiety can be a motivational influence at low to moderate levels and can prompt creativity, athletic accomplishments, and test performance. At high levels, anxiety can interfere with normal functioning and can be highly unpleasant. Individuals with autism may experience extreme anxieties and show associated physiological signs. *See also* antianxiety medications, antidepressant medications, obsessive-compulsive disorder (OCD), social phobia.
Jennifer M. Gillis

applied behavior analysis (ABA)

An applied science that develops methods of changing behavior and a profession that provides services to meet diverse behavioral needs. ABA is based on the scientific study of principles of operant and respondent conditioning and has a well-respected research literature that has accumulated over decades. ABA is applied (the outcome has practical significance), behavioral (behavior itself is of interest), analytical (functional relationships can be established), technological (procedures are described, so replication of an intervention is possible), conceptually systematic (procedures are derived from basic theoretical principles), effective (interventions are socially valid), and generalized (behavior changes are evident over time and in different settings) (Baer, Wolf, & Risley, 1968). Interventions using ABA that have been found to be effective for individuals with autism (New York State Department of Health, Early Intervention Program, 1999a) include analysis of verbal behavior (AVB) and Discrete Trial Training (DTT). ABA is the only therapeutic/educational approach for children with autism that is deemed effective by the Surgeon General of the United States. *See also* analysis of verbal behavior (AVB), behavior modification, behavior principles, behaviorism, discrete trial training, operant conditioning, respondent conditioning, social validity, verbal behavior (VB).
Gerald L. Shook

apraxia

A disorder of performing skilled motor actions despite intact motor and sensory functioning. In adults, apraxias are presumed to result from acquired head injuries to the left hemisphere. Adults with apraxia have language and motor planning impairments. In children, research and evaluation of apraxia has been less systematic and rigorous. The term *developmental dyspraxia* has been used to describe children with motor coordination and/or motor planning problems (thus, it is often difficult to distinguish between studies evaluating impairments in gross and fine motor skills from those evaluating impairments in planned motor movements). Treatments for children diagnosed with developmental dyspraxia are often based on sensory integration (SI) methods and may address skills hypothesized to be related to motor planning impairments (e.g., body awareness). The relevance of apraxia to autism relates to the difficulty individuals with autism have in performing gestural imitation tasks (Smith & Bryson, 1998). The broadly defined terms used in the study of motor planning in children, however, limit evaluation of motor planning in autism. Support for motor planning impairments in autism exists in a limited literature base. Further research distinguishing motor planning from motor coordination impairments, evaluating apraxia in low- and high-functioning individuals with autism, and evaluating apraxia in longitudinal designs is needed to better understand the role of motor planning in autism. *See also* fine motor skills, gross motor skills, sensory integration (SI).

Latha V. Soorya

AS

See Asperger syndrome.

ASD

See autism spectrum disorder.

ASL

See American Sign Language.

Asperger syndrome (AS)

Also called *Asperger disorder.* One of the conditions considered a pervasive developmental disorder (PDD), AS is characterized by marked and sustained social and behavioral impairment but no significant cognitive or language delays. Individuals with AS have difficulties with transitions or changes and a desire to maintain sameness. Individuals often have obsessive routines and may be preoccupied with a particular subject of interest. These individuals have difficulty reading nonverbal cues (body language); difficulty determining proper body space; and may be sensi-

tive to sounds, tastes, smells, and sights. Individuals with AS have average to above average IQ, and many (although not all), exhibit exceptional specific skills or talents. However, individuals with AS can be extremely literal and have difficulty using language in a social context. Frequently, motor awkwardness or clumsiness is evident. There is a great deal of debate concerning how to classify AS; it is presently described as part of the autism spectrum with clear overlap of autism and AS characteristics (Szatmari, 1992). Some experts contend that AS is the same as high-functioning autism, while others state that it is better described as a non-verbal learning disability or pervasive developmental disorder-not otherwise specified (PDD-NOS). Many individuals have been incorrectly diagnosed or remained undiagnosed. An interesting difference between autism and AS that has been noted is the apparent inability of children with autism, per se, to provide insights into or be introspective concerning their own condition (Sacks, 1995). Named for Viennese physician Hans Asperger, Asperger syndrome was added in 1994 to the *Diagnostic and Statistical Manual of Mental Disorders, Fourth Edition* (DSM-IV; American Psychiatric Association), and only in the past few years has AS been recognized by professionals and parents. *See also* autism spectrum disorder (ASD), pervasive developmental disorder (PDD), high-functioning autism, social impairment.
John T. Neisworth & Pamela S. Wolfe

assessment

The process of gathering information to evaluate the functioning of an individual. This process typically includes direct interaction with the individual and family members, how the person functions in typical settings, standardized testing, review of records, and interviews. Types of assessment include developmental, neuropsychological, psychoeducational, psychiatric, personality, socioemotional, speech and language, and occupational and physical therapy. Assessment, which is also sometimes referred to as *evaluation,* is a close and comprehensive appraisal of the child's status, whereas screening is a rapid procedure to identify whether a child should receive assessment. Assessment of autism and pervasive developmental disorders (PDDs) typically includes evaluation of verbal and nonverbal communication, adaptive and cognitive functioning, repetitive and stereotypical behaviors, sensory processing, and social relatedness (Halgin & Whitbourne, 2003; see also Appendix A). *See also* informal assessment, screening, standardized tests.
Julie Wolf & Jessica Lord

assistive technology (AT)

AT is a broad term that includes a wide range of devices *and* services that have the potential to help individuals with disabilities perform specific tasks, improve their functional capabilities, and become more independent (Parette, 1997; Technology-Related Assistance for Individuals with Disabilities Act of 1988, PL 100-407; Technology-Related Assistance for Individuals with Disabilities Act Amendments of 1994, PL 103-218). More generally, AT includes anything needed by individuals with disabilities to do things that they could not do without the AT. *See also* assistive technology (AT) device, assistive technology (AT) service.
Phil Parette

assistive technology (AT) device

Any item, piece of equipment, or product system used to increase, maintain, or improve functional capabilities. Such devices include hardware, software, and other devices. AT devices may be categorized as either low- or high-technology. Low-technology (or light-technology) devices are simple and inexpensive (e.g., a flexible drinking straw for a person who has limited physical ability). High-technology devices are more complex in design and cost (e.g., a voice output communication aid). These devices may also be categorized by the type of assistance: 1) daily living, 2) augmentative and alternative communication (AAC), 3) computer applications, 4) environmental control systems, 5) home or worksite modifications, 6) prosthetics and orthotics, 7) seating and positioning, 8) aids for vision and/or hearing, 9) mobility aids, and 10) vehicle modifications. *See also* assistive technology (AT), assistive technology (AT) service.
Phil Parette

assistive technology (AT) service

Any service that directly assists an individual with a disability in the selection, acquisition, or use of an AT device (Technology-Related Assistance for Individuals with Disabilities Act Amendments of 1994, PL 103-218). Often AT devices cannot be effectively identified, purchased, modified, customized, or implemented without certain services being available. It is important to evaluate the specific needs of a person, including the customary environments (Parette & McMahan, 2002). During evaluation, it may be determined that a particular AT device may need to be selected, designed, fitted, customized, adapted, applied, retained, repaired, or replaced. Another important AT service is the training and/or technical assistance that would be provided

directly to the person with a disability and/or the person's family, as well as professionals, employers, or others who may be substantially involved in the life of the person. Once identified, a device must be obtained and implemented using as many services as necessary to ensure that the potential of the AT device is fully realized. *See also* assistive technology (AT), assistive technology (AT) device.
Phil Parette

association method

An instructional technique intended to increase the understanding and use of oral language; improve articulation, co-articulation, and speech fluency; and teach reading and written composition skills. The method is systematic, incremental, phonetically based, and multisensory in the purest sense. The method was originally conceived and outlined by Mildred McGinnis (1963) and expanded and explained in a later publication (DuBard & Martin, 1994). Publications explain the principles on which the method was devised, its distinctive features (e.g., cursive writing, Northampton Symbols, color coding), its instructional levels, and the accompanying correlative programs.
Anne Sullivan

AT

See assistive technology; *See also* assistive technology (AT) device, assistive technology (AT) service.

attachment disorder

Pertaining to any of several types of dysfunctional patterns that infants display relating to their caregivers (e.g., avoidant, resistant, disoriented). Typical attachment pattern involves the infant's use of the caregiver as a base from which to explore the environment and to return for safety. A disorder related to attachment identified in the *Diagnostic and Statistical Manual of Mental Disorders, Fourth Edition* (DSM-IV; American Psychiatric Association [APA], 1994), is *reactive attachment disorder of infancy or early childhood*. The disorder begins before 5 years of age and is marked by disturbed and developmentally inappropriate social interactions across contexts. The disorder is classified as inhibited if the child's social interactions are characterized by excessive inhibition, vigilance, or ambivalence and contradiction. If the child is not selective in social interactions and lacks the skill to form attachments that are selective and appropriate, he or she is classified as having the disinhib-

ited form of the disorder. For a person to be diagnosed with the disorder, the symptoms must not result exclusively from a developmental delay and the criteria for a pervasive developmental disorder (PDD) must not be met. The disorder is thought to be rare (APA, 1994). *See also* infantile autism.
Ellen R. Borsuk

attention-deficit/hyperactivity disorder (ADHD)

A disorder characterized by patterns of inattentive and/or hyperactive-impulsive behavior that is not typical for the average person at that developmental level (American Psychiatric Association [APA], 2000). While a person may be diagnosed with ADHD much later in life, at least some of the symptoms causing the diagnosis must have been present before the age of 7. The impairment caused by the symptoms of ADHD must occur in two or more settings, such as school and home, and this impairment must be clearly evident in the person's social, academic, or occupational functioning. The fifth and final criterion is that ADHD cannot be diagnosed if the symptoms occur only as a result of a pervasive developmental disorder (PDD) or other psychiatric disorder in the APA's (2000) diagnostic classification. Treatment of choice includes applied behavior analysis (ABA) and pharmacological agents. *See also* applied behavior analysis (ABA), psychopharmacology.
Leah Bucknavage

atypical antipsychotic medications

See antipsychotic medications.

atypical behavior

Unusual action or conduct, including specific behavior that is of immediate concern or that may signal subsequent and more pervasive developmental and health problems. Atypical behaviors do not usually refer to delays in skills but rather refer to behavioral deficiencies or excesses or displays of behavior at inappropriate times and places. Atypical behavior may include body rocking; spinning; self-injury; sleeping or eating problems; and abnormal sensitivities to sights, sounds, and touch. Children with autism or other pervasive developmental disorders (PDDs) characteristically evidence atypical behavior, and such behavior is assessed as part of a diagnosis. *See also* pica, stereotypic behavior.
John T. Neisworth & Pamela S. Wolfe

audiologist

An entry-level hearing and health care professional who has completed at least a master's degree from an accredited university plus 1 year of internship. An audiologist deals with hearing loss, tinnitus (noises in the ear), equilibrium disorders, and central auditory processing impairments and is trained in identifying medical pathologies such as diseases involving the hearing and balance mechanism. Individuals having hearing loss are seen by an audiologist to determine the appropriateness of amplification with which hearing instruments and which circuits would be most appropriate. An audiologist may also recommend assistive listening devices such as alerting systems or counsel the patient regarding the appropriateness of cochlear implants. Audiologists work cooperatively with other professionals such as physicians, physical therapists (PTs), optometrists, teachers, and speech-language pathologists (SLPs). The American Speech-Language-Hearing Association (ASHA) offers the Certificate of Clinical Competence in Audiology (CCC-A). To obtain the CCC-A, a clinician must hold a master's degree, pass a national examination, and complete a supervised fellowship year. *See also* audiology.

John T. Neisworth & Pamela S. Wolfe

audiology

A branch of science dealing with hearing; specifically, the assessment and therapy of individuals having impaired hearing. *See also* audiologist.

John T. Neisworth & Pamela S. Wolfe

auditory acuity

See acuity.

auditory integration therapy (AIT)

AIT is based on the assumption that some children with autism may have sensitive hearing especially to specific sounds or tones (Scott, Clark, & Brady, 2000). This method of treatment is a type of auditory training that is being used in the treatment of individuals with autism. Children may cover their ears to keep the environment from being too noisy and overwhelming. To "recalibrate the student's auditory processing systems" (Tharpe, 1999), a child undergoing AIT listens to music through headphones that have been specially processed to filter selected frequencies. Initially an audiogram (hearing test) is conducted to isolate the frequencies to which the child seems to experience hypersensitivity. These fre-

quencies are filtered out, dampened, modulated, and presented to the individual during training through the headphones. The training takes place during two 30-minute sessions per day for 10 days. Theoretically, the therapy strengthens muscles in the middle ear, which, in theory, prevents sensory overload. There are no published research studies that meet scientific standards to support or refute the validity of AIT (Berkell, Malgeri, & Streit, 1996). AIT is an invasive procedure that could possibly cause harm to the patient (through prolonged exposure to certain sounds) if not administered properly (Berkell et al., 1996; New York State Department of Health, Early Intervention Program, 1999a). *See also* auditory training, hyperresponsiveness, sensory integration (SI) therapy.
Jamie Capri Barbarich

auditory processing disorder

See central auditory processing disorder (CAPD).

auditory training

A type of sensory training based on the theory that individuals with autism fail to integrate auditory information. Auditory training is a category of treatments based on the assumption that the body can be retrained to integrate auditory information. When an individual who has auditory hypersensitivity experiences certain tones, frequencies, and sounds at an intense rate, these sounds may cause pain and impair functioning. Auditory training centers attempt correcting auditory hypersensitivity. First, an audiogram, or hearing test, is conducted to isolate the frequencies that are a problem (Berkell, Malgeri, & Streit, 1996). Once sounds are isolated, the auditory training is used to "exercise the middle ear muscles and auditory nervous system in much the same way as one conducts physical therapy on an injured elbow" (Tharpe, 1999, p. 379). There are several approaches to auditory training, all relatively new to the United States. There is little or no empirical research to support auditory training (New York State Department of Health, Early Intervention Program, 1999a). *See also* auditory integration therapy (AIT), hyperresponsiveness.
Jamie Capri Barbarich

augmentative and alternative communication (AAC)

Nonverbal communication methods used to promote communication and language development in individuals who have little or no vocal ability. Primary AAC methods include use of manual signs, visual communication (e.g., eye gaze), and communication devices (e.g., communication board, voice output communication aid). Given reports that children with autism do not attain functional use of verbal language, AAC methods are often helpful (Sigafoos & Drasgow, 2001). Little data exist to suggest the utility of one AAC method over another. Most findings suggest wide individual differences in acquisition and functional use of AAC methods for individuals with autism (Mirenda, 2001). An individual can use AAC communication temporarily or permanently. *See also* assistive technology, communication board, visual schedule.

Latha V. Soorya & Fan-Yu Lin

autism

A developmental disorder characterized by marked difficulty in communication and social relations and by the presence of atypical behaviors such as unusual responses to sensation, repetitive movements, and insistence on routine or sameness (American Psychiatric Association, 2000; Assistance to States, 2003, § 300.7[1]). Autism is evidenced between 18 and 36 months, although it is sometimes not formally diagnosed until 5 years of age. Diagnosis is based on behavioral rather than medical, anatomic, or genetic markers. Leo Kanner (1943) first identified and differentiated autism from childhood schizophrenia (and other disorders) and named the syndrome *autism* (from the Greek *autos,* meaning *of or for oneself*) based on the social disregard or avoidance shown by these children. Speculation on causes of autism have included Bettelheim's (1967) now-rejected psychoanalytic contention regarding cold, distant mothering (*refrigerator mothers*). Rimland's landmark 1964 book refocused attention to biological factors and the current consensus of a biological-neurological basis that may be triggered by environmental stressors. Originally considered a rare disorder (4 in 10,000 children), recent incidence studies report 10 in 10,000 children (Bryson, 1997; Wing, 1993). The U.S. Department of Education reported a total of 118,669 school-age children with autism for 2002–2003 (IDEAdata.org, 2002) (as compared with the 1992–1993 report of about 16,000). The reported incidence may be due to greater vigilance in early detection, a broader definition, or a real increase (Feinberg & Beyer, 1998). A number of environmental stressors have been suggested as responsible for triggering autism in people with a predisposition for the disorder who otherwise might not show signs of the disorder. Major approaches to treatment include intensive applied behavior analysis (ABA), classroom-based behavioral programs, and methods based on social developmental theory (Marcus, Garfinkle, & Wolery, 2001). Several formal definitions of autism for purposes of classification and diagnosis are available (e.g.,

American Psychiatric Association, 2000; World Health Organization, 1992). *See also* applied behavior analysis (ABA); core deficits, *Diagnostic and Statistical Manual of Mental Disorders, Fourth Edition, Text Revision (DSM-IV-TR)*; environmental stressors; infantile autism; *The International Statistical Classification of Diseases and Related Health Problems, Tenth Revision (ICD-10)*.
John T. Neisworth & Pamela S. Wolfe

autism spectrum disorder (ASD)

Term used to refer to any disorder in the array of pervasive developmental disorders (PDDs). Not a formal diagnostic classification, the term ASD is used by professionals in two ways. First, as in this book, ASD is used synonymously with PDD to refer to any of these developmental disorders, including autism, Rett syndrome, childhood disintegrative disorder (CDD), hyperlexia, Asperger syndrome (AS), and pervasive developmental disorder-not otherwise specified (PDD-NOS) (Siegel, 1996). Second, ASD is used to refer to any of these disorders except autism (i.e., when children who do not fully meet the criteria for autism) (Szatmari, 1992). *See also* autism, Asperger syndrome (AS), childhood disintegrative disorder (CDD), hyperlexia, pervasive developmental disorder (PDD), pervasive developmental disorder-not otherwise specified (PDD-NOS), Rett disorder.
John T. Neisworth & Pamela S. Wolfe

autism-like

Pertaining to symptoms and/or characteristics that resemble those exhibited by a child with autism but that are not of sufficient intensity or frequency to meet criteria for a formal diagnosis of autism, such as certain stereotypies or other atypical behavior (e.g., rocking, twirling, preoccupation with a string). Children with mental retardation may evidence autism-like behaviors. *See also* stereotypic behavior.
John T. Neisworth & Pamela S. Wolfe

autistic disorder

See autism.

AVB

See analysis of verbal behavior.

B₆ and magnesium therapy

See vitamin B_6 and magnesium therapy. *See also* dimethylglycine (DMG), vitamin therapy.

BACB®

See Behavior Analyst Certification Board®.

baseline

The repeated measurement of a behavior before the introduction of an intervention (independent variable). Baseline data can be used to compare the effects of the systematic application of a treatment. For example, a teacher can record the number of times a child screams in the classroom over 5 days. The teacher can then try a procedure (e.g., response cost; continue to collect data and then compare the number of screams with the baseline data). *Baseline* does not mean the absence of behavior; rather, it is the environment absent of an intervention or introduction of an independent variable (Cooper, Heron, & Heward, 1987). Baselines can have different patterns: stable, unstable, descending, or ascending. *See also* single subject.
Richard M. Kubina, Jr.

BCABA®

See Board Certified Associate Behavior Analyst™.

BCBA®

See Board Certified Behavior Analyst™.

bed wetting

See enuresis.

behavior

Any activity of a living thing. To be considered *behavior,* the activity must be detectable and/or measurable. Both verbal and nonverbal behaviors are important aspects in the analysis and treatment of autism. *See also* antecedent-behavior-consequence (ABC) analysis, applied behavior analysis (ABA). *John T. Neisworth & Pamela S. Wolfe*

behavior analysis

See antecedent-behavior-consequence (ABC) analysis, applied behavior analysis (ABA).

Behavior Analyst Certification Board® (BACB®)

A not-for-profit corporation providing professional credentials for practitioners of applied behavior analysis (ABA). Credentials are issued for Board Certified Behavior Analyst™ (BCBA®) and Board Certified Associate Behavior Analyst™ (BCABA®). Certificants must meet specific degree, coursework, and experience requirements and pass a professionally developed written examination. Once certified, individuals must maintain their credential by obtaining continuing education. The BACB® has developed eligibility, renewal, and recertification standards; guidelines for responsible conduct; professional disciplinary standards; and a certificant registry and approves university course sequences that meet BACB® requirements. *See also* applied behavior analysis (ABA), Board Certified Associate Behavior Analyst™ (BCABA®), Board Certified Behavior Analyst™ (BCBA®). *Gerald L. Shook*

behavior modification

Refers to both a field of psychology and methods that lead to the analysis and modification of human behavior (Miltenberger, 1997). Behavior modification can decrease nonproductive behaviors and increase positive and adaptive behaviors (Kazdin, 2001). While some professionals use *behavior modification* as synonymous with *applied behavior analysis (ABA)* (Miltenberger, 1997), most others broaden the scope of *behavior modification* to include cognitive-behavioral strategies and pharmaceutical interventions. Like ABA, behavior modification procedures have a wide purview and can accommodate human behavior in many fields (e.g., industrial, academic, sports) and with the full range of human behavior (e.g., typically developing children, individuals with disabilities, older adults). *See also* applied behavior analysis (ABA), behavior therapy. *Richard M. Kubina, Jr.*

behavior plan

An outline designed to increase skills or decrease undesirable behaviors based on assessment data such as functional analysis. Behavior plans may include strategies such as ecologic or setting events, predictors, teaching, and consequence (O'Neill et al., 1997). Behavior plans should include data collection measures and be consistently implemented in each individual setting. *See also* functional behavior assessment (FBA), individualized education program (IEP), setting events.
Catherine R. Meier

behavior principles

Statements regarding the reliable and predictable relationships between behavior and environmental circumstances. Reinforcement (positive and negative), punishment (positive and negative), extinction, and stimulus control are examples of principles that have been formulated and refined through experimental and applied research. Behavior principles are the basis for operant and respondent learning and the profession of applied behavior analysis (ABA)—a major approach to understanding and helping individuals with autism or another pervasive developmental disorder (PDD). *See also* applied behavior analysis (ABA), extinction, punishment, reinforcement, stimulus control.
John T. Neisworth & Pamela S. Wolfe

behavior rehearsal

A method to improve skills (e.g., assertiveness) or to eliminate problems that cause distress and personal maladjustment (e.g., fears). A therapist using the procedure begins by identifying a clinical objective; for example, an individual will interact more effectively with peers, colleagues, and family members. Positive interactions are described and then demonstrated by the therapist. In the case of an individual who has difficulty controlling anger, desirable interpersonal behaviors might be maintaining a low voice volume, projecting a calm demeanor, and refraining from making negative comments. After observing several demonstrations, the individual then responds similarly while the therapist guides performance through instruction, direction, and corrective feedback. Once skills are acquired in this context, the individual is encouraged to use them in the real-world situations in which he or she has encountered problems. *See also* desensitization, shaping.
James K. Luiselli

behavior therapy

Use of techniques based on behavioral (both operant and respondent) and cognitive approaches in the treatment of behavior disorders. While these procedures are also effective in instruction, therapeutic use has been successful for helping with depression, phobias, self-injurious behavior (SIB), obsessive-compulsive disorder (OCD), and other such difficulties. Behavior therapy is useful both for individuals diagnosed with a recognized syndrome and for individuals who are stressed or otherwise in need of therapy. Behavior therapy differs from psychoanalysis and related approaches based on presumed unconscious processes because it uses principles of learning and conditioning that permit objective assessment and manipulation. *See also* operant conditioning, respondent conditioning.
John T. Neisworth & Pamela S. Wolfe

behavioral health rehabilitation (BHR) services

Also called *wraparound services*. A process within mental health systems designed to provide service delivery within school and community agencies. Using a team of family and friends, as well as professionals, a plan is developed that is needs driven and family based. A child with autism who attends an inclusive preschool, for example, may require and obtain the help of therapeutic support staff (TSS) personnel who attend to the child during the day and provide noneducational support, such as positive behavior support (PBS). These services may also be available to the child in the home and in community settings. *See also* therapeutic support staff (TSS) worker.
Christopher Jones

behavioral objective

A description of what a learner should be able to do as a result of instruction or intervention. A behavioral objective states what the learner will do and the criterion for success. The terms *terminal behavior, desired behavior,* or *performance objective* are sometimes used interchangeably with *behavioral objective*. Behavioral objectives address three specific questions: What behavior will the learner exhibit (behavior)? Under what conditions will the learner exhibit the specified behavior (conditions)? and How well will the learner exhibit the behavior (criteria)? For example, when introduced to someone new (condition), the learner will extend a hand and say, "I'm pleased to meet you," while looking at the new acquaintance (behavior) correctly over four trials (criteria). Behavioral objectives are used in a number of instructional and/or therapeutic approaches, especially those based on

applied behavior analysis (ABA). *See also* applied behavior analysis (ABA), behavior, individualized education program (IEP).
Kathy Ruhl

behavioral phenotyping
See psychobiology.

behaviorism
A philosophical position that asserts that behavior, including human behavior, can be subject to scientific analysis. Behavior is seen as important in its own right and can be described, predicted, and controlled. The study of behavior is seen as akin to the disciplines of physics, chemistry, geology, and other natural sciences.
John T. Neisworth & Pamela S. Wolfe

best practice guidelines
See clinical practice guidelines.

BHR services
See behavioral health rehabilitation services.

bias
The influence of an observer on the collection of data or on data that have been collected (McCall, 2001). An observer influences results in different ways. Experiences or beliefs (personal bias) or knowledge of a study and its possible effects (observer expectancy) can bias observations, ratings, or reports (Gall, Borg, & Gall, 1996). One way to try to minimize biases and the distortion of information is to use observers who do not know the purpose of the study or who do not know whether the student being observed is part of the experimental group or the control group (blind observers) (McCall, 2001). It is sometimes impossible to control for all biases (e.g., past experiences the observer has had). Bias can be minimized through certain methods for gathering information, such as through direct observation and recording (counting and recording frequency of behavior) and interrater reliability training and testing. It is important that the accuracy of observations be stressed and accurate observations recorded during training and actual observation (Salvia & Ysseldyke, 2001). *See also* assessment, informal assessment, validity.
Janelle Matesic

bipolar disorder

A mood disorder (previously known as *manic-depressive disorder*) characterized by episodes of mania and, in many cases, episodes of depression. A manic episode is defined as a period during which the individual experiences an elevated, expansive, or irritable mood (American Psychiatric Association, 2000). For example, the person may feel an inflated sense of self-esteem or grandiosity and have little need for sleep. Individuals experiencing manic episodes may be distractible and agitated. They may attempt to start multiple large projects as well as engage in behaviors that have dangerous consequences (e.g., spending money recklessly, having unsafe sex, driving recklessly). Unlike adults, children with bipolar disorder do not appear to have sudden onsets and clear offsets of mania and depression. In children, the disorder can be difficult to differentiate from attention-deficit/hyperactivity disorder (ADHD); in fact, most children with bipolar symptoms also meet criteria for ADHD (Cassano, McElroy, Brady, Nolen, & Placidi, 2000). In addition, mood disorders such as bipolar disorder are often confused with autism, and some children may be diagnosed with autism and a mood disorder. *See also* attention-deficit/hyperactivity disorder (ADHD), depression, mania.
Laura M. Arnstein

Board Certified Associate Behavior Analyst™ (BCABA®)

The BCABA® conducts descriptive behavioral assessments and is able to interpret the results and design ethical and effective behavior analytic interventions for clients. The BCABA® designs and oversees interventions in familiar cases (e.g., similar to those encountered during their training) that are consistent with the dimensions of applied behavior analysis (ABA). He or she obtains technical direction from a Board Certified Behavior Analyst™ (BCBA®) for unfamiliar situations. The BCABA® is able to teach others to carry out interventions after demonstrating competency with the procedures involved under the direct supervision of a BCBA®. The BCABA® may assist a BCBA® with the design and delivery of introductory level instruction in behavior analysis. It is strongly recommended that the BCABA® practice under the supervision of a BCBA® and that the applicable regulatory governmental entities require this supervision. *See also* applied behavior analysis (ABA), Behavior Analyst Certification Board® (BACB®), Board Certified Behavior Analyst™ (BCBA®).
Gerald L. Shook

Board Certified Behavior Analyst™ (BCBA®)

An independent practitioner who also may work as an employee or independent contractor for an organization and who conducts descriptive and systematic behavioral assessments, including functional analyses, and provides behavior analytic interpretations of the results. The BCBA® designs and supervises behavior analytic interventions. The BCBA® is able to effectively develop and implement appropriate assessment and intervention methods for use in unfamiliar situations and for a range of cases. The BCBA® seeks the consultation of more experienced practitioners when necessary. The BCBA® teaches others to carry out ethical and effective behavior analytic interventions based on published research and designs and delivers instruction in behavior analysis. It is strongly recommended that the BCBA® supervise the work of Board Certified Associate Behavior Analysts™ (BCABA®) and others who implement behavior analytic interventions. *See also* applied behavior analysis (ABA), Behavior Analyst Certification Board® (BACB®), Board Certified Associate Behavior Analyst™ (BCABA®), functional behavior assessment (FBA).
Gerald L. Shook

bowel problems

See constipation, diet therapy, dysbiosis, encopresis, leaky gut syndromes, secretin.

brain imaging

See neuroimaging.

brushing

See deep pressure proprioception touch technique.

CA

See chronological age.

CAPD

See central auditory processing disorder.

case manager

See service coordinator.

case study

Nonexperimental design involving a small number of participants (usually one or two). There is no experimental manipulation of variables to test for effects, thus limiting the usefulness or validity of results. Case studies are commonly used in emerging research, but without systematic control of variables, their contribution to the research field is limited and results cannot be clearly interpreted (i.e., identification of the effective factors is difficult). *See also* experimental design, testimonial.

John T. Neisworth & Pamela S. Wolfe

casein

A chemical found in milk that is sometimes related to allergic reactions. Casein *allergy* should not be confused with lactose *intolerance*. Most people who have difficulty digesting milk are lactose intolerant, meaning that they produce too little lactase enzyme to break down milk sugar (lactose). A casein allergy can also be just an allergy. It may manifest as breathing difficulty, hives and rashes, or serious pain in the gut and may lead to inability to get nourishment from food and dangerous weight loss. *See also* diet therapy, food intolerance.

John T. Neisworth & Pamela S. Wolfe

CBA
See curriculum-based assessment.

CCC-A
Certificate of Clinical Competence in Audiology. *See* audiologist.

CCC-SLP
Certificate of Clinical Competence in Speech-Language Pathology. *See* speech-language pathologist (SLP).

CDD
See childhood disintegrative disorder.

central auditory processing disorder (CAPD)
Difficulties in comprehending auditory information not attributable to hearing impairment per se. Children who exhibit CAPD may also be considered as having attention-deficit/hyperactivity disorder (ADHD), in which case both diagnoses may be given. Instructional and management strategies are similar for either diagnosis.
John T. Neisworth & Pamela S. Wolfe

Certificate of Clinical Competence in Audiology (CCC-A)
See audiologist.

Certificate of Clinical Competence in Speech-Language Pathology (CCC-SLP)
See speech-language pathologist (SLP).

certified behavior analyst
See Board Certified Behavior Analyst™ (BCBA®); *see also* Board Certified Associate Behavior Analyst™ (BCABA®).

certified rehabilitation counselor (CRC)
Professional who assists with rehabilitation, client assessment, planning and service delivery, counseling and interviewing, and job development and placement (Parker & Szymanski, 1998). CRCs in the United States or Canada

are certified by the Commission on Rehabilitation Counselor Certification. *See also* vocational evaluator.
Lynn Atanasoff

chaining

A set of sequenced behaviors linked together to produce a result (often used with task analyses when a series of behaviors are chained together). Forward and backward chaining represent two methods for producing a behavior chain. With forward chaining, a child learns the first step of the chain (e.g., holding the shoelaces when tying a shoe) and then each successive step up to the last. Conversely, with backward chaining, the child learns the last link of the chain (e.g., pulling the loops of the laces accurately) and each step in backward order. When forward chaining is difficult, reverse or backward chaining may be successful because the child practices the last step right before the end, which functions as a reinforcer. The links in the chain can function both as discriminative stimuli and reinforcers. *See also* task analysis.
Richard M. Kubina, Jr.

challenging behavior

Actions that significantly interfere with the quality of life of individuals engaging in these behaviors and those with whom they live or work. These behaviors can include aggression (e.g., hitting, biting, scratching others); self-injury (e.g., head banging, hand biting, face slapping); tantrums (e.g., screaming, destroying objects); stereotyped body movements (e.g., hand flapping, rocking); and bizarre, psychotic speech. Behaviors such as these are obstacles when individuals are in community, employment, or educational settings and are disruptive to family life. Challenging behaviors may be precipitated by communication difficulties and may actually be behavioral adaptations necessitated by the abilities of an individual and the limitations of his or her environment. Challenging behaviors may serve a useful function to the individual, and it is important to assess this function (Durand & Crimmins, 1992). *See also* functional behavior assessment (FBA), functional communication training (FCT), functional equivalent alternative behavior.
Melissa L. Zona, Kristin V. Christodulu, & V. Mark Durand

chelation

Chelation represents binding of heavy metals or other toxins in the blood using drugs with a high affinity for these compounds. This technique can remove a toxin from sites in the body in which it is stored and cause its excretion by the liver and kidneys. Chelation has been used for many years, especially for children with high blood levels of lead, a known brain toxin. Protocols for lead chelation are available with specific guidelines based on blood lead level.

It has been suggested that some children with autism are affected by mercury toxicity from exposure to vaccines containing thimerosal, a preservative used in some vaccines until the late 1990s. It is theorized that some children are susceptible to neurological impairment from low levels of exposure to heavy metals, especially mercury. There are similarities between the general symptoms of mercury exposure and those of autism, including sensory disturbance; movement disorder (e.g., hand flapping, toe walking); and cognitive impairment, specifically in verbal and auditory memory. Proponents of this theory have supported the use of chelation to treat children with autism to remove mercury. The drug used as the chelating agent, meso-2,3-dimercaptosuccinic acid (DMSA), can have significant side effects (Chisolm, 2000). Side effects can include liver toxicity and upset stomach with abdominal pain and vomiting. Chelation for children with autism remains controversial because a clear link between thimerosal and autism has not been shown; indeed, in 2004, the Institute on Medicine released a report that "favors rejection of a causal relationship between thimerosal-containing vaccines and autism" (p. 1). *See also* heavy metals, mercury, thimerosal, toxicology.
Jeanette C. Ramer

childhood disintegrative disorder (CDD)

Formerly called *disintegrative psychosis* or *Heller syndrome*. A rare condition first described by Theodore Heller in 1908 (as *dementia infantilis*) as the formal diagnosis of *autism*. Children with CDD develop symptoms resembling autism but do so after a period of normal development—minimally 2 years—with an age of onset prior to 10 years. Typically, onset is between ages 3 and 4 years and may be gradual or abrupt. Early signs include increased motor activity, irritability, and anxiety, followed by intellectual impairment with withdrawal from communication and other social interactions, including loss of previously acquired skills. Developmental delay may be mild for an extended period, followed by continued decline. Research suggests that CDD occurs 60 times less frequently than other forms of autism, and it usually results in severe mental retardation. The cause of CDD currently is unknown. As with autism, CDD is more common among boys than girls. *See also* Asperger syndrome (AS), autism, pervasive developmental disorder (PDD), regression.
Curtis K. Deutsch

childhood-onset schizophrenia (COS)

Also called *early-onset schizophrenia* or *prepubertal schizophrenia*. A very rare and serious mental disorder characterized by specific abnormalities in thinking, perception, and emotion, COS involves the early appearance (before age of 12) of positive and negative symptoms of the adult form of schizophrenia (National Institute of Mental Health, 2003). These symptoms may be more prominent for children than for adults with this disorder, although delusions may be less in depth than they are in adults with schizophrenia (American Psychiatric Association, 2000). Common symptoms include disorganized speech and disorganized behavior. There is controversy in the child psychopathology field as to whether COS should be classified as a separate entity, discontinuous of adult schizophrenia. (Autism was previously regarded as a form of childhood schizophrenia before it was differentiated as an entirely separate syndrome). *See also* schizophrenia.
Judith H. Chan

chronological age (CA)

The child's actual age from birth date in months or years. If a child was born prematurely, CA will sometimes be reported as *corrected* for prematurity (e.g., if 2 months premature, 2 months may be subtracted from CA, yielding the same physical age as children born 2 months later). This correction is generally done only for the first 2 years of life. Because children are typically grouped by CA, correcting for prematurity permits greater similarity of social and cognitive skills. CA is sometimes used to compare a child with a normative sample of children of the same CA. *See also* developmental age (DA), developmental quotient (DQ), mental age (MA).
Deborah Fein

circle of communication

Term used in the Developmental, Individual-Difference, Relationship-Based (DIR) model or floortime approach (Greenspan & Weider, 1997) to refer to a procedure to facilitate communication. A circle begins with a child's initiation. Then, the adult responds and, in turn, the child responds to the adult. *See also* Developmental, Individual-Difference, Relationship-Based (DIR) model; floortime.
John T. Neisworth & Pamela S. Wolfe

circle of friends

Also called *Circles of Friends*. A process developed to promote the inclusion of children with disabilities in a general education classroom. The process

begins with typical peers identifying their own natural support systems to create a "circle of friends" network for a classmate who has a disability (Forest & Lusthaus, 1989; Snow & Forest, 1987). *See also* inclusion, peer-mediated intervention.
Linda Crane Mitchell

classic antipsychotic medications
See antipsychotic medications.

classical conditioning
See respondent conditioning.

The Classification of Child and Adolescent Mental Diagnoses in Primary Care: Diagnostic and Statistical Manual for Primary Care (DSM-PC) Child and Adolescent Version

A system to classify, manage, and refer childhood and adolescent developmental and behavior difficulties. Developed by the American Academy of Pediatrics in close collaboration with related professionals (e.g., psychologists, psychiatrists), the *DSM-PC Child and Adolescent Version* is compatible with and can be linked to the *Diagnostic and Statistical Manual of Mental Disorders, Fourth Edition* (American Psychiatric Association, 1994), and other systems, such as the *Diagnostic Classification of Mental Health Disorders of Infancy and Early Childhood* (*DC: 0-3;* ZERO TO THREE Diagnostic Classification Task Force, 1994). The approach shares some features with the *DC: 0-3* system in its recognition of childhood issues, avoidance of pathologic labels, and focus on observable difficulties, rather than inferred underlying conditions. The *DSM-PC Child and Adolescent Version* offers several features that make it a system of choice among many pediatricians:

- A wide range of childhood developmental and behavior difficulties are described as presenting problems and organized within 10 domains (e.g., impulsivity/hyperactivity, inattention; negative/antisocial behavior; emotions and mood difficulties; atypical behavior).
- Difficulties and presenting problems are judged in relation to three levels of intensity: *normal variation* (expected within typical development and manageable through less intense treatments, e.g., counseling, parent education), *problem* (serious enough to impair developmental progress and/or occasion excessive parental distress and may be man-

aged by the primary care provider or be referred to other medical or early intervention professionals), or *disorder* (more severe difficulties defined and classified within the standard *DSM* system).

- Eleven groups of "situations" (environmental stressors, e.g., parent–child separation; domestic violence, poverty, chronic health issues) can used for diagnosis and treatment, in recognition that life circumstances can cause or contribute to childhood difficulties.

DSM-PC Child and Adolescent Version may be a gateway to early recognition and services for real childhood problems that may otherwise go undetected or as not meeting the full diagnostic criteria required by DSM system. Finally, with *DSM-PC Child and Adolescent Version,* symptoms and signs may be identified and services made available at an early age, when professionals may be reluctant to employ *DSM* labels (e.g., Autistic Disorder, Asperger's Disorder). *See also Diagnostic and Statistical Manual of Mental Disorders, Fourth Edition, Text Revision (DSM-IV-TR); Diagnostic Classification of Mental Health Disorders of Infancy and Early Childhood (DC: 0-3).*
John T. Neisworth & Pamela S. Wolfe

clinical assessment

A process that involves varied procedures, instruments, and multiple sources of information to form an evaluation of developmental and psychological characteristics (Simeonsson & Rosenthal, 2001). The critical feature of clinical assessment is that the clinician, rather than the test, is at the center of the assessment process (Murphy & Davidshofer, 1991). *See also* assessment, clinical opinion, diagnosis, standardized tests.
Valerie J. Postal

clinical opinion

An outcome of clinical assessment (informed clinical opinion) based on qualitative and quantitative information to determine difficult-to-measure aspects of a child's current developmental status and intervention needs (Shackelford, 2002). Clinical opinion is especially important when standardized testing procedures are not appropriate. Part C of the Individuals with Disabilities Act (IDEA) Amendments of 1997 (PL 105-17) requires that assessment be based on informed clinical opinion (Early Intervention Program, 1999, §303.322[c][2]) and used to establish eligibility for services (Early Intervention Program, 2003, §303.300). *See also* assessment, clinical assessment, diagnosis, Individuals with Disabilities Education Act (IDEA).
Janice H. Belgredan

clinical practice guidelines

Also called *best practice guidelines*. A set of standards for care that informs consumers and service providers about the status of accepted practice parameters for specific conditions or disorders. An accepted methodology for evaluating treatments was formalized by the U.S. Department of Health and Human Services, Agency for Health Care Policy and Research (now called the Agency for Healthcare Research and Quality). The clinical practice guideline methodology uses specific principles for developing practice guidelines as recommended by the Institute of Medicine (within the National Academy of Sciences). The methodology is considered to be the standard for developing evidence-based clinical practice guidelines (Eddy & Hasselblad, 1994; Holland, 1995; Schriger, 1995; Woolf, 1991, 1994) and has been applied to autism spectrum disorders (ASDs). The New York State Department of Health, Early Intervention Program (1999b), used this methodology to develop evidence-based clinical practice guidelines regarding young children with autism (the guidelines are available at http://www.health.state.ny.us/nysdoh/eip/menu.htm).
Raymond G. Romanczyk

clinical significance

See treatment effectiveness.

clinical social worker

A professional who addresses treatment and prevention of psychosocial dysfunction, disability, or impairment, including emotional and mental disorders. Services consist of assessment, diagnosis, treatment (including psychotherapy and counseling), client-centered advocacy, consultation, and evaluation. At least a master's degree in social work and current state license or certification are required as well as 2 years of post–master's degree clinical social work experience and supervision. *See also* service coordinator, team models.
Grace E. Peters

clinical trial

A research method used to appraise the effectiveness and safety of a new intervention or diagnostic procedure. (The U.S. Food and Drug Administration [FDA] requires clinical trials for drugs and medical devices.) A trial typically refers to use of the new drug, device, therapy, or other intervention with some persons while others receive placebo treatment or an older treatment. Both short- and long-term outcomes are monitored. Clinical trials often include four

phases: Phase I typically uses a small number of people (e.g., 50) to assess safety and possible side effects; Phase II consists of continued trials using a greater number of participants (e.g., several hundred); Phase III uses perhaps several thousand participants to determine effectiveness with larger populations and in comparison with older treatments; and Phase IV, done after FDA approval, consists of continued intervention monitoring to assess long-term effects.
John T. Neisworth & Pamela S. Wolfe

Clostridium tetani

The organism responsible for tetanus. *Clostridium tetani* is hypothesized to have caused autism in a large subset of individuals with autism whose onset of autistic behaviors occurred after antibiotic use for chronic infections and who demonstrate increased levels of urine phenolic metabolites and persistent loose bowel movements (Bolte, 1998). In immature intestines, disruption of normal or indigenous intestinal bacteria, especially by antibiotic use or chronic diarrhea, permits *Clostridium tetani* colonization of the lower intestinal tract. The neurotoxin elaborated by this organism travels to the central nervous system (CNS) along the vagus nerve, effecting the major behavioral abnormalities associated with autism. *Clostridium tetani* also elaborates a cytotoxin that damages the intestinal wall, enhancing absorption of neuroactive peptides, and generates ammonia and several other neurotoxic phenolic compounds. Evidential support for this hypothesis includes the following: Clostridial species are known to pathologically colonize immature intestines (*Clostridium botulinum,* which can cause infant botulism) and intestines of older individuals with antibiotic-altered intestinal microflora (*Clostridium difficile,* which can cause antibiotic-associated colitis). In experimental animals, intracerebral tetanus neurotoxin causes stereotypical behavioral abnormalities and can be shown to travel to the central nervous system from the intestine via the vagus nerve. The "fixed smile," difficulty in swallowing foods (dysphagia), rigidity, and muscle spasms seen in many children with autism are all clinical symptoms of tetanus. High levels of phenols and phenolic metabolites (potential neurotoxins) are found in the urine of many children with autism. Quantitative and qualitative clostridial species counts are significantly higher in children with autism compared with controls (Finegold et al., 2002), and antibiotics effective against *Clostridium tetani* dramatically improve behaviors associated with autism in certain subjects, although regression is common when the antibiotics are stopped. See *also* constipation, dysbiosis, peptide.
Robert A. Da Prato

cognitive processes

Mental constructs such as memory, language, visuospatial skills, attention, imagery, processing of emotional information, and executive functions that refer to the way people perceive, process, understand, and respond to information. Cognitive processes are often (but not always) assessed as uneven in autism, with relative strengths in visuospatial skills and visual memory and relative weaknesses in language, verbal memory, attention, and processing of emotional information (Frith, 1992; Frith, Morton, & Leslie, 1991). *See also* executive functions, intelligence tests.
Jamie M. Kleinman

collaborative team

See team models.

communication board

A system of communication for individuals with severe speech difficulties. Communication boards display pictures, symbols, or words and may or may not be electronically operated. A communication board helps an individual to communicate by pointing to symbols or pictures. For example, a child may communicate needing a cup or toothbrush by pointing with his or her hand or with a stick or a pointer attached to his or her head. To use this system efficiently, an individual must be able to associate pictures with objects, events, or needs. *See also* alternative communication, augmentative and alternative communication (AAC), low-technology device, visual strategies.
Devender R. Banda

communication disorder

A disruption in the process of exchanging information and conveying ideas. Disruption can affect language (words, sentences), speech (sound production), fluency (ease of flow of speech and language), voice production (quality of a person's voice), and reception (comprehension) (Bernstein & Tiegerman-Farber, 2002). For example, a person with a limited vocabulary or limited sentence formation can be described as having a communication disorder. A communication *disorder* is different from a communication *difference,* which is a difference in speech or language production affected by a person's cultural-linguistic background or experiences. *See also* augmentative and alternative communication (AAC), pragmatics, prosody, speech-language pathologist (SLP).
Lynn Adams

community-based instruction
See service delivery model.

comorbid
See co-occurring; *see also* morbidity.

compliance
See guided compliance.

concrete language
Specific, literal word usage rather than metaphorical or figurative language. Individuals with autism characteristically interpret figurative expressions (e.g., *slept like a log, it's raining cats and dogs*) literally and do not understand them. Children with autism need systematic instruction in communication, especially in colloquial, pragmatic language. *See also* figurative language, pragmatics.
John T. Neisworth & Pamela S. Wolfe

concurrent validity
See validity.

confidentiality
The protection of personal information and the assurance that names and other identifying information (e.g., gender, ethnicity, medical information, physical characteristics) will be kept private. Professional associations and federal and state law impose procedural safeguards on businesses and institutions (e.g., school districts), requiring them to protect personal information. Protected information, such as assessment results, may only be shared among a child's team members and others providing services or consultation. Institutions may follow different procedures to protect privacy in addition to those required by federal law. Information related to child endangerment does not fall under legal confidentiality provisions, and individuals involved with certain crimes may lose their rights to certain forms of confidentiality. *See also* ethics.
Britta Saltonstall

consent
A legal right of an individual to participate or not participate in a treatment plan, activity, or research. The right of consent requires several elements,

including capacity (the individual is competent to make decisions), information (the individual is informed of the nature of and benefits and risks of procedures), and voluntariness (the individual is not coerced into giving consent). Minors cannot give consent; instead, parents or legal guardians can give consent, preferably with the child's assent when feasible. *See also* Americans with Disabilities Act (ADA) of 1990 (PL 101-336), due process, procedural safeguards.

John T. Neisworth & Pamela S. Wolfe

consequence

An external or internal event that immediately follows a behavior or response. Consequences are key elements in skill acquisition: They provide feedback, communicating to the recipient the accuracy and/or suitability of a behavior, and serve to reward or punish a behavior, altering the probability that the behavior will or will not occur again. In an instructional setting, consequences may take the form of teacher attention, praise, the end of an activity, peer response, or the attainment of a preferred object (Wolery, Bailey, & Sugai, 1988). Therapy and instruction for children with autism frequently involves extensive and intensive planning and management of consequences. *See also* antecedent, antecedent-behavior-consequence (ABC) analysis, operant conditioning, punishment, reinforcement.

Marcia L. Schatz

constipation

Difficulty in passing stools, including incomplete or infrequent passage of hard stools. Symptoms can include a hard, formed stool; a palpable rectal mass; straining at stool; decreased bowel sounds; reported feeling of abdominal or rectal fullness or pressure; and passing a less-than-useful amount of stool. A person who is constipated may also experience nausea, abdominal pain, reduced appetite, back pain, headache, and interference with daily living. There are numerous causes and related factors, including inadequate fluid, food, or fiber intake; less than adequate physical activity; side effects of medication; neuromuscular or musculoskeletal impairment; pain on defecation; lack of privacy; weak abdominal musculature; and emotional status (Anderson, Anderson, & Glanze, 1998). Some research studies have found an increased frequency of gastrointestinal symptoms such as constipation, diarrhea, and abdominal bloating in children with autism (Wakefield et al., 2000). *See also* secretin.

Julie L. FitzGerald

construct validity
See validity.

content validity
See validity.

contingency
The relation between a behavior and its associated consequences. A contingency exists when an event is consistently presented, removed, or withheld following the occurrence of a specific behavior. A contingency can be contrived (e.g., a piece of good given for answering a question correctly) or may occur naturally (Ferster, 1965) (e.g., putting on a sweater, with a consequence of warmth). Contingencies exist for positive or negative reinforcement and positive or negative punishment (Lattal, 1995). *See also* antecedent-behavior-consequence (ABC) analysis, contingency contracting, punishment.
Michael E. May & Craig H. Kennedy

contingency contracting
Reciprocal agreements between the learner and teacher or therapist that specify behavior to be changed, how it will change, and the contingencies associated with the behavior change. Contingency contracting typically delineates the responsibilities and rewards for all participants. There are both informal and formal contracts. Contingency contracting is an application of the Premack principle: A behavior that has a high rate of occurrence can be used to increase a behavior with a low rate of occurrence (Premack, 1965). Preferred, higher frequency behavior can be made contingent upon performance of less preferred, lower frequency behavior. Contracts specify the following elements: target behavior, performance criteria, reinforcement and payoff ratios between behavior and reinforcement, time and place where reinforcement is provided, possible bonuses for near perfect performance of target behavior, possible punishment for breaking the contract, and methods to determine that criteria are met (Homme, Csanyi, Gonzales, & Rechs, 1969). Contingency contracting is often part of interventions for individuals with autism to promote self-regulation of behavior, as the contracts include negotiation and commitment among the participants and self-monitoring and self-evaluation procedures. *See also* contingency, Premack principle, reinforcement.
Robert H. Zabel

control condition

A condition used for demonstrating experimental control. In a scientific experiment, the treatment or instructional conditions are manipulated to test effects. For example, if interested in examining the effects of a new therapy, the teacher may implement a condition in which the therapy is used. In the control condition, the therapy will not be used (and the other circumstances are kept the same). The experimental and control conditions may be alternated. *See also* empiricism, experimental design, single subject.
Thomas P. Kitchen

co-occurring

Also called *comorbid*. Referring to additional symptoms or problems that often accompany a diagnosis. Often co-occurring with Down syndrome, for example, are respiratory and heart problems. Mental retardation and certain medical problems, such as bowel problems, often co-occur with a diagnosis of autism and its primary indicators.
John T. Neisworth & Pamela S. Wolfe

coprolalia

See Tourette disorder.

core deficits

Also called *triad of impairments*. The three areas of behavior and developmental concern common for all children with autism: social behavior (social phobias, avoidance, or awkwardness); absence of spoken language or notable qualitative differences in communication; and the presence of atypical behavior such as repetitive actions, narrow interests, insistence on routine and sameness, and frequent aversions to sights, sounds, and textures. Cumulative research indicates the primacy of social relatedness as a central deficit of autism. Early markers of social deficits include limited eye contact, failure to initiate play or to make other social contacts, little interest in or even avoidance of being held or touched, and little stranger anxiety. Children with autism may relate better to adults than to peers. Difficulties in sharing perspectives, empathy, and social reciprocity are often evident. Communication problems include lack of functional spoken language or loss of language (at about age 2) after initial typical language development. Needs and wants may be communicated through challenging behaviors (e.g., hitting, screaming) that allow the child to obtain desired outcomes, to escape unwanted circumstances, or to express frustration. Means of nonverbal communication

(gestures, body position, facial expression, eye contact) are typically not used by young children with autism. When spoken language is used, there are peculiarities, including immediate or delayed repetition of what has been heard (echolalia); pronoun confusion; and atypical rate, inflection, and qualities (e.g., volume, intonation) of speech (prosody). Children with autism may exhibit behaviors such as rocking, spinning, hand regard, finger flicking, and head banging. Ritualistic, compulsive, or repetitive behavior is often evident. Play is rarely imaginative. Reaction to sights, sounds, and textures may be almost absent or excessive. Hyperactive and anxious behaviors are often characteristic. *See also* atypical behavior; autism; *Diagnostic and Statistical Manual of Mental Disorders, Fourth Edition, Text Revision (DSM-IV-TR)*; pervasive developmental disorder (PDD); prosody; social impairment.
John T. Neisworth & Pamela S. Wolfe

corrected age
See chronological age (CA).

COS
See childhood-onset schizophrenia.

CRC
See certified rehabilitation counselor.

criterion
A standard of judging; any approved or established rule or test by which facts, principles, opinions, and conduct are tried in forming a correct judgment respecting them. For example, to receive a diagnosis of autism, a child must satisfy three criteria: inadequate communication, ineffective social skills, and stereotypic behavior. *See also* criterion-referenced assessment.
Christopher Jones

criterion-referenced assessment
An assessment or test related to set standards or expected mastery. The expected standards or criteria can be determined through several procedures, including expert consensus, job or task analysis, or simply the demands of a setting (e.g., criteria for enrollment in kindergarten include being able to wait in line, being toilet trained, and so forth). Often, instruction in specific skills is continued until the child's skill reaches an agreed-on criterion. The agreed-on skills are behaviors that are functionally useful to the child

and that are developmentally and educationally important (e.g., uses a spoon to eat, walks up steps, can delay obtaining something wanted). Curriculum-based assessment (CBA) is one form of criterion-based measurement. Often the criteria are stated in terms of *what* gets accomplished, that is, functions (e.g., gets across the room), rather than in terms of *how* it gets done (topography). Criterion-referenced assessment is most useful for planning and monitoring instruction; in contrast, norm-referenced assessment is based on group norms and assessment items that are often not considered to be educationally worthwhile (e.g., stands on one foot for 30 seconds, places pegs in holes, looks for small object under small plastic cup). Published materials for therapy in autism and other pervasive developmental disorders (PDDs) are often criterion referenced and target important social and communication skills and functions of particular pertinence to children with autism (see Appendix A). *See also* criterion, curriculum-based assessment (CBA), fluency.
John T. Neisworth & Pamela S. Wolfe

curriculum

A set of instructional objectives, usually sequenced from easier to more advanced, used to plan child programs and monitor progress. Most curriculum packages include descriptions of strategies for teaching to the objectives. Some practices that may be useful to consider in developing appropriate curricula for students with autism include language acquisition and growth strategies, behavior management interventions, and social interaction strategies. *See also* behavioral objective, curriculum-based assessment (CBA).
Holly Williams

curriculum-based assessment (CBA)

Materials and procedures to appraise a person's attainment within an organized set of educational and/or therapeutic objectives (i.e., a curriculum). There are numerous developmental and disability-specific curricula with corresponding assessment materials. CBA is used to provide an initial profile of capabilities, to identify feasible objectives, to monitor individual progress, and to evaluate treatment effect. Published CBA materials are available specific to children with autism or other pervasive developmental disorders (PDDs) (see Appendix A). *See also* assessment, norm-referenced assessment, standardized tests.
John T. Neisworth & Pamela S. Wolfe

DA
See developmental age.

daily living skills
See activities of daily living (ADLs). *See also* adaptive skills.

DAP
See developmentally appropriate practice.

DAS
Developmental apraxia of speech. *See* apraxia.

data
The "quantitative results of deliberate, planned and usually controlled obser-vation" (Johnston & Pennypacker, 1980, p. 327). Data can be collected in many forms, including anecdotal reports, frequency counts, interviews, or videotapes. Furthermore, the data can be organized and graphically displayed to show patterns and trends. Data are useful to inform diagnosis, program development, and an individual's progress. *See also* anecdotal report, assess-ment, direct observation, empiricism.
Dana J. Stevens

DC: 0-3
See Diagnostic Classification of Mental Health Disorders of Infancy and Early Childhood.

deep pressure proprioception touch technique
Also called *brushing* or *Wilbarger protocol.* A technique in which a specially designed brush is used in sensory integration (SI) therapy, typically by

occupational therapists (OTs). Some professionals believe that many of the behaviors evidenced in individuals with autism (e.g., toe walking, hand flapping) are attempts by the individual to deal with SI issues.

The technique uses firm strokes with a soft brush on the back, arms, and legs. Brushing is often combined with joint compression, in which elbows and other joints are pushed together firmly in succession. Although the technique is frequently used, it has no current evidence base acceptable to the scientific community. *See also* occupational therapist (OT), sensory integration (SI), sensory integration (SI) therapy.
Devender R. Banda

delayed echolalia
See echolalia.

dementia infantilis
See childhood disintegrative disorder (CDD).

depression
A psychological/emotional syndrome that involves a range of behavioral and physical symptoms experienced over time. Symptoms include saddened affect, change in sleep patterns, change in appetite and/or weight, lack of motivation, feelings of helplessness and hopelessness, crying episodes, difficulty with memory and concentration, loss of pleasure in activities, and irritability (American Psychiatric Association, 2000). Causes of depression are currently considered to include a combination of genetic, biochemical, and psychosocial factors (Malkoff-Schwartz et al., 1998). Study has demonstrated the co-occurrence of depression and autism. Evidence suggests that depression is the most common psychiatric disorder that occurs for individuals with autism and Asperger syndrome; these individuals also experience other mood disorders and anxiety disorders at a higher rate than other people (Ghaziuddin, Ghaziuddin, & Greden, 2002). *See also* psychoactive medications, psychopharmacology, serotonin.
Britta Saltonstall

desensitization
The gradual reduction of feared stimuli so that the learner increasingly tolerates the presence of such stimuli. One of the most effective ways to accomplish desensitization is to pair the aversive stimulus with reinforcing stimuli and to provide gradually increased exposure to what is aversive (e.g., a child who is fearful of a swimming pool is reinforced first when approaching the

pool, then when a foot is put into the water, and finally when fully in the pool). It is considered to be one of the most acceptable treatment procedures available to treat fears and phobias (King & Gullone, 1990). *See also* behavior therapy, phobias.

Thomas P. Kitchen

desired behavior
See target behavior; *see also* behavioral objective.

detoxification
A practice purported to remove poisons from the body in order to improve functioning and/or reduce symptoms related to the presence of heavy metals or other poisons in the body. Until recently, vaccines contained a preservative (thimerosal) that contained the heavy metal mercury, which has been thought by some to be associated with symptoms of autism. Detoxification is not presently supported by convincing empirical research. *See also* chelation, heavy metals, mercury, thimerosal, toxicology.

John T. Neisworth & Pamela S. Wolfe

developmental age (DA)
A number that expresses, in years and months, the child's attainment of developmental skills in a certain domain or domains; this number is equivalent to the chronological age (CA) of other children who have similar skills (Coleman, 1999). For example, a child may be 5 years old but have the social skills of a 3-year-old (CA = 5, social DA = 3). Various DAs can be described for a child, including mental, social, emotional, or neurological. While not typically used in formal assessment reports, DA and mental age (MA) are sometimes more meaningful to parents than normative comparisons that involve standard deviation scores. *See also* chronological age (CA), developmental quotient (DQ), mental age (MA).

Janelle Matesic

developmental apraxia of speech (DAS)
See apraxia.

developmental delay
Failure to demonstrate skills and behaviors, or *developmental milestones,* within the same age range as most other children; an ongoing, significant delay in the anticipated sequence of development (not a slight or temporary lag).

Delays may be exhibited in one or more developmental domains: cognitive, communication, adaptive, socioemotional, and physical (including vision and hearing). Developmental delays are distinguished from disordered development, which is characterized by a nonsequential pattern of development and which is of particular concern for children with autism spectrum disorders (ASDs) (McConnell, 1998). Developmental delays are often described as percentages. For instance, a child with a chronological age (CA) of 24 months whose most competent communication skills are typically seen in children of 18 months would be described as having a 25% delay in communication development. Delays are frequently expressed as standard deviations (*SD*) from the mean (average) attainment of typical development. A majority of states use developmental delay as a disability category for at least a portion of eligible students ages 3 through 9. States determine their own criteria (what percentage delay or *SD*) for what constitutes an eligible developmental delay. The developmental delay eligibility category serves several purposes: 1) It is used to identify young children who might go unserved due to the challenges of using traditional disability categories early in life, 2) it can avoid the premature categorization or miscategorization of young children into traditional disability categories, and 3) it supports the development of program plans based on individual need rather than on disability label (Division for Early Childhood, 2001). *See also* developmental milestones, diagnosis, disability, early intervention (EI), eligibility.
Janice H. Belgredan

developmental dyspraxia
See apraxia.

Developmental, Individual-Difference, Relationship-Based (DIR) model
Intervention approach based on the theory that individuals with autism have biologically based processing difficulties that affect their ability to have relationships with others (Greenspan & Weider, 1997). The approach emphasizes developmental level, individual differences, and affect and relationships. The DIR model includes a technique referred to as *floortime* because parents and others are asked to interact with the child on the floor in play settings to develop relationships. The approach encourages parents and therapists to follow the child's lead and then expand on what the child is doing. The DIR approach centers on developmentally appropriate practices in play settings and includes some behavioral aspects. Bonding and establishing affective relationships are seen as central to helping children with multisystem devel-

opmental disorder (MSDD; ZERO TO THREE's Diagnostic Classification Task Force, 1994). Elements of a comprehensive program based on the DIR model include floortime (home-based developmentally appropriate interactions and practices), speech-language therapy (3 or more times per week), sensory integration therapy (2 or more times per week), an educational program (daily), and biomedical treatments (including possible medication).

Currently, there is not a sufficient research data base (controlled studies) to support the DIR approach; however, DIR does include best practice elements such as family involvement and individuality (New York State Department of Health, Early Intervention Program, 1999a). Future research is anticipated. *See also* circle of communication; developmentally appropriate practice (DAP); *Diagnostic Classification of Mental Health Disorders of Infancy and Early Childhood (DC: 0-3);* floortime; multisystem developmental disorders (MSDD).
John T. Neisworth & Pamela S. Wolfe

developmental milestones

Important skills or behaviors typically evident at given age ranges (e.g., walking at 9–15 months). Developmental milestones can be divided into several categories: gross motor, fine motor, language, cognitive, and socioadaptive. Delayed development can be identified when there is a delay in achievement of developmental milestones. Culture and ethnicity should be taken into account when determining whether a child's development is delayed (Kalesnik, 1999). *See also* developmental delay, disability, early intervention (EI).
Ellen R. Borsuk

developmental quotient (DQ)

A child's developmental age (DA) divided by that child's chronological age (CA) and multiplied by 100. DQ may be used as a way to communicate more simply the relative status of a child's functioning (e.g., it may be more easily understood than standard scores), but DQ is not psychometrically or statistically a sound metric and is not recommended for use in formal decision making. *See also* chronological age (CA), developmental age (DA).
John T. Neisworth & Pamela S. Wolfe

developmental surveillance

Monitoring of a child's developmental status, from a few weeks to perhaps a year or more, depending on the risk factors present. Parent report/interviews,

screening tests of overall development, and observations may be used and discussed with parents. Delays in attaining age-appropriate developmental milestones, presence of unusual behaviors, risk factors, and parent concerns can be used to direct attention to more focused assessment. (See Appendix A for screening tests.) *See also* assessment, clinical opinion, early signs.
John T. Neisworth & Pamela S. Wolfe

developmentally appropriate practice (DAP)

The body of early childhood professional standards related to environmental arrangements, materials, activities, and teaching methodologies that are suitable or appropriate to a child's level of development. DAP guidelines are published by the National Association for the Education of Young Children (NAEYC; Bredekamp & Copple, 1997) and have three domains: age appropriateness, individual appropriateness, and cultural appropriateness. NAEYC requires the use of DAP in its early childhood program accreditation system. DAP is seen by some to be in opposition to the more teacher-driven structured practices often deemed necessary for helping children with autism. *See also* best practice guidelines, early intervention (EI).
John T. Neisworth & Pamela S. Wolfe

diagnosis

A procedure to identify a relevant label for a set of characteristics, symptoms, or markers and to inform treatment. A diagnosis is generally required for eligibility for services for individuals with autism. A formal diagnosis is typically conducted using a variety of instruments by a team of professionals. The term *assessment* is typically used by nonmedical professionals but refers to the same process. *See also* clinical assessment, clinical opinion, differential diagnosis.
John T. Neisworth & Pamela S. Wolfe

Diagnostic and Statistical Manual of Mental Disorders, Fourth Edition, Text Revision (DSM-IV-TR)

The *DSM-IV-TR* (2000) is published by the American Psychiatric Association (APA),[1] the professional membership organization representing psychiatrists in the United States. The *DSM-IV-TR* contains a listing of disorders and corresponding diagnostic codes. Each disorder in the manual is accompanied by a set of diagnostic criteria and text containing infor-

---

[1]The American Psychological Association is also referred to as APA but is not a part of the American Psychiatric Association.

mation about the disorder, such as associated features; prevalence; familial patterns; age-, culture-, and gender-specific features; and differential diagnosis. Previous editions include the DSM-I, DSM-II, DSM-III, DSM-III-R, and DSM-IV (1952, 1968, 1980, 1987, and 1994, respectively). DSM-V is scheduled for publication in 2010. *See also Diagnostic Classification of Mental Health Disorders of Infancy and Early Childhood (DC: 0-3); The International Statistical Classification of Diseases and Related Health Problems, Tenth Revision (ICD-10);* psychiatrist.
Marley W. Watkins

Diagnostic Classification of Mental Health Disorders of Infancy and Early Childhood (DC: 0-3)

Like the American Psychiatric Association's and World Health Organization's diagnostic systems, *DC: 0-3* (ZERO TO THREE's Diagnostic Classification Task Force, 1994) is designed to help organize and communicate observations, to assess and monitor change, and to inform intervention. *DC: 0-3* differs, however, in several ways. First, it exclusively focuses on the mental health and developmental needs of children birth through 3 years of age and is sensitive to dimensions of early developmental concern, such as self-regulation, childhood depression, and early social development, among others. Second, *DC: 0-3* emphasizes presenting problems; that is, it describes what children do and do not do (e.g., has exaggerated startle response, shows disinterest in relationships, shows panic without clear precipitant), rather than specifying presumed underlying explanatory pathologies (e.g., mental retardation, psychosis). The system is not to be used to provide diagnostic labels for the child (e.g., schizophrenia, autism, oppositional-defiant disorder). Rather, problematic behavior/functioning is identified (e.g., problems in self-regulation, such as in sleeping or in eating; disorders in relating and communicating; problems in modulating reactions to sensations). Third, because of the functional orientation of the system, *DC: 0-3* is relevant to intervention, helping professionals to identify feasible and accessible educational and therapeutic variables. The system is intended not to replace other systems but to supplement them, especially when those systems do not address issues of early childhood or the early onset of problems identified in later childhood.

A child who would be given an autism diagnosis according to the American Psychiatric Association's criteria might be designated with *DC: 0-3* as evidencing multisystem developmental disorder (MSDD). The MSDD criteria (ZERO TO THREE's Diagnostic Classification Task Force, 1994,

p. 44) include 1) significant difficulties in (but not complete absence of) relating to a primary caregiver; 2) communication impairment, including gestural, verbal, and symbolic language impairment; 3) marked impairment in perception and comprehension; and 4) significant dysfunction in sensory processing (hypo- or hyperreactivity). It should be noted that MSDD is not a fixed diagnosis; rather, it is a description of a child's current functioning, subject to change, including improvement. *DC: 0-3* offers advantages to early interventionists who seek assessment systems that generate goals rather than global pathology labels. *See also Diagnostic and Statistical Manual of Mental Disorders, Fourth Edition, Text Revision (DSM-IV-TR); The International Statistical Classification of Diseases and Related Health Problems, Tenth Revision (ICD-10);* multisystem developmental disorder (MSDD).
John T. Neisworth & Pamela S. Wolfe

diet therapy

A therapeutic modality involving reduction or elimination of specific foods from the diet. Numerous dietary constituents have been implicated in contributing to the observed signs and patient-reported symptoms of autism (Lucarelli et al., 1995). Pathophysiologic mechanisms of symptom relief from elimination diets include reductions in exposure to neuroactive digestive products (e.g., opiate peptides from milk, excitatory amino acids); proteins damaging intestinal mucosal structures (e.g., gliadin from wheat), allowing absorption of digestive fragments and bacterial toxins that are usually excreted; and dietary components responsible for the myriad symptom complexes attributed to food intolerance (Page, 2000). Although by convention diet therapy refers to elimination of selected foods, the concept can incorporate therapeutically reducing or eliminating food additives and synthetic contaminants such as artificial dyes, pesticides, and herbicides if neuroactive effects are suspected. Further supporting a gut–brain axis (relationship) in autism is the remarkably high incidence of various forms of gastrointestinal pathology, such as increased intestinal permeability (leaky gut), esophagitis, colitis, enzyme deficiencies, intestinal dysmotility, as well as quantitative and qualitative changes in intestinal microflora. Although there is literature support for improvement in behaviors associated with autism with dietary modification (Knivsberg, Reichelt, Hoien, & Nodland, 2002), it is not plausible that foods present in the diet for many generations would be the primary cause of autism. More likely the fundamental central nervous system (CNS) abnormalities that lead to symptoms and signs of autism also adversely affect CNS integration of the digestive processes.

This disruption allows normally safely processed foods to become pathogenic in various ways and to contribute secondarily to the overall spectrum of autism. Benefits from elimination diets must be balanced against the social stress of eating differently, the psychological stress of viewing foods as threatening to health, and the importance of preventing nutrient deficiency. *See also* allergy, amino acid, antiyeast therapy, antigluten therapy, leaky gut syndromes.

Robert A. Da Prato

differential diagnosis

A process of attempting to distinguish the most apt diagnosis when signs and symptoms might be considered for two or more syndromes. For example, it may be important to differentiate between autism and pervasive developmental disorder-not otherwise specified (PDD-NOS), or between high-functioning autism and Asperger syndrome (AS). (Often, educational and behavioral interventions are not dependent on precise diagnosis.)

John T. Neisworth & Pamela S. Wolfe

differential reinforcement

A procedure wherein a reinforcer is delivered after a certain behavior or in the presence of a certain circumstance rather than another. Differential reinforcement is used to decrease problematic behaviors through several strategies. Differential reinforcement of other behavior (DRO) involves reinforcing any behavior except the inappropriate behavior targeted for reduction (e.g., giving a child a sticker while she is in her seat and *not* hitting herself). A reinforcer is delivered contingent on the individual's engaging in behavior other than the unwanted behavior during an interval. DRO is also sometimes referred to as *omission training;* that is, reinforcement is delivered for omission rather than commission of the target behavior (e.g., a timer may be set and rewards given at the end of 5 minutes when no disruptive behavior has occurred). DRO can be very effective, although one drawback is that the *other* behaviors that are reinforced may not be the most appropriate for that individual in a given setting. Differential reinforcement of alternative behavior (DRA) ensures that the behavior targeted for reduction is replaced with an appropriate functionally equivalent alternative (e.g., using a signal for "I need a break" instead of screaming and hitting people). In DRA an appropriate behavior that serves the same function (purpose) as the inappropriate behavior is identified and reinforced while reinforcers are withheld

for the inappropriate behavior. The appropriate behavior generally increases because it now helps the individual acquire reinforcers, whereas the inappropriate behavior no longer accomplishes this purpose. Differential reinforcement of incompatible behavior (DRI) strengthens a behavior that is physically incompatible with the inappropriate behavior. By increasing the appropriate behavior, the inappropriate behavior is reduced automatically (e.g., sitting and standing are incompatible behaviors—they cannot occur at the same time; if sitting behavior is increased through reinforcement, the incompatible behavior of standing will decrease). Differential reinforcement of low rate of behavior (DRL) and differential reinforcement of high rate of behavior (DRH) are used to encourage low and high rates of behavior, respectively. For example, asking "What time is it?" 20 times in 1 hour is clearly inappropriate. The individual's unwanted behavior can be systematically reduced to more appropriate levels. A DRL program might begin by delivering a reinforcer when a student keeps the number of questions about the time to fewer than 15 in a 1-hour period. The criterion for reinforcement can be systematically reduced until the question is asked at progressively lower levels. A DRH program could also be used. For example, to increase the rate of a child's social initiations, which at first may be at a low level, a child may learn to initiate social contact once every half-hour. A higher rate of social contact is thus required for reinforcement; there is a gradual shift in the required rate of social initiations toward higher levels until an acceptable rate is achieved. *See also* extinction, functional behavior assessment (FBA), functional communication training (FCT).
David L. Lee

dimethylglycine (DMG)

A naturally occurring substance similar in structure to the B vitamins. DMG is classified by the U.S. Food and Drug Administration as a food, has been used since the 1960s, and is widely available. In 1965, two Russian investigators, Blumena and Belyakova (as cited in Rimland, 1990), reported the benefits of DMG in 12 of 15 children with mental retardation and speech impairment. In the United States, there have not been studies of this compound used specifically with children with autism. Reported improvements in some individuals include improved language skills and enhanced behavioral control. DMG has been used many times in individuals with autism with no clear side effect. Changes can occur within days to 4–6 weeks. There are many proponents of its use, along with strong anecdotal evidence of some positive effects. The lack of scientifically supervised studies of this compound has led to skepticism of its efficacy in the medical com-

munity. It is one of a large number of food additives and vitamins considered alternative therapies (Shaw, 1998). *See also* vitamin B$_6$ and magnesium therapy, vitamin therapy.
Jeanette C. Ramer

DIR model
See Developmental, Individual-Difference, Relationship-Based model.

direct instruction
A highly structured and systematic approach for teaching important and complex skills (e.g., language, reading, math, writing, science methods). Extensive research often determines the structure and sequence of content. Major characteristics of direct instruction include one-to-one or small-group instruction; teacher modeling of expected responses; required frequent responding from students (students say or write something several times per minute); immediate teacher feedback, typically positive; highly scripted lessons; use of positive and negative examples by the teacher; adequate practice for students to achieve mastery at each step; guided assistance that is faded as appropriate; and a pace of instruction that is brisk but is adjusted for each learner. Due to its high structure and explicit nature, direct instruction is extremely useful for children with autism (New York State Department of Health, Early Intervention Program, 1999a). Direct instructional materials are available for teaching readiness to learn (e.g., paying attention, responding when asked, engaging in tasks, taking turns) and for teaching preacademic and academic content (e.g., language, reading, math). (See Appendix A for curriculum materials.)
John T. Neisworth & Pamela S. Wolfe

direct observation
The watching and recording of an individual's behavior, typically in natural settings. Direct observation is often used to assess a student's level of functioning to identify needed skills or monitor progress. Factors to consider when conducting direct observations include potential biases of the observer as well as drift (changes over time in how the observer might describe what is seen). Direct observation is particularly useful for assessing young children or individuals with severe disabilities for whom formal testing may not be developmentally appropriate or feasible. *See also* bias, data, informal assessment, reliability.
Britta Saltonstall

disability

A restriction or lack of ability (resulting from an impairment) to perform a major activity in the manner or within the range considered typical. A disability may be temporary or permanent but typically produces difficulties in the conduct of major life activities. For a person with autism, disability may refer to a loss of participation in activities with peers due to social and communication challenges. A disability is considered to reside with the individual, whereas a handicap is considered to be the burden imposed on the person by the environment. *See also* handicap, impairment.
Lisa A. Ruble

discrete trial training

An instructional strategy to teach children with autism or other pervasive developmental disorders (PDDs) that emphasizes distinct and repeated practice of correct responding to a signal, followed by reinforcement. A single trial is defined as a signal, the child's response, and the consequent feedback (e.g., "touch *your* nose," the child touches his or her nose, then the teacher says, "Good, that is *your* nose"). It is a discrete trial because it has a clear beginning and end. Lovaas employed discrete trials in his research and developed a more formal and structured set of procedures based on discrete trial instruction over years of clinical experience; this formalized use of discrete trial instruction is sometimes referred to as *Discrete Trial Training* (note capitalization). The term *Discrete Trial Training* (or *DTT*) may be used to refer to the use of discrete trial teaching as specified and formalized by Lovaas and colleagues through years of use and refinement. The use of these specific discrete trial procedures is so central to the Lovaas approach that the term *Discrete Trial Training* is often used synonymously with the term *Lovaas approach*. *See* applied behavior analysis (ABA), Lovaas approach, massed practice.
Devender R. Banda

discrimination

A process of responding differently to two or more stimuli. Discrimination training is important in early language instruction, in teaching children to read social cues, and for many other educational and therapeutic goals. It is also useful in helping a child who has difficulty with pronoun use (touch *my* nose versus touch *your* nose) and is taught through differential reinforcement and prompt-and-fade methods. Instruction and practice in making correct discriminations (e.g., telling the difference between situations

in which it is okay to be noisy and those in which it is not; knowing the difference between a sad facial expression and one that is not sad) are central to behavior analytic approaches. *See also* differential reinforcement, discrete trial training.
Richard M. Kubina, Jr.

discriminative stimulus (S^D)

See Lovaas approach, response latency.

disintegrative psychosis

See childhood disintegrative disorder (CDD).

distributed practice

A strategy in which the student distributes effort over time rather than concentrating that effort within a short interval (Ausubel & Youssef, 1965). Spaced presentation and practice yields greater meaningful learning and helps the student better retain information (e.g., learning to tie a shoe when dressing each day rather than tying or untying a shoe repeatedly in succession) (Dempster, 1989). *See also* massed practice, trial.
Devender R. Banda

DMG

See dimethylglycine.

Doman/Delacato approach

Also referred to as *patterning,* this treatment is based on the assumption that failure in neurological organization affects subsequent development (Delacato, 1966; Doman, 1974). The theory states that the developing organism proceeds through the same successive stages of development as did the species progressing from lower to higher forms of life (fish, reptiles, mammals, human). According to the approach, the best way to treat children is to begin by practicing more primitive modes of functioning. A series of intensive primitive exercises, including crawling and creeping, are practiced to retrain and establish neurological development in children with disabilities. The approach has a questionable theoretical base and no controlled research studies to demonstrate therapeutic effects. It is controversial and rarely used today (American Academy of Pediatrics, 1982; Creaghead, 1999).
Devender R. Banda

dopamine

A neurotransmitter that is thought to be at higher levels in individuals with autism and that may be related to self-injurious and stereotypic behaviors. Dopamine is also thought to be related (with atypically lower levels) to attention-deficit/hyperactivity disorder (ADHD). *See also* neurotransmitter, self-injurious behavior (SIB), stereotypic behavior.
John T. Neisworth & Pamela S. Wolfe

double blind

A research procedure in which neither the person receiving a treatment nor the person delivering and assessing the treatment effectiveness knows whether the experimental treatment, an alternate treatment, or a placebo is being delivered. Double-blind procedures are designed to minimize possible bias and influence on the perception of treatment effectiveness.
John T. Neisworth & Pamela S. Wolfe

DQ

See developmental quotient.

DRA, DRH, DRI, DRL, DRO

Differential reinforcement of alternate behavior, of high rate of behavior, of incompatible behavior, of low rate of behavior, and of other behavior, respectively. *See* differential reinforcement.

DSM-IV–TR

See Diagnostic and Statistical Manual of Mental Disorders, Fourth Edition, Text Revision.

DSM-PC

See The Classification of Child and Adolescent Mental Diagnoses in Primary Care: Diagnostic and Statistical Manual for Primary Care Child and Adolescent Version.

DTT

See discrete trial training, Lovaas approach.

due process

A legal concept by which fairness is ensured in disputes between the government and citizens. There are two primary forms of due process: substan-

tive and procedural. Substantive due process places an outer limit on what a government may do (Turnbull, 2002). Procedural due process is access to fair procedures. The Individuals with Disabilities Education Act (IDEA) Amendments of 1997 (PL 105-17) and its regulations (Assistance to States, 2003, §§ 300.503–300.511) specify a set of procedural due process requirements, including consent, notice, information, and due process hearings. *See also* Education of the Handicapped Act (EHA) of 1970 (PL 91-230), Individuals with Disabilities Education Act (IDEA).
James K. McAfee

dysbiosis

An intestinal complication related to the reduction of helpful bacteria and the presence of harmful organisms. Typically, more than 400 species of helpful bacteria live in the intestine and provide digestion, detoxification, and the production of vitamins (symbiosis). Reduction of harmful organisms produces a great improvement in health and disposition. Dysbiosis can result from repeated or long-term use of antibiotics. Antibiotics kill not only unwanted, pathogenic bacteria but also the natural, helpful bacteria needed in the intestine. Children with autism are often treated for bowel problems (e.g., constipation that may sometimes be the result of dysbiosis due to frequent antibiotic use). *See also Clostridium tetani,* constipation.
John T. Neisworth & Pamela S. Wolfe

dysphasia

Loss of speech, understanding, or retrieval of words typically related to brain lesions, stroke, or head trauma. Aphasia can be either congenital or acquired. *See also* communication disorder.
John T. Neisworth & Pamela S. Wolfe

early infantile autism

See infantile autism; *see also* autism.

early intervention (EI)

Services and supports provided to children younger than 3 years of age and their families that are designed to preempt or minimize developmental difficulties of the young children. EI programs are provided by state agencies (e.g., maternal and child health bureaus) and/or private agencies. Eligibility for public-supported EI varies across states but typically involves a diagnosis/ assessment to document eligibility criteria. EI is considered important for children with autism or other pervasive developmental disorders (PDDs); early detection and services are preferred. EI providers include a variety of professionals who often work collaboratively, especially important in autism. EI services can be delivered in special centers and/or in the child's natural environment (e.g., the home). A broader description of EI includes children up to the age of 8 (Sandall, McLean, & Smith, in press); special services for children ages 3–5 are administered through state educational agencies (SEAs). *See also* developmental delay, individualized family service plan (IFSP), state educational agency (SEA), team models.
John T. Neisworth & Pamela S. Wolfe

early signs

Reports of past concerns or observations of current atypical or absent/ delayed behaviors that may be clinical clues ("red flags") of autism and other pervasive developmental disorders (PDDs). Some evidenced-based clinical clues are marked delay or absence of speech, lack of pretend play, little interest in peers, failure to show joint attention or social gaze, abnormal sensory reactions, and insistence on routines (New York State Department of Health, Early Intervention Program, 1999b, pp. III-20, III-24). No one clue

or group of clues is definitive, but each can trigger closer assessment and diagnosis (see Appendix A for screening tests). *See also* clinical opinion, core deficits, developmental surveillance.
John T. Neisworth & Pamela S. Wolfe

early-onset schizophrenia
See childhood-onset schizophrenia (COS).

echoic
See verbal behavior (VB).

echolalia
The repetition of someone's words, intonation, accent, or other sounds heard from the speech of others. Common in children with autism, an estimated 75% of verbal children with autism exhibit echolalic speech at some time (Scott, Clark, & Brady, 2000). Echolalic utterances can be classified as immediate, delayed, or mitigated. Immediate echolalia is the exact repetition of a word or phrase soon after it is heard. Delayed echolalia occurs when the repetition begins hours, days, or even weeks after the spoken model was first heard. Mitigated echolalia is immediate repetition that contains minor alterations in structure from the original model. Once thought to be nonfunctional, echolalia is now believed perhaps to serve communicative purposes (e.g., blocking unwanted communicative overtures of others, gaining or maintaining attention, obtaining wanted objects or activities) (Wetherby & Prizant, 1989). *See also* atypical behavior.
Kathryn Craig

ecological approach
An approach used to evaluate the relationship between an individual and his or her environments. Individuals with autism have difficulty generalizing skills; the ecological approach aids in generalization because skills are taught in natural settings. Educational objectives are also derived from natural environments. In the ecological approach, assessment, instruction, and therapy are conducted in natural contexts, rather than in decontextualized, contrived circumstances. Students with skill needs may either be taught a skill, an adaptation, or a related skill (e.g., how to communicate their choice of meal, how to use their communication device to order, how to prompt a peer to place their orders for them). *See also* embedded skills, natural environment, naturalistic interventions.
Lisa A. Ruble

ecological inventory

Type of informal assessment conducted in natural settings from which instructional objectives can be derived. Steps typically include identification of curricular domains (e.g., community), environments (e.g., restaurant), subenvironments (e.g., counter for placing order, seating, restrooms), activities (e.g., waiting in line, placing an order, finding a seat), skills (e.g., waiting, communicating choice of meal), and how skill needs may be taught. *See also* ecological approach, informal assessment.
John T. Neisworth & Pamela S. Wolfe

ecology of human performance (EHP)

Ecological framework outlining the relationships among people, activities, performance, and the contexts for performance (Dunn, Brown, & Youngstrom, 2003) for interpreting behavior and developing interventions. A person's skills and interests are considered within daily contexts. Interventions include environmental adaptations (e.g., moving a child's desk to a less active location in the room), adjustments in the demands of activities (e.g., simplifying personal hygiene routine), or changes in the selection of contexts for performance (e.g., changing a preschool program to better match a child's needs). *See also* activities of daily living (ADLs), ecological approach.
Winnie Dunn

Education for All Handicapped Children Act of 1975 (PL 94-142)

See Individuals with Disabilities Education Act (IDEA).

Education of the Handicapped Act (EHA) of 1970 (PL 91-230)

The first federal law enacted by Congress to provide specific protections and services to school-age children with disabilities. The law was a precursor to the Education for All Handicapped Children Act of 1975 (PL 94-142) that subsequently became the Individuals with Disabilities Education Act (IDEA) of 1990 (PL 101-476). EHA provided funding for programs for students with disabilities and created the federal Bureau for Education of the Handicapped. EHA set the initial framework for the right to education for children with disabilities. The EHA Amendments of 1986 (PL 99-457) resulted in a substantial increase in federal support for early intervention and preschool programs for young children with disabilities (birth to 5). In the IDEA Amendments of 1997 (PL 105-17), which amended and reau-

thorized PL 99-457 and IDEA, changes in the law focused on disciplinary provisions such as suspension, expulsion, and changes in placement. *See also* individualized education program (IEP), Individuals with Disabilities Education Act (IDEA), least restrictive environment (LRE).
James K. McAfee

educational placement
See inclusion, least restrictive environment (LRE), mainstreaming, notice of recommended educational placement (NOREP).

EEG
See electroencephalogram.

effective treatment
See treatment effectiveness.

EHA
See Education of the Handicapped Act of 1970 (PL 91-230).

EHP
See ecology of human performance.

EI
See early intervention.

electroencephalogram (EEG)
A medical test that records the electrical activity emanating from the cortex of the brain. This activity is recorded with metal disks that are placed in a specific pattern on the scalp. A typical EEG records brain waves for about 20 minutes and may use techniques such as hyperventilation and exposure to strobe lights to induce selected types of abnormal patterns. The test is painless but may be difficult for children with autism to tolerate, especially if they have sensory sensitivities. Sedation is sometimes given to induce sleep and diminish movement that can interfere with the interpretation of the study. Children with autism have a significantly increased incidence of abnormalities noted on EEG (up to 62% in some studies). *See also* seizures.
Jeanette C. Ramer

eligibility

Identification of students who are qualified for special education and related services based on meeting specified state and federal criteria for a specific disability. According to federal guidelines based on the Individuals with Disabilities Education Act (IDEA) Amendments of 1997 (PL 105-17), students ages 3 through 21 with at least one of the following disabilities are eligible for special education if the disability negatively affects their educational performance: mental retardation, hearing impairments (including deafness), speech or language impairments, visual impairments (including blindness), emotional disturbance, orthopedic impairments, autism, traumatic brain injury, other health impairments, specific learning disabilities, deaf-blindness, multiple disabilities, or developmental delay (Assistance to States, 2003, § 300.7). In addition, each state has specific eligibility criteria and laws based on the definitions adopted by that state educational agency (SEA); therefore, the labels used to refer to special education categories in each state may differ from those specified in federal law. Some children ages 3–21 who have Asperger syndrome (AS) or other pervasive developmental disorders (PDDs) may not qualify under the autism category as defined by the federal regulations but may qualify under the other health impairments category. Infants and toddlers (birth to 3) may be declared eligible for early intervention (EI) services based on less specific categories (e.g., developmental delay) and less reliance on norm-referenced standardized testing. See also diagnosis, disability, early intervention (EI), norm-referenced assessment, special education.
Catherine M. Marcell

elimination diet

See diet therapy, food intolerance.

embedded skills

Skills within naturally occurring activities that allow opportunities to practice goals and objectives that are included in naturally occurring activities (e.g., to practice counting, children could count the number of students present each day). Embedding can occur within routines or within child-initiated, teacher-directed, or planned activities. See also ecological approach, naturalistic interventions.
Nancy P. Rapp

emotional support

Assistance received through family relationships, friendships, and partnerships with professionals who specialize in therapeutic support and human services. Professional support can be provided by social workers, medical doctors, counselors, or psychologists. Emotional support can be provided to individuals with disabilities by their caregivers. *See also* positive behavior support (PBS), respite care, Sibshops.
Britta Saltonstall

empiricism

Reliance on experience and factual information, rather than theory, authority, or testimonials. Other related terms include *evidence-based practice* and *empirically validated treatments* (Kazdin, 2001). Empirical, objective observation is the basis for scientific study. Empirical studies typically include controlled methodologies (e.g., subjects are randomly selected and/or observers are trained) and offer stronger evidence of an intervention's effectiveness than those that are nonempirical. Numerous methods proposed for treating autism do not have an empirical evidence basis and are not generally accepted by the professional community. *See also* data, evidence based, pseudoscience.
John T. Neisworth & Pamela S. Wolfe

encopresis

Repeated passages of formed or semiformed stool in a child's clothing, on the floor, or other inappropriate places. Encopresis is most often involuntary, but occasionally the behavior appears to be intentional. To be diagnosed with encopresis, the child must be at least 4 years of age and the behavior cannot be due to a medical condition. The frequency of the inappropriate behavior must occur at least once per month for at least 3 months (Geroski & Rodgers, 1998). Encopresis can be classified as primary or secondary. Primary encopresis occurs when the child with encopresis has reached age 4 without having bowel control for at least 1 year. Secondary encopresis occurs when the child has had at least 1 year of bowel control before the current episode of encopresis began (Peterson, Reach, & Grabe, 2003). Treatments include medical intervention (e.g., use of laxatives, high-fiber diets) and applied behavior analysis (ABA) (e.g., prompting, shaping, reinforcement). *See also* enuresis.
Janelle Matesic

engagement

Engagement is "sustained attention to an activity or person" (National Research Council, Division of Behavioral and Social Sciences and Education,

Committee on Educational Interventions for Children with Autism, 2001, p. 160). Researchers have evaluated the effects of instructional strategies for children with autism on engagement and have documented increased academic and task engagement with use of specialized methods, such as photographic activity schedules, self-monitoring, and cooperative group learning. Researchers have also evaluated social and language strategies and have shown that social stimulation, peer-directed pivotal response training, peer tutoring, peer imitation, script fading, and choice making increase social and language engagement. Despite the recognition of active engagement as critical, why only about 50% of children with autism benefit from specialized early intervention (EI) approaches is unclear; therefore, efforts in engagement research may improve outcomes for all children with autism. *See also* direct instruction, fluency.
Lisa A. Ruble

entrepreneurial model
Model of employment in which manufacturing services or subcontract operation arrangements are owned or operated by individuals with disabilities. *See also* supported employment program.
Lynn Atanasoff

enuresis
Repeated passage of urine during the day or at night into the bed, clothes, or other inappropriate places. Enuresis is most often involuntary and may occur when the child is asleep, awake, or both. To be diagnosed with enuresis the child must be at least 5 years of age and the voiding cannot be due to any organic dysfunction. The frequency of inappropriate voiding must occur two times per week for at least 3 months or must cause clinically significant distress or impairment in functioning (Geroski & Rodgers, 1998). There are two main types of enuresis: nocturnal and diurnal. Nocturnal enuresis, commonly known as bed wetting, is the involuntary passage of urine during the night while asleep. Diurnal enuresis is the involuntary passage of urine when awake during the day. It is not uncommon for children to have both types of enuresis (e.g., mixed nocturnal and diurnal enuresis). In addition, enuresis is typically divided into two categories: primary and secondary. With primary enuresis, the child has never had a significant period of dryness since birth. Secondary enuresis is the return of inappropriate voidance after at least 6 months of dryness (Klein, 2001). The majority of children diagnosed with enuresis display both primary and noc-

turnal forms. Medical assessments typically are conducted to rule out biological causes such as infections. Treatment can include medications or applied behavior analysis (ABA). *See also* encopresis.
Janelle Matesic

environmental stressors

Physical factors that elicit an integrated hormonal, immunologic, neurological, and behavioral stress response to reduce potentially injurious or aversive effects of the stressor. Detectable biological or behavioral illness occurs when a stressor exceeds an individual's adaptive capabilities by quantity, by quality (e.g., route of intake, chemical makeup), or by duration. Resistance to disease is a complex summation of genetic endowment, experiential factors, and the nature and context of stressor presentation. For example, as mercury exposure increases in a population, the susceptibility to mercury toxicity is determined by genetics (e.g., variability in proteins such as enzymes affecting absorption, excretion, biochemical sequestration, tissue vulnerability), experiential factors (e.g., vitamin deficiencies and supplementation, previous exposures to other heavy metals), and the current context of exposure (e.g., age, concurrent illness, chelation intervention, the chemical form of mercury). When an environmental stressor is present at a low level, individuals react in greatly variable ways; when the stressor is much greater, more individuals are affected and are affected in more similar ways. Both primary stressors and an organism's attempt to adapt to them may lead to physiological and behavioral changes that allow previously harmless or mildly noxious substances to become secondary stressors with amplified toxicity (e.g., stress-caused damage to the blood–brain barrier and intestinal mucosal surfaces permit increased opioid peptide absorption and access to central neurons, effectively turning certain foods, such as wheat, into environmental stressors). The complex central nervous system (CNS) dysfunctions underlying the behaviors associated with autism very likely extend to other critical CNS integrative activities, including distortions in the recognition of and response to stressors, and the creation of multiple secondary stressors (which may partially explain why the hypotheses of what causes autism are so numerous). Even though doing so may not address the fundamental cause or causes of autism, it is reasonable to reduce or eliminate the burden of environmental stressors if the amelioration of symptoms substantially outweighs the effort and social stress of environmental change.
Robert A. Da Prato

EO
See establishing operation.

epidemiology
The study of the origin of, determinants of, distribution of, trends in, and protective factors related to disease. Groups of affected individuals are studied in order to identify plausible contributors and deterrents to a disease. The epidemiology of autism remains unclear, but investigations of reported higher-incidence locales of autism and possible relationships to environmental stressors or genetic links are underway or proposed. *See also* environmental stressors, genetic factors, incidence, prevalence.
John T. Neisworth & Pamela S. Wolfe

epilepsy
A pattern of recurrent seizures with characteristic electroencephalogram (EEG) findings. A seizure is a sudden and excessive discharge of electrical energy in the brain that affects consciousness and/or motor and sensory functioning (Freeman, 1979). Seizures are thought to be genetically based (Curatolo, Arpino, Stazi, & Medda, 1995). Seizures may vary with regard to duration, frequency, onset (triggered by an unexpected stimulus or by a predictable stimulus), movements (e.g., major convulsions, minor tics), causes (e.g., brain infection, trauma), associated disabilities, or control (full or partial control from medications). There are various epilepsy syndromes, which involve seizures of different types. Seizures can be divided into two basic types: partial, or focal, seizures and generalized seizures (Freeman, 1979). Seizures are more common in children with autism than in typical age peers and are associated with increased severity of autism (Gilberg, 1991). *See also* electroencephalogram (EEG), psychoactive medications, seizures.
Kathryn Craig

equinus gait
See toe walking.

error correction
Systematic provision of consequences following incorrect or undesired responses, particularly incorrect responses to instructional stimuli. Effective error-correction procedures promote more rapid, accurate, enduring, and fluent skill acquisition. Error-correction procedures fall into two general categories: *errorless* methodologies, in which students are always provided with

prompting to ensure a correct response, and methodologies that involve specific consequences for incorrect responses, such as no-no-prompt (NNP) procedures, in which the first two incorrect responses are followed by a flatly stated *no*, the absence of reinforcement, and a termination of the learning trial. Proponents of errorless methods suggest that these methods are more reinforcing and do not permit students to learn an error. Proponents of NNP procedures suggest that errorless methods may lead to prompt dependency. Hybrid approaches to error correction use errorless methods during skill acquisition and then implement NNP procedures as skill acquisition progresses. *See also* fluency, prompting.
Thomas P. Kitchen

escape training

Training that occurs when an increase of behavior succeeds in terminating an aversive event. For example, if a child escapes an unwanted instructional demand by having a tantrum or by hitting, those escape behaviors will be strengthened. Many maladaptive behaviors (e.g., self-injury, aggression) are produced or maintained through unintentional escape training. Escape training has been used to motivate children to acquire constructive behavior (e.g., release from a time-out condition contingent on the child stating the rule that was violated). *See also* functional behavior assessment (FBA).
John T. Neisworth & Pamela S. Wolfe

establishing operation (EO)

Any change in the environment that alters the strength of a reinforcer and thus the strength of the behavior that is supported by the reinforcer. *Establishing operation* is a more technical term than and subsumes the older term *setting event*. EOs center on the relationship between motivation and behavior. The reinforcing effect of consequences can be enhanced or diminished (thereby changing the probability of behavior) by manipulating a relevant EO. The term is synonymous with *motivating operation*. For example, a person's request for food is likely to be greater several hours before, instead of immediately following, a meal; in this case, food deprivation is an EO for the behavior that results in getting food. A child who displays challenging behaviors to gain attention from adults may do so more in a group situation if he or she had previously been alone for a long time. In this case, the EO is social isolation. EOs are related to states of deprivation (reinforcer value increases) and satiation (reinforcer value decreases). In educational environments, manipulation of an EO can be viewed as an antecedent intervention

(Luiselli & Cameron, 1998). *See also* antecedent-behavior-consequence (ABC) analysis, reinforcement, setting events.
James K. Luiselli

ESY services
See extended school year services.

ethics
In the helping professions, rules, moral standards, and principles that govern professional conduct (Kenyon, 1999). Ethical decisions may occur in the course of work with individuals with disabilities, such as ensuring human rights. Professional organizations (e.g., American Speech-Language-Hearing Association [ASHA], Behavior Analyst Certification Board® [BACB®]) typically have statements of ethics and ethical conduct that set standards for their members. *See also* best practice guidelines.
Britta Saltonstall

etiology
The science and study of the causes of diseases and disorders. The etiology of autism and other pervasive developmental disorders (PDDs) is not clear, but accumulating evidence suggests a neurological basis that may relate to inheritable factors. Environmental stressors are also implicated as possibly contributing to the etiology of autism and other PDDs, in that stressors may trigger PDDs in individuals with otherwise subthreshold predispositions for the disorders. *See also* environmental stressors, epidemiology.
Devender R. Banda

evaluation
See assessment.

evaluation report
Report of a multidisciplinary evaluation (MDE) of a child, including demographic information, reason for referral, educational history, information from the family, behavioral observations, assessment results, present levels of performance, recommendations (including educational needs of the child, areas of delay, and skill needs), conclusions (including disability category), and signatures of all who provided assessment data, including parents. The evaluation report is completed before an individualized education program

(IEP) is written and periodically thereafter. *See also* individualized education program (IEP), multidisciplinary evaluation (MDE).
Donna Meloy

evidence based

Pertaining to practices or materials that have been subjected to objective, publicly verifiable examination of their effectiveness with specified people or groups. Judgments of what research reports or information constitute evidence are a complex matter and involve much professional agreement based on rigorous and clear criteria. Specific methodologies for gathering, analyzing, and summarizing existing research literature are available in a variety of fields of inquiry. For example, the Early Intervention Program of the New York State Department of Health (DOH) used

> An evidenced-based, multidisciplinary consensus panel approach. The methodology used for these guidelines was established by the Agency for Health Care Policy and Research (AHCPR [now the Agency for Healthcare Research and Quality]). The DOH selected the AHCPR model for this effort because it is an effective, scientific, and well-tested approach to guideline development. (1999a, p. xi)

It may be the case that some treatments do not pass muster as scientific evidence but may sometimes be effective with some individuals; however, consumers of interventions should be wary of treatment claims and should seek the evidence base (empirical data) for such claims. *See also* empiricism, experimental design, pseudoscience, single subject, testimonial.
John T. Neisworth & Pamela S. Wolfe

exceptionality

Any significant departure from typical development that is recognized as making the individual eligible for special services and/or therapy. Exceptionality can encompass lower than average development (lower IQ in the mental retardation range) or higher than average development (higher IQ in the intellectually gifted range). Typically, exceptionality is identified through multidimensional assessment, which includes standardized assessment, direct observation, and caregiver interviews. Federal law does not require states to provide special education services for children who are identified as gifted but does require states to provide services for children identified as having lower-than-average development. *See also* assessment, diagnosis, eligibility.
John T. Neisworth & Pamela S. Wolfe

executive functions

Higher-order cognitive abilities such as planning with regard to long-term consequences, choosing and initiating goal-directed behaviors, sustaining and dividing attention, correcting and modifying behaviors in response to environmental changes, generating multiple response alternatives, and organizing. While it has been suggested that executive function deficits are evident in individuals with autism, the literature remains mixed as to the nature of the specific deficits and whether or not these deficits are central to autism (Hughes, 2001). Neuroimaging research (e.g., some of the research being conducted by the federally funded Collaborative Programs of Excellence in Autism [CPEA] network; see Appendix B) is designed to explore further the role of executive function in individuals with autism. *See also* cognitive processes.

Garland Jones

experimental design

Plan for examining the effects of a variable (e.g., a procedure, set of materials, medication). Some designs help to make interpretation of results more clear than other designs. A simple before–after design is fraught with problems in interpreting results: There is no control or comparison condition and no manipulation of the experimental variable. For example, taking a pill when experiencing fatigue then feeling more energetic does not provide convincing evidence that the pill itself was responsible for the change. Numerous reports of improvement in behaviors associated with autism have been based on before–after designs (e.g., rub a secretin compound on a child's hands, then observe whether there is improved behavior). The credibility of interventions is also compromised by how results are measured and reported. Biases, expectations, and incentives may alter actual observations. When feasible, experimental designs should allow participants to be randomly assigned to treatment groups or control groups, for the control group to be given a placebo (that appears to be the treatment but is not, e.g., a sugar pill), for observers to be "blind" to who is actually getting treatment or placebo, and for results to be objectively appraised. Both single-subject and group designs are available that help to reduce or rule out threats to the validity of results. Field research in autism is difficult, and experimental designs are often compromised due to the realities of real-life circumstances. Nevertheless, parents and professionals should carefully examine the experimental design and evidence basis for any explicit or implicit claims concerning the efficacy of an intervention. Autism treatment suggestions, unfortunately, often rest on sus-

pect, dubious, nonexperimental reports. *See also* bias, control condition, pseudoscience, single subject, validity.
John T. Neisworth & Pamela S. Wolfe

expressive language

The production (output) of language that serves to communicate with others. Expressive language may be verbal (spoken) and/or nonverbal (gestures, use of symbols, pictures). Development expressive language almost always follows receptive language development. Typically, children at 18 months express about 50 recognizable words; at 24 months, about 200. Most of these words refer to concrete things that serve to operate on the social environment (e.g., "No!" "Mommy," "juice"). About 75% of children with autism do not evidence socially accepted expressive language but develop actions or vocalizations that function to obtain or avoid things or events. In these cases, a child's actions, often challenging behaviors such as hitting, screaming, and so forth, do indeed serve to communicate and thus may be seen as a form of expression. *See* challenging behavior, receptive language.
John T. Neisworth & Pamela S. Wolfe

extended school year (ESY) services

Special education or related services provided at no cost to the parents outside of the standard schedule of approximately 180 school days per year for the purpose of ensuring a free appropriate public education (FAPE) to an eligible student (Assistance to States, 2003, § 300.9). The Individuals with Disabilities Education Act (IDEA) Amendments of 1997 (PL 105-17) mandate that ESY services be considered annually for every school-age child with a disability. Each child's individual education program (IEP) team determines the child's eligibility for ESY services. The ESY program does not have to be a continuation of the student's school program, nor is it required for every student. Eligibility is individually determined. *See also* free appropriate public education (FAPE), individualized education program (IEP), Individuals with Disabilities Education Act (IDEA).
Michele M. Trettel

extinction

Weakening or cessation of a behavior resulting from the absence of reinforcement that has been responsible for supporting the behavior. If a person's behavior is no longer reinforced, that behavior eventually weakens. While extinction can be an effective way to reduce undesirable behaviors, it can be difficult to accurately identify the reinforcer and withhold it; furthermore, there may be multiple reinforcers for a given behavior, and withholding only one of several reinforcers will not decrease the unwanted behavior. (It should be noted that extinction is the withholding, *not the removing*, of a reinforcer; removing reinforcer is a form of negative punishment sometimes referred to as *response cost*. Finally, behavior on extinction typically intensifies before diminishing. *See also* punishment, reinforcement, reinforcer, response cost.

Raphael Bernier

eye gaze

The intentional direction of visual attention, or looking behavior. Eye gaze is studied using a variety of methods, such as monitoring looking behavior during interactions, coding videotapes, and using sophisticated technology to record the movements of an individual's eyes. Eye gaze has been studied primarily within the context of social interactions (social gaze, eye contact). Individuals with autism often exhibit great difficulty in making or keeping eye contact, often refusing to maintain eye contact or a gaze at anyone or at anything (Volkmar, 1996). Some individuals with autism evidently make great use of their peripheral vision, completing tasks without apparently looking at them. Eye contact problems are especially evident in joint attention situations (Mundy, Sigman, Ungerer, & Sherman, 1986). Lack of eye gaze constitutes a significant difficulty in nonverbal communication and social relations. Such problems with eye gaze are not to be confused with reticence or extreme shyness. Some children with autism and other pervasive developmental disorders (PDDs) do make spontaneous eye contact. Furthermore, appropriate eye contact skills can be taught. Some research has addressed more basic properties of eye gaze within this group. Individuals with autism have been shown to exhibit abnormal frequencies of eye movement during looking behavior and difficulties during orienting, disengaging, and shifting of visual attention. *See also* joint attention, social gaze.

James McPartland

face recognition

The skill to discriminate specific faces even though the basic featural config-
uration of all faces is the same. An area of the brain (right fusiform gyrus)
has been identified as the *fusiform face area* (FFA) due to its specialized role in
the processing of faces (Puce, Allison, Gore, & McCarthy, 1995). Individuals
with autism have considerably greater difficulty recognizing faces than individuals with typical development and individuals with other developmental
delays. Hypoactivation of the FFA in individuals with autism spectrum disorders (ASDs) is one of the first replicated neurofunctional markers of ASD
(Schultz et al., 2000). Impairment in face processing is part of the broader
impairments in social relatedness observed in individuals with autism. *See also*
eye gaze, fusiform gyrus, social gaze, social impairment.
Diana L. Robins

face validity

See validity.

facial gyrus

See fusiform gyrus.

facilitated communication (FC)

A communication method in which a child's hand is supported by a facilitator to type out messages on a keyboard or other communication device. A
hand-over-hand position is often used, with a facilitator holding the child's
hand with the child's index finger extended; occasionally the support is as
minimal as touching the child's elbow or shoulder. The theory is that children with autism, even those who test as having severe mental retardation,
may have normal cognitive and communication abilities that they cannot
express due to motor problems and that FC unlocks their ability to communicate (Biklen, 1993). Controlled experiments do not support this

position (Mostert, 2001) and generally show that communication signifi-cantly above what the child can do through other modalities originates from the facilitator and not the child. It should be noted, however, that some individuals with autism comprehend and express more through writing than speaking. *See also* communication disorder.
Deborah Fein

fading

The gradual reduction of prompts or cues over time or trials with the goal that prompts are no longer needed to elicit a correct response. For example, a child traces a letter depicted by a dark, heavy line; gradually the line may be made thinner until the child writes the letter independently. Instruction for individuals with autism should address how fading will occur to avoid prompt dependency. *See also* prompt hierarchy, prompting.
Valerie J. Postal

false-belief paradigm

Task used to assess theory of mind (ToM) in children during early childhood. ToM involves the ability to infer the thoughts, desires, emotions, and inten-tions of oneself and of others that motivate people into action. In the false-belief task, a child is told about or sees someone who hides an object in one location and then momentarily leaves the room. While the first person is out of the room, a second person moves the object to a different location. When the first person returns to the room, the child is asked where he or she thinks that first person believes the object is. For a child to respond correctly, he or she must differentiate between where he or she knows the object is (in its new location) and where the first person believes the object is (where the character originally hid it) (Harris, 2000a). When a child successfully com-pletes the false-belief task, he or she is thought to be aware that different individuals can have different beliefs about a situation or, more specifically, that one's belief can be different from someone else's. Between the ages of 3 and 5 years, an increasing proportion of typically developing children are able to successfully complete this false-belief task. Individuals with autism have great difficulty in understanding and reading the emotions of others and are unable to take another's perspective and thus have difficulty with the false-belief paradigm. *See also* mindblindness, theory of mind (ToM).
Judith F. Chan

FAPE

See free appropriate public education.

FBA
See functional behavior assessment.

FC
See facilitated communication.

FCT
See functional communication training.

Feingold diet
A diet free of salicylates, food colorings, and artificial flavoring intended for treating hyperactivity. The notion that food can have an effect on behavior grew popular in 1973 when allergist Benjamin F. Feingold, M.D., published *Introduction to Clinical Allergy,* which discussed the Feingold diet. Feingold's diet did not eliminate sugar specifically but focused on food additives. Refined sugar, however, also has been typically excluded as part of the diet. There is no convincing evidence supporting the use of the Feingold or other special diets for autism treatment; to the contrary, such diets may be deficient in nutrients and may be costly. *See also* diet therapy.
John T. Neisworth & Pamela S. Wolfe

figurative language
Expressions that use words or phrases that create an impression or represent an abstract concept but that cannot be interpreted literally. For example, the expression *James ran his heart out* cannot be accepted at face value. Figurative expressions cannot be learned as part of a rule system; they are instead acquired through continual use with their meanings inferred from the context. Types of figurative language include idioms (*It is raining cats and dogs*), metaphors (*He often hatched new ideas*), similes (*She could run like the wind*), and proverbs (*People who live in glass houses should not throw stones*). Children with autism have great difficulty with figurative expressions and usually interpret them as literal statements. *See also* concrete language.
Lynn Adams

fine motor skills
Movements that require the use of small muscles necessary for dexterity in tasks requiring precision such as grasping and manipulating small items

(e.g., holding a pencil, using scissors, using fasteners for dressing activities) and other tasks of daily living. *See also* activities of daily living (ADLs), gross motor skills, occupational therapy (OT), visual-motor.
Denise Lynn Schilling

floortime

An approach originally designed to build affective relationships between caregivers and children who have multisystem developmental disorder (MSDD; ZERO TO THREE's Diagnostic Classification Task Force, 1994), which consists of communication and/or social difficulties like those found in autism (Greenspan, 1992a, 1992b). Several steps are described in the floortime approach to support a child's social and affective development. Adults get down on the floor, follow the child's lead, play with the child to elaborate and enhance pretend play, and establish mutual respect and interpersonal warmth. Floortime is both a philosophy and an approach. The goals of floortime are encouraging attention and intimacy, two-way communication, expression and use of feelings and ideas, and logical thought. *See also* circle of communication; Developmental, Individual-Difference, Relationship-Based (DIR) model; *Diagnostic Classification of Mental Health Disorders of Infancy and Early Childhood (DC: 0-3)*; multisystem developmental disorder (MSDD).
John T. Neisworth & Pamela S. Wolfe

fluency

Performance of a behavior or series of behaviors with high degrees of accuracy and speed. Three critical learning outcomes occur with fluency or fluent behavior: retention, endurance, and application (Binder, 1996). Behaviors are practiced until they are fluent have both clinical and educational significance. New skills taught to children with autism can be brought to fluency to ensure greater retention and utility of the skills in natural settings. For example, individuals with autism may be taught multiplication facts and then practice until they are fluent. Fluency training can occur with a variety of skills and domains (e.g., greetings, domestic skills, academics). *See also* generalization.
Richard M. Kubina, Jr.

fMRI

See functional magnetic resonance imaging.

food intolerance

Adverse effects attributed to foods that are not caused by immune system mechanisms. By convention, *food intolerance* is distinguished from *food allergy*, a term which is restricted to adverse reactions to foods mediated solely by immune system components, such as antibodies. Although there is anecdotal support for the concept of foods as aggravating factors in autism, professional acceptance is minimal. This is partially due to the mechanisms causing food intolerance, which, unlike those of food allergy, are mostly unknown or controversial, and partially due to the highly idiosyncratic reactions attributed to patient-specific combinations of foods, which do not lend themselves to confirmation by group studies. There are many sources available that describe food elimination methods of testing for food intolerances. Although conceptually simple, in practice the diagnosis of food intolerance is tedious, and adherence to various food prohibitions carries its own social and nutritional stresses. Improvement in behaviors related to autism should be obvious, marked, and sustained to justify rigid dietary restrictions. *See also* allergy, diet therapy.

Robert A. Da Prato

fragile X syndrome

An X-linked chromosomal disorder resulting from a break at the distal end of the X chromosome, visible only with special laboratory techniques. Children with fragile X syndrome often have temperament qualities similar to individuals with autism, with some differences. Language delay and dysfunction, especially echolalia, are evident, as are shyness; avoidance of gaze; stereotypic hand flapping; impaired social interaction; hyperactivity; poor attention focus; anxieties; and obsessive behaviors, including skin picking (Wassink, Piven, & Patil, 2001). Physical characteristics include a large head circumference, narrow face, prominent forehead, large ears, hyperextensibility of joints, and decreased muscle tone. Cognitive skills for boys are usually mildly to moderately impaired. Girls are usually not as severely affected because the abnormal X chromosome is partly balanced by the unaffected X. Skill levels in individuals with fragile X syndrome range from mild cognitive impairment to above average, with specific impairments in math skills and, often, a predisposition to anxiety and depression in adulthood.

The overlap between fragile X syndrome and autism is well recognized. While only a few children with autism have fragile X syndrome, a significant proportion of children with fragile X syndrome meet some or all of the diagnostic criteria for autism (Meyer & Batshaw, 2002). Most

clinicians note a similarity in behavioral characteristics, but they are distinguishable by physical examination or behavioral qualities. Although boys with fragile X syndrome exhibit gaze avoidance, giving the impression of shyness, they are often quite easily engaged and are rarely as aloof as most children with autism. *See also* genetic factors.
Jeanette C. Ramer

free appropriate public education (FAPE)

Special education and related services that meet the standards of the state educational agency (SEA), are provided in conformity with the individualized education program (IEP), and are provided at public expense to preschool through high school students (Assistance to States, 2003, § 300.13). The term *appropriate* means that the education that a student with a disability receives addresses specific educational needs; therefore, FAPE may be different for each student with a disability because what is considered appropriate for one student may not be considered appropriate for another (National Information Center for Children and Youth with Disabilities, 1997). The regulations for the Individuals with Disabilities Education Act (IDEA) Amendments of 1997 (PL 105-17) indicate that FAPE must thus be based on a student's unique needs, not on a disability label or category (Assistance to States, 2003, § 300.300[a][3][ii]). *See also* Individuals with Disabilities Education Act (IDEA), least restrictive environment (LRE), state educational agency (SEA).
Catherine M. Marcell

functional behavior assessment (FBA)

An approach that incorporates a variety of techniques and strategies to diagnose the causes (functions) and identify likely interventions to address challenging behaviors (Durand, 1990). FBA generally is considered a team problem-solving process that relies on a variety of techniques and strategies to identify the purposes of specific behavior and to help individualized education program (IEP) teams to select appropriate interventions to directly address them. A major objective is to learn how best to promote student behavior that serves the same function as current behavior but that is more socially acceptable and responsible. FBA looks beyond the behavior itself and focuses on identifying significant social, sensory, physical, affective, cognitive, and/or environmental factors associated with the occurrence (and nonoccurrence) of specific behaviors (Nelson, Roberts, & Smith, 1998). Assessments include structured interviews, observations, motivational scales, checklists,

and recording situational factors surrounding a problem behavior (e.g., antecedent and consequent events). Once a function has been identified, behaviors and skills are taught to the student that serve the same function but are more socially acceptable. FBA is often a highly informative procedure (and required as part of the IEP) for identifying the functions of challenging behaviors of children with autism so that alternative behaviors may be taught. *See also* antecedent, consequence, functional communication training (FCT), functionally equivalent alternative behavior, individualized education program (IEP).
Lisa A. Husar

functional communication training (FCT)

A procedure used to reduce challenging behaviors by assessing the consequences maintaining the challenging behaviors then providing the same consequences for a different constructive behavior. The procedure is a form of functional behavior assessment (FBA) but focuses on communication. It is assumed that if individuals can gain access to desired consequences more effectively with the new acceptable behavior, they will use the new behavior and reduce their use of the undesirable one (Durand, 1999; Durand & Carr, 1992). For example, if an individual bangs his head and this results in escape from a task, a functionally equivalent alternative response would be to teach the child to request a break. Depending on the verbal ability of the individual, this could take a number of forms (e.g., pointing to the word *break,* saying "break," signing BREAK). The second component of functional communication training involves making the problem behavior nonfunctional by not intervening in any way when the individual engages in the problem behavior, resulting in the loss of effect on others of the unwanted behavior. This procedure in particular and FCT in general are useful in reducing problematic social behavior with children with autism and in replacing it with socially functional behavior. Communication training should be applied simultaneously to achieve optimal success. FCT is an empirically validated intervention that has been successfully used with individuals displaying a wide array of problem behaviors (e.g., self-injurious behavior [SIB], aggression, psychotic talk) (Mirenda, 1997; Reichle, York, & Sigafoos, 1991). *See also* challenging behavior, functional behavior assessment (FBA), functionally equivalent alternative behavior.
Melissa L. Zona, Kristin V. Christodulu, & V. Mark Durand

functional goals

Outcomes that support the child's ability to function independently in natural environments (e.g., sorting colored blocks may be nonfunctional,

whereas sorting clothes of different colors may be functional in order to learn laundry skills). *See also* activities of daily living (ADLs), age appropriate.
Marilyn Hoyson

functional limitations

Problems engaging in everyday activities that are of importance to an individual. People can have limitations in their abilities without those limitations interfering with daily functions. For example, a person might have poor endurance that limits speed of walking. If it does not matter how fast the person gets to a destination, this limitation would not interfere with function. If being on time is important to the daily activity, however, poor endurance could contribute to reduced function and be considered a functional limitation. *See also* activities of daily living (ADLs), functional outcomes.
Winnie Dunn

functional magnetic resonance imaging (fMRI)

A method used to display brain function by displaying changes in chemical composition of brain areas or changes in the flow of fluids that occur over time spans of seconds to minutes. FMRI is often done as part of the assessment of children with autism and/or with seizures. The method can also be used to study the physiology of other organs (studying blood flow to pathological organs, thus helping us to understand the disease process). In the brain, blood flow is presumably related to neural activity, so fMRI, like other imaging techniques such as positron emission tomography (PET), can be used to monitor the brain functions when people perform specific tasks or are exposed to specific stimuli. *See also* magnetic resonance imaging (MRI), positron emission tomography (PET).
Devender R. Banda

functional outcomes

Results that indicate progress and have utility for the person and his or her family. Outcomes are deemed functional by the individual and family. Outcomes are not considered functional if, although progress is indicated, they do not have an apparent impact on the individual's participation in daily life. A person can have a measured increase in strength or range of motion in a limb without these changes being enough to affect function (e.g., not enough range of motion in the ankle to take a step). *See also* activities of daily living (ADLs), functional limitations, social validity.
Winnie Dunn

functional protest training

Teaching an individual an appropriate way to protest an activity or condition that is undesired by the individual. Functional protest training, for example, can be teaching someone to request a temporary break from an activity. This type of training is especially helpful for children whose functional analyses indicate that their behavior is maintained by negative reinforcement (escape). *See also* escape training, reinforcement.
Thomas P. Kitchen

functionally equivalent alternative behavior

A behavior that is taught to replace an unwanted behavior that has the same function as the unwanted behavior. When the function of the behavior is determined, an alternate behavior is chosen. The replacement behavior can be verbal or nonverbal (Durand & Carr, 1992). For example, if a student's challenging behavior (e.g., pulling his or her hair) is assessed and found to be maintained by escape from a difficult task, a functionally equivalent alternative behavior would be a verbal request for assistance with the task (e.g., "I need help"). *See also* challenging behavior, functional behavior assessment (FBA), functional communication training (FCT).
Melissa L. Zona, Kristin V. Christodulu, & V. Mark Durand

functions of behavior

There are two central functions of behavior: to get or obtain (e.g., objects, sensory input) or to avoid or escape (e.g., settings, people, tasks). For example, if a child purposely falls off a chair in class, the behavior may function to obtain social attention. The goal of functional behavioral assessment (FBA) and analyses is to identify the functions of behavior so that behavior can be understood and a replacement behavior or skill can be taught. *See also* functional behavioral assessment (FBA), functional communication training (FCT).
Mark T. Harvey & Craig H. Kennedy

functions of communication

Uses or purposes of communication. Functions of communication include requesting (e.g., "I want the ball"), attracting attention (e.g., "Look at me"), greeting or closing (e.g., "hello," "goodbye"), regulating others (e.g., "Give me a cookie"), commenting (e.g., "I like your shirt"), and protesting (e.g., "No!"). *See also* functional communication training (FCT), functions of behavior.
Lynn Adams

fusiform gyrus

Also called the *facial gyrus*. The part of the brain, extending over the temporal and occipital lobes, that recognizes the facial area. Individuals with autism often have difficulty in face recognition, which is critical for interpersonal relationships. Some research has indicated that individuals with autism fail to engage the fusiform face area (FFA) during face discrimination tasks (Schultz et al., 2000). FFA activation level may predict the degree of social impairment and can distinguish individuals with autism from those with Asperger syndrome (AS) and pervasive developmental disorder-not otherwise specified (PDD-NOS). *See also* amygdala, face recognition.
John T. Neisworth & Pamela S. Wolfe

Gg

general case programming (GCP)

A generalization strategy that involves the use of numerous and varied examples of a wanted behavior to ensure students will be able to perform the behavior in various circumstances. For example, teaching students how to use only one type of vending machine may not result in their being able to operate all vending machines with which they come into contact. When students are provided instruction with a variety of machines, they are more likely able to operate other and different machines not included in the instruction. GCP has been used for individuals with autism (Baer, 1999). *See also* generalization.

Charles A. Hughes

generalization

Effects of training beyond the conditions in which training took place. This is contrasted with *discrimination,* in which behaviors occur only in the presence of specific conditions. Individuals with autism often have difficulty generalizing skills when training takes place in settings that are controlled and restricted. Thus, teaching skills across settings (generalization) is an exceedingly important part of instruction for individuals with autism. *See also* discrimination, general case programming (GCP).

Richard J. Cowan

genetic factors

Factors related to the parental hereditary material contributed at conception. There is considerable evidence to support a genetic hypothesis for the etiology of some forms of autism. Genetic epidemiology studies, which base their quantitative models on the family patterns of autism, indicate that autism is passed from generation to generation; among these are twin studies that strongly support the presence of heritable factors. Specific genes for autism, however, have not yet been confirmed, nor have subtypes of autism with different causes been identified, although significant molecular genetic research

is focusing on these issues. It is likely that many genes come into play in the etiology of autism and other pervasive developmental disorders (PDDs), and that there are distinct subtypes with different causal factors. Indeed, there are several recognized medical conditions that share behavioral symptoms of autism (e.g., Rett disorder, childhood disintegrative disorder [CDD]). A defect in a single gene might not necessarily result in a full expression of autism or another PDD per se, but rather in a less extreme form of the disorder (e.g., perhaps Asperger syndrome [AS]). *See also* Asperger syndrome (AS), childhood disintegrative disorder (CDD), heredity, pervasive developmental disorder (PDD), Rett disorder, twin studies in autism.
Curtis K. Deutsch

genotype

Units of heredity (genes) that are arranged on chromosomes (normally 46 chromosomes in the human). Each person's genotype is different (identical twins have essentially the same). Numerous disorders (e.g., Down syndrome) are related to gene abnormalities; however, there is no current evidence that autism is a genetic disorder, nor are there genetic markers or signs for autism. There appears to be some research regarding the heritability of autism characteristics, that is, a familial association wherein parents or grandparents of children with autism are likely to show some aspects of autism (Piven, Palmer, Jacobi, Childress, & Arndt, 1997). *See also* phenotype.
John T. Neisworth & Pamela S. Wolfe

giftedness

Exceptional performance in one or more areas of human activity characterized by *precocity* (i.e., earlier than average acquisition of skills or knowledge and faster than average learning) and *high level of motivation* (e.g., interest and intense focus in the area of interest). There are two kinds of giftedness: *global* (manifested in exceptional general mental ability and outstanding academic performance) and *specific* (manifested in exceptional ability in specific domains, e.g., athletics, mathematics, dance). Giftedness is usually based on standardized measures of intelligence (i.e., IQ of 135 and higher), scores from domain-specific achievement tests, and teacher rating scales. Assessment of giftedness in specific domains outside academics (e.g., arts, athletics) is also based on observation and analysis of products and performance in tasks representative of the specific domain. A small number of individuals who have subaverage IQ may also evidence remarkable specific ability. The terms *gift-*

edness and *talent* are often used interchangeably. Children with autism may exhibit giftedness and talent (Heller, Mönks, Sternberg, & Subotnik, 2000). *See also* intelligence tests, savant syndrome, splinter skills.

Ljiljana Vuletic

Gilles de la Tourette syndrome

See Tourette disorder.

gluten free

Pertaining to food products that do not contain gluten, or proteins found in wheat. A person who is allergic to gluten may experience upset stomach, rash, hay fever, asthma, and even anaphylaxis after eating foods containing gluten and thus should avoid consuming any products with gluten (Grayson, 2004). Processed foods may contain wheat flour. Labels should be checked as manufacturers occasionally change recipes. Many gluten-free products are now available and are often labeled as such. *See also* antigluten therapy, diet therapy.

John T. Neisworth & Pamela S. Wolfe

graduated guidance

A technique combining physical guidance and fading in which the instructor's physical guidance is gradually faded according to the student's responsiveness (Foxx, 1982). *Graduated guidance* and *physical prompting* or *physical assistance* are different in that *graduated guidance* refers to adjustment of the amount or degree of the instructor's physical assistance (hand pressure or contact) from moment to moment, depending on the student's behavior at that time. The amount of physical assistance can vary in location (e.g., shoulder, elbow, wrist) or intensity (e.g., firm grip, gentle grip). Shadowing is a component of graduated guidance. In shadowing, the physical guidance is faded until the instructor has no physical contact with the student but is prepared to reapply graduated guidance if the desired behavior slows down or stops. The instructor shadows the student's hands by keeping his or her hands within 1 inch of the student's hands throughout the entire behavioral sequence. Graduated guidance is used to increase or decrease behavior. For example, graduated guidance is used extensively to teach dressing and toileting skills and as an integral part of the use of overcorrection to decrease toileting accidents (Foxx & Azrin, 1973). Its greatest application is in self-help skills training programs. *See also* fading, overcorrection, prompting.

Richard M. Foxx & Kimberly A. Schreck

gravitational insecurity

Overreaction to moving through space and the relationship of head position with gravity, especially when the feet are no longer in contact with the floor. Maintaining contact with the ground may be extremely important to some individuals in order to feel secure. Having an inverted, tilted head position or moving backward through space may be anxiety producing to some individuals. This is considered to be a sensory modulation disorder. Treatments can include desensitization procedures and sensory-based interventions. *See also* phobia, sensory processing.
E. (Rocky) Landers

Greenspan approach

See Developmental, Individual-Difference, Relationship-Based (DIR) model.

gross motor development quotient

An index of gross motor development equivalent to gross motor age divided by chronological age multiplied by 100. Gross motor (locomotor) development concerns muscle activity in the arms, legs, and trunk. A child's gross motor skills are assessed on developmental scales and are summarized as a gross motor age, a number equivalent to the chronological age of children who exhibit equivalent gross motor skills. Children with autism are usually well developed in gross motor areas, although some of these children may be clumsy. *See also* gross motor skills, physical therapy (PT).
Britta Alin Åkerman

gross motor skills

Movements that require the use of large muscles, including such skills as crawling, walking, running, jumping, skipping, and climbing. *See also* fine motor skills, gross motor development quotient, physical therapy (PT).
Denise Lynn Schilling

guided compliance

A technique of gradually increasing prompting based on an individual's response to compliance training. An instruction is given once. If a correct response is given, the individual is positively reinforced. If the individual does not provide the correct response, the instruction is repeated and accompanied by a greater physical prompt. (A full physical prompt may then be used.) Most-to-least prompt hierarchies are similar to guided compliance, but the goal in the latter is compliance. A large body of literature suggests that guided compliance is highly effective in reducing noncompliance in individuals with developmental disabilities (Smith & Lerman, 1999) and in remediating skill needs (Handen, Parrish, McClung, Kerwin, & Evans, 1992). Some people consider guided compliance to be an intrusive, restrictive procedure (Miltenberger & Lumley, 1997) and may argue for a less intrusive intervention. *See also* graduated guidance, prompt hierarchy, prompting. *Rachel L. Loftin*

habit reversal

A multiphase treatment procedure to help teach an individual a new behavior to replace a problematic habit. The first phase promotes awareness by teaching an individual to describe his or her own behavior and the situations in which it occurs and then to practice detecting the behaviors (self-monitoring). The next phase involves the individual's learning a new or competing behavior that is physically incompatible with the habit. A variety of motivational techniques are then used to encourage the individual's practice of the replacement behaviors. Finally, attempts are made to help the individual take the replacement behaviors from the instructional setting to school or other public settings where training has not occurred (i.e., generalization). Research has demonstrated that habit reversal procedures can be effective in treating a variety of simple and complex tics and habits sometimes seen in individuals with autism, including motor tics (e.g., head jerks), vocal tics (e.g., grunting), hair pulling, thumb sucking, nail biting, skin picking, and bruxism (i.e., teeth grinding) (Miltenberger, Fuqua, & Woods, 1998). Habit reversal procedures have not been widely investigated as a means of controlling repetitive, stereotypic behaviors (e.g., hand flapping). *See also* behavior modification, generalization.

Keith Allen & Richard J. Cowan

hair analysis

Measurement of mineral content of hair. Proponents claim that it is useful for evaluating a person's general state of nutrition and health, mineral deficiencies, mineral imbalances, or heavy metal pollutants in the body. Hair analysis is not an established or validated method. The American Medical Association opposes the use of hair analysis.

Sharise Wilson

hand regard

Repeated, continual examination of one's hand. This may be seen at an age much older than 20 weeks in a child with developmental delay (and may also occur in a blind child). Hand regard is a stereotypic behavior sometimes evidenced by individuals with autism. *See also* atypical behavior, perseveration, stereotypic behavior.

John T. Neisworth & Pamela S. Wolfe

handicap

A socially or environmentally imposed disadvantage for a given individual, resulting from impairment or a disability, that limits or prevents the fulfillment of a role that is normal. For autism, handicap occurs when participation is not allowed due to a lack of supports (adaptations and modifications) that allow for participation or when decisions are made based solely on the label of autism rather than on the child's specific, individual needs. Disallowing a child to participate in activities with other children because of the diagnosis is handicapping; furthermore, removing the child from activities due to challenging behaviors and a lack of social and communication supports is handicapping. *See also* disability, impairment.

Lisa A. Ruble

hand-over-hand assistance

A form of prompting that uses full physical assistance to show the individual how to move his or her hands or body through a task (e.g., in teaching a young child to put on a hat, the child's father might put his hand over the child's hand and gently guide her to pick up the hat and put it on her head). Individuals who are taught using only hand-over-hand assistance may become prompt dependent and may not perform desired behaviors independently. When faded out systematically, however, hand-over-hand prompting has been demonstrated to be an effective teaching strategy for individuals with autism. *See also* prompt dependence, prompt hierarchy, prompting.

Britta Saltonstall

head circumference

A measure of the greatest distance between the *glabella* (the most protrusive point between the eyebrows) and the *opisthocranion* (the most protrusive point at the back of the head, also known as the occiput) (Deutsch & Farkas, 1994). This measurement is a general indicator of development and is often

assessed during routine pediatric checkups. A tape measure is used, and normative data are used to adjust for age, sex, and ethnicity. Because head circumference is correlated with whole brain volume, head circumference is sometimes used as a marker of neural development (Aylward, Minshew, Field, Sparks, & Singh, 2002). Studies of autism have revealed an overrepresentation of both extremes—microcephaly (smaller than normal head circumference) and macrocephaly (larger than normal). Research indicates an increase in head circumference in children with autism that begins postnatally, with a subsequent deceleration in growth, resulting in normal head circumference at maturity (Courchesne, Carper, & Akshoomoff, 2003). *See also* diagnosis, psychobiology.
Curtis K. Deutsch

heavy metals
Metallic elements that have a relatively high density, are toxic at low concentrations, and tend to bioaccumulate (tissue levels continue to increase as an organism ages). Unlike metals such as iron (chemical symbol: Fe), copper (Cu), and zinc (Zn), heavy metals have no known useful biologic functions and can show toxic effects at levels attainable environmentally and medically. The most clinically important metals in this category are cadmium (Cd), lead (Pb), and mercury (Hg). The possible relevance to autism is the synergistic toxicity to the central nervous system (CNS) of heavy metals and the multiple sources of exposure to them: environmental (e.g., food, water), occupational (e.g., dust inhalation, skin contact), and medical (e.g., mercury–silver dental amalgams, organic mercury preservatives in vaccinations). The primary treatment for heavy metal toxicity is chelation, the use of various agents that preferentially bind to the metal and permit an increased rate of excretion. *See also* chelation, mercury, thimerosal, toxicology.
Robert A. Da Prato

Heller syndrome
See childhood disintegrative disorder (CDD).

heredity
The transmission of traits from one generation to the next through the genetic material of a parent. Autism and other pervasive developmental disorders (PDDs) appear to be inherited, but currently no clearly defined genetic basis is known. *See also* genetic factors, twin studies in autism.
Curtis K. Deutsch

high-functioning autism

A form of autism in which the individual's intellectual functioning is at least within the average range (i.e., IQ greater than 85). It is estimated that 20% of children with autism may be classified as having high-functioning autism (Fombonne, 1999). There is significant debate as to whether high-functioning autism (not a formal diagnosis) and Asperger syndrome (AS) are distinct. While the two disorders may be distinct regarding historical variables such as early language, behavior, and symptomatology, such differences may become insignificant in childhood and adolescence (Ozonoff, South, & Miller, 2000). *See also* Asperger syndrome (AS).
Laura Arnstein

high-technology device

Assistive technology (AT) devices that use electronic or mechanical parts. The devices can be used to perform many functions (e.g., for communication, for daily living) and may require training before use. Selection of high-technology devices should take into consideration how, where, and when the device should be used, portability, if training is necessary, and whether it is user friendly. High-technology devices are contrasted with low technology systems that do not use electronic or mechanical parts (Turnbull, Turnbull, Shank, & Smith, 2004). Individuals with autism may use high-technology devices, particularly for communication (e.g., voice output communication aids). *See also* assistive technology (AT), low-technology device.
John T. Neisworth & Pamela S. Wolfe

hippocampus

A limbic structure in the temporal lobe of the brain that governs short-term memory for facts and events, affects spatial perception and the comprehension of spatial relations, and is implicated in fear and anxiety responses. Myriad studies have examined the relations among autism spectrum disorders (ASDs), the size of the hippocampus, and the pattern of interconnections among the hippocampus and other brain structures. Results from these studies are inconsistent (Casaccia-Bonnefil et al., 1997; Dawson, Klinger, Panagiotides, Lewy, & Castelloe, 1995). For many individuals with autism, the hippocampus is atypically small and the neurons in the structure are packed densely. The number of connections to other areas of the brain is reduced as compared with the number of connections in individuals without autism. Given these conditions, some researchers link the cortical dysfunctions often associated with the disorder to the abnormal pattern of

connections between the hippocampus and the cerebral cortex. These differences, however, are not present in all individuals who exhibit behaviors associated with autism. *See also* amygdala, metallothionein.
J. Michael Pickle

home visitor
See mobile therapist.

home-based services
Early intervention (EI) services (birth to 3 years old) provided in the child's home or other natural environments, as mandated by the Individuals with Disabilities Education Act (IDEA) Amendments of 1997 (PL 105-17). The child's team, including teachers, therapists, and family members, develops a list of priorities to be worked on at home during weekly or monthly home visits as determined by the individualized family service plan (IFSP). Some examples of priorities (also known as *outcomes* on the IFSP) may be to lengthen the child's attention span, to assist the child in tolerating a variety of textures, or to encourage the child to play appropriately with toys. Home-based services are one choice along the continuum of how best to provide supports to a child with special needs and are alternative to center-based services. *See also* early intervention (EI), individualized family service plan (IFSP), Individuals with Disabilities Education Act (IDEA).
Susan Wuchenich Parker

hormone therapy
Use of hormones, or substances that simulate hormonal effects, to treat a disease or dysfunction (e.g., insulin to treat diabetes). Hormone therapy has been proposed by some as a possible treatment for autism. The two hormones suggested for use in treatment are secretin and adrenocorticotropic hormone (ACTH). Secretin is produced by the pancreas and aids in digestion. ACTH is produced in the pituitary gland and is a growth hormone. The hormones may be administered by injection or in tablet form. Hormone therapy is not recommended for individuals with autism (New York State Department of Health, Early Intervention Program, 1999a). *See also* secretin.
Julie L. FitzGerald

hug machine
A large box in which an individual lays face down on an inclined plane with the head resting outside the box and elevated with relation to the feet. Using

a lever, the individual can pull the panels toward the sides of the body to apply deep pressure. The machine (originally developed by Temple Grandin) is designed to apply deep pressure to the entire body. The theory is that deep pressure may be calming for individuals with autism, especially those who display high levels of anxiety. Research on the efficacy of the device is limited (New York State Department of Health, Early Intervention Program, 1999a). *See also* sensory integration (SI), touch pressure.
Dana J. Stevens

hyperactivity

Behavior that is characterized as excessively energetic, intense, misdirected, and inappropriate (Mash & Wolfe, 1999). The four main components of hyperactivity are 1) inattention and distractibility, 2) overarousal and excessive activity, 3) impulsiveness, and 4) difficulty with rewards. Typical hyperactive behaviors include fidgeting, having problems in concentrating, acting impulsively, and constantly moving. Although some stereotypic behavior such as hand flapping might be viewed as hyperactivity, there is no known link between hyperactivity and the stereotypic behaviors observed in autism. *See also* attention-deficit/hyperactivity disorder (ADHD), stereotypic behaviors.
Janelle Matesic

hyperlexia

A significant discrepancy between an individual's word recognition skills and his or her reading comprehension or cognitive ability, with the former being superior (Snowling & Frith, 1986). Hyperlexia is noted most frequently in individuals with autism spectrum disorders (ASDs) (Grigorenko et al., 2002), although it has also been observed in individuals with other developmental disorders, especially those involving language and communication difficulties, such as speech-language impairment (Cohen, Hall, & Riccio, 1997), Williams syndrome (Bellugi, Birhle, Neville, Jernigan, & Doherty, 1992), Turner syndrome (Temple & Carney, 1996), and mental retardation having no known cause (Snowling & Frith, 1986). These precocious reading skills are self-taught and often develop during preschool years. Despite its precocity, hyperlexia is rarely designated as a savant skill. Word recognition skills eventually cease to be outstanding because of a natural ceiling on ability. It remains unclear how or why individuals develop hyperlexia. Weak central coherence, the propensity to preferentially focus on details, sometimes to the detriment of overall, global meaning, may pro-

vide one explanation (Welsh, Pennington, & Rogers, 1987). *See also* savant syndrome, weak central coherence.
Gregory L. Wallace

hyperresponsiveness

Also called *hyperresponsivity* or *overresponsiveness*. Larger, more intense responses than expected. The nervous system receives both excitatory and inhibitory messages and must balance these competing inputs for adaptive responding. Hyperresponsiveness is assessed by observing behavior in a specific context (Dunn, 1997b). For example, a child who cringes and covers his or her ears during group instruction may be exhibiting hyperresponsiveness to the sounds in the classroom. *See also* sensation avoiding, sensory sensitivity, somatosensory.
Winnie Dunn

hyporesponsiveness

Also called *hyporresponsivity* or *underresponsiveness*. Smaller, less intense responses than expected. The nervous system receives both excitatory and inhibitory messages, and must balance these competing inputs for adaptive respond-ing. Hyporesponsiveness is assessed by observing behavior in a context (Dunn, 1997b). For example, a child who seems oblivious to his or her family's activ-ities during family fun night may be exhibiting hyporesponsiveness to the movement, sounds, and visual stimuli of the family activities. *See also* sensa-tion seeking, sensory sensitivity, somatosensory.
Winnie Dunn

ICD-10

See The International Statistical Classification of Diseases and Related Health Problems, Tenth Revision.

icon

A symbol, representation, or pictogram (e.g., a stick figure of a girl on a girl's restroom door). Icons are often used in communication systems (e.g., communication boards) for individuals with autism. *See also* communication board, Picture Exchange Communication System (PECS), visual strategies. *John T. Neisworth & Pamela S. Wolfe*

IDEA

See Individuals with Disabilities Education Act.

idiosyncratic language

Language usage peculiar or unique to an individual; patterns of language or specific usage of words that makes sense only to the individual or those familiar with his or her communication style. These types of words or phrases might be based on loose associations that the individual may have made at some point in time (e.g., saying "a red" when he or she wants to play with a red toy). Extensive use of idiosyncratic language is a symptom of impairment in communication identified by the *Diagnostic and Statistical Manual of Mental Disorders, Fourth Edition, Text Revision* (*DSM-IV-TR;* American Psychiatric Association, 2000), as one diagnostic criterion of autism. *Teresa Babula*

idiot savant

See savant syndrome.

IEP
See individualized education program.

IFSP
See individualized family service plan.

IgA, IgD, IgE, IgG, IgM
See immunoglobulin.

imagination
The production of ideas, especially in the form of mental images, of what is not present or has not been experienced. Imagination involves recombining former experiences to solve unexpected or unusual problems in a flexible, resourceful, and creative manner. Imagination includes mental creative ability (e.g., pretend play, storytelling, creative writing, poetry, art, drama, music composition) (Wolfberg, 1999, 2003). Harris (2000b) suggested that children's ability to imagine hypothetical and counterfactual possibilities makes a continuing contribution to their cognitive and emotional development.

Autism is characterized by qualitative impairments in imagination, which when linked with difficulties in the development of reciprocal social interaction and communication, form a *triad of impairments* (American Psychiatric Association, 2000; Wing & Gould, 1979), or core deficits. An early sign that imagination is affected in autism is a failure to develop spontaneous pretend play. Individuals with autism tend to engage in rituals that reflect stereotyped patterns of behavior, interests, and activities, including preoccupations with objects or amassing information about arcane subjects. The capacity to recognize and understand mental states (e.g., feelings, desires, intentions, beliefs) in oneself and others, also known as *theory of mind* (ToM) (Baron-Cohen, 1995; Harris & Leevers, 2000), is also impaired in individuals with autism. On a related point, people with autism tend to be very literal as opposed to flexible and creative in their thinking, particularly with regard to deciphering meaning in social situations. There is strong evidence to suggest that with specialized intervention, children on the autism spectrum are capable of improving their imaginative capacities (Wolfberg, 1999, 2003; see also Howlin, Baron-Cohen, & Hadwin, 1999). *See also* core deficits, spontaneous play, stereotypic behavior, symbolic play, theory of mind (ToM).
Pamela J. Wolfberg

imitation

Also called *modeling*. Imitation occurs when a person observes another individual and subsequently makes his or her own behavior similar in form to the observed model. Imitation may be vocal (i.e., saying what the model says) and/or motor (i.e., doing what the model does). Imitation can also involve an individual making the products of his or her behavior similar to the products of the model. A preschool-age child might draw a circle on the paper after watching a teacher do the same. Individuals who lack social awareness or who have not been rewarded for making their behavior look like others will not be as likely to imitate. Imitation training is important for children with autism who have difficulty in learning and engaging in (i.e., imitating) needed skills. A learner is likely to attend to and maintain focus on models who are perceived as similar to him- or herself or who have valued attributes (Hosford & Johnson, 1983).
Richard J. Cowan & Keith Allen

immediate echolalia

See echolalia.

immunoglobulin

Also called *immune serum globulin*. Antibodies that are produced by the immune system in response to the presence of antigens, foreign microorganisms, bacteria, fungi, and viruses. Immunoglobulins act as a defense mechanism and aid in fighting infections. There are five distinct immunoglobulins present in the serum and external secretions of the body (IgA, IgD, IgE, IgG, and IgM). *See also* immunologic therapy, immunological tests.
Julie L. FitzGerald

immunologic therapy

Also called *immunotherapy*. Use of knowledge of the immune system and its components to prevent and treat disease. Advocates of immunologic therapy as a treatment for autism often cite research studies that have shown that some children with autism may have abnormal or dysfunctional immune systems (Gupta, Aggarwal, & Heads, 1996; Singh, Fudenberg, Emerson, & Coleman, 1988). The immunologic therapy described in current literature is founded on the idea that treatment with intravenous immunoglobulin (IVIG) may correct certain immune deficiencies or abnormalities. Research on immunologic therapy is mixed (DelGiudice-Asch, Simon, Schmeidler, Cunningham-Rundles, & Hollander, 1999; Gupta, 2000); more convincing evidence of its

effectiveness as a treatment for autism is needed before it is accepted as a treatment option. *See also* immunoglobulin, immunological tests.
John T. Neisworth & Pamela S. Wolfe

immunological tests

Analysis of a sample of blood to measure the levels of the different elements present in a person's immune system. The reason for immunological testing in individuals with autism is to determine if their immune status is different from people without autism. Some researchers believe that immunological factors may contribute to the symptoms and possibly to the development of autism (Gupta, Aggarwal, & Heads, 1996). *See also* immunoglobulin, immunologic therapy.
Julie L. FitzGerald

immunotherapy

See immunologic therapy.

impairment

Any loss or abnormality of psychological, physiological, or anatomical structure or function. For an individual with autism, impairment refers to personal challenges that relate to the diagnosis and includes qualitative impairments in social and communication development (World Health Organization, 1992). *See also* disability, handicap.
Lisa A. Ruble

inattention

See attention-deficit/hyperactivity disorder (ADHD).

incidence

The rate of occurrence of *new* cases of a specific disease or disorder in a population. Incidence is computed by dividing the number of cases identified by the number of individuals screened for the disorder and is usually expressed as number of cases per 1,000, 10,000, or 100,000. The term is often incorrectly used interchangeably with *prevalence,* which is the estimated *total* number of cases present in the general population. Incidence rates for autism vary due to the diagnostic criteria used and the population representativeness of the sample screened. Incidence estimates for autism range from 4.5 per 10,000 to 20 per 10,000, and estimates for autism spectrum disorders (ASD) are as high as 60 per 10,000 (Charman, 2002). *See also* prevalence.
Raymond G. Romanczyk

incident report
See anecdotal report.

incidental teaching
A variety of methods for teaching skills in typical environments. In autism, incidental teaching is most commonly associated with increasing and generalizing language skills (e.g., generalizing skills from a structured discrete trial format to the natural environment). Incidental teaching of language, for example, typically involves the following steps (Fenske, Krantz, & McClannahan, 2001; Hart & Risley, 1982):

1. The child indicates a desire or makes a request.
2. The parent or therapist confirms what the child is requesting.
3. The parent or therapist prompts a more elaborate response using shaping or chaining if necessary.
4. The child responds to the parent's or therapist's prompt.
5. The parent or therapist confirms and elaborates on the child's response.
6. The child receives the requested object(s) as a reinforcer.

See also chaining, generalization, maintenance, prompting, shaping.
Kimberly A. Schreck & Richard M. Foxx

inclusion
Education of children with disabilities in general education classrooms with typical same-age peers. Curricula and activities are adapted to permit the individuals with disabilities to participate as independently as possible. The term is often used interchangeably with *mainstreaming.* Inclusion in the general education classroom is sometimes (but not always) the least restrictive environment (LRE) for a child receiving special education and related services, depending on his or her needs. *See also* least restrictive environment (LRE), mainstreaming, service delivery model.
J. David Smith

individualized education program (IEP)
Comprehensive document designed to ensure that 1) students with disabilities receive the services they need to benefit from an education, 2) parents are fully involved in the decision-making process, 3) educators understand their obligations to the individual child, 4) the effectiveness of services is evaluated, 5) the child's needs are viewed from multiple vantage points, and 6) the child is provided with services to support the move to adult independence. The Individuals with Disabilities Education Act (IDEA) Amendments of 1997 (PL 105-17) mandates that every qualified child with a dis-

ability, age 3 through 21, have an IEP. Every IEP must contain specific information, including the following (Assistance to States, 2003, §§ 300. 340–300.350):

- A statement of the child's present levels of educational performance
- Measurable annual goals
- Special education and related services and supplementary aids and/or services to be provided to the child
- Program modifications or supports for school personnel that will be provided for the child
- The extent, if any, to which the child will not participate with children without disabilities in the general education curriculum
- Any individual modifications in the administration of state- or district-wide assessments of student achievement that are needed for the child to participate in the assessment
- Projected date for the beginning of the services and modifications and the anticipated frequency, location, and duration of those services and modifications
- How the child's progress toward the annual goals will be measured
- How the child's parents will be regularly informed (e.g., through periodic report cards) of their child's progress toward the annual goals
- The extent to which that progress is sufficient to enable the child to achieve the goals by the end of the year

See also due process, Education of the Handicapped Act (EHA) of 1970 (PL 91-230), eligibility, Individuals with Disabilities Education Act (IDEA).
James K. McAfee

individualized family service plan (IFSP)

A statement that addresses both the developmental needs of the child, birth to 3 years of age and the needs of the family that are deemed important in supporting the child's development. Like the individualized education program (IEP), the IFSP also specifies expected outcomes (goals) to be attained and the intervention plan. The focus on family as essential to child progress and support and the empowering of family members as decision makers are notable features mandated under federal law. *See also* early intervention (EI), home-based services, Individuals with Disabilities Education Act (IDEA).
John T. Neisworth & Pamela S. Wolfe

individualized plan for employment (IPE)

Formerly called *individualized written rehabilitation plan (IWRP)*. A central document for any person found to be eligible for state and/or federal vocational rehabilitation services. Typically, IPEs are created for individuals 18 years or older. Based on input from the individual, his or her family, and the vocational rehabilitation counselor, the IPE sets forth in writing the vocational goals and corresponding services pursuant to the vocational goals. *See also* Rehabilitation Act of 1973 (PL 93-112).

Lynn Atanasoff

individualized transition plan (ITP)

A formal plan for transition for a child with a disability, detailing needed services, responsible agency staff, and expected outcomes. The ITP, often included as part of the child's individualized education program (IEP), is designed to facilitate transfer from public school to adult living. It should include a coordinated set of activities for the individual with a disability, including instruction, community experiences, and development of employment and other postschool adult living objectives. *See also* early intervention (EI), individualized education program (IEP), Individuals with Disabilities Education Act (IDEA).

John T. Neisworth & Pamela S. Wolfe

individualized written rehabilitation plan (IWRP)

See individualized plan for employment (IPE).

Individuals with Disabilities Education Act (IDEA)

Federal statute that guides the provision of special education services to children with disabilities, ages 3 through 21, and early intervention services to infants and toddlers (birth to 3) with disabilities. The original legislation, the Education for All Handicapped Children Act of 1975 (PL 94-142), guaranteed children with disabilities ages 6 through 21 a free appropriate public education (FAPE), the development of an individualized education program (IEP), and the right to due process. PL 94-142 included most of the current provisions of federal law for education of children with disabilities, such as right to a public education, individualized education programs (IEPs), due process, and parent involvement.

The Individuals with Disabilities Education Act (IDEA) of 1990 (PL 101-476) reauthorized the original special education law. At that time, two new categories of eligibility for special education were also added, autism and traumatic brain injury, and transition procedures were outlined. The IDEA Amendments of 1997 (PL 105-17), which amended and reauthorized IDEA and related legislation, shifted the focus of special education to the involvement of children with disabilities within the general curriculum. The

pending reauthorization of IDEA (H. Res. 1350, 2004) closely aligns its provisions with those of the No Child Left Behind Act of 2001 (PL 107-110) and emphasizes accountability and improving educational results for children with disabilities. *See also* due process, Education of the Handicapped Act (EHA) of 1970 (PL 91-230), free appropriate public education (FAPE), individualized education program (IEP), least restrictive environment (LRE), special education.
Linda Crane Mitchell

infantile autism

An early designation for what is now known as *autistic disorder* or *autism* (Kanner, 1943). The term *infantile autism* implied that the disorder only affected children, rather than being a lifelong disability. The terms *autistic disorder, infantile autism,* and *early infantile autism* are still used interchangeably by the general public and professionals to describe the same syndrome. *See also* Asperger syndrome (AS), autism, autism spectrum disorder (ASD).
Laura Arnstein

informal assessment

Evaluation or data collection by means other than standardized tests (Salvia & Ysseldyke, 2001), including criterion-referenced tests (teacher-made and districtwide), observations, interviews, review of records, academic samples and personal documents, and curriculum-based tests or procedures. The information gained through informal assessment is a valuable supplement to standardized, norm-referenced tests; however, informal assessment procedures have unknown reliability and validity and should therefore be interpreted cautiously (Sattler, 2001). *See also* assessment, criterion-referenced assessment, curriculum-based assessment (CBA).
Catherine M. Marcell

instrumental activities of daily living

See activities of daily living (ADLs).

Integrated Play Groups (IPG) model

An approach to address peer relations and play of children with autism. The IPG model supports children with autism (novice players) in mutually enjoyed play experiences with typical peers and siblings (expert players) in natural play environments (Wolfberg, 1999, 2003; Wolfberg & Schuler,

1993). Small groups of children regularly play together under the guidance of an adult facilitator (play guide). The model includes an observation framework and corresponding assessment tools that document social play styles, cognitive/symbolic and social dimensions of play, communication functions and means, play preferences, and diversity of play. *See also* imagination, social play, spontaneous play, symbolic play.
Pamela J. Wolfberg

intelligence tests

Measure of cognitive functioning, typically a standardized test, yielding an intelligence quotient (IQ). The construct of intelligence is composed of many elements, including communication, reasoning, and concept formation. Widely used standardized measures of intelligence tests include the Wechsler Intelligence Scale for Children–Third Edition (WISC-III; Wechsler, 1991) and the Stanford-Binet Intelligence Scale–Fourth Edition (Thorndike, Hagen, & Sattler, 1986). Intelligence tests are often part of a formal diagnosis of mental retardation. Their use in diagnosis, however, is limited due to characteristics of disability (e.g., the inability of some individuals to communicate) and the measures themselves (e.g., their failure to meet the cultural or linguistic differences of individuals). Some professional organizations (e.g., American Association on Mental Retardation) stress that intelligence tests should be used in conjunction with assessment of adaptive skills. Intelligence tests can be useful to assess cognitive ability and differentiate autism from mental retardation (although the two diagnoses often co-occur). Due to core deficits (e.g., impaired communication and social interaction; restricted, repetitive behavior), individuals with autism often score lower on intelligence tests. For example, the standardized testing demands (e.g., sitting at a table, talking with an unfamiliar test administrator, verbally communicating answers) may make it difficult to obtain an accurate assessment for an individual with autism. Thus, intelligence tests are recommended as only one part of an assessment that includes a variety of instruments (particularly those indexed to natural environments). *See also* assessment, core deficits, diagnosis, executive functions.
John T. Neisworth & Pamela S. Wolfe

interdisciplinary team
See team models.

The International Statistical Classification of Diseases and Related Health Problems, Tenth Revision (ICD-10)

The World Health Organization's (1992) classification of health and behavior disorders morbidity (disorders, pathologies, and presenting problems) and mortality data throughout the world. The classification system is divided into 21 chapters that describe diagnostic groups; related signs, symptoms, and etiology; and other relevant information. Each diagnosis is listed as a 3-digit alphanumeric code that can be followed by additional numerals providing additional specificity within the diagnosis. For example, the *ICD-10* diagnostic code for Childhood Autism is F84.0 and Pervasive Developmental Disorder, Unspecified, is F84.9. The *ICD-10* is used by some professionals as an alternative to the *Diagnostic and Statistical Manual of Mental Disorders, Fourth Edition, Text Revision (DSM-IV-TR;* American Psychiatric Association, 2000) or other classification systems. *See also Diagnostic and Statistical Manual of Mental Disorders, Fourth Edition, Text Revision (DSM-IV-TR); Diagnostic Classification of Mental Health Disorders of Infancy and Early Childhood (DC: 0-3).*
Raphael Bernier

interobserver agreement; interrater reliability
See reliability.

intestinal problems
See constipation, diet therapy, dysbiosis, encopresis, leaky gut syndromes, secretin.

IPE
See individualized plan for employment.

IPG
See Integrated Play Groups model.

IQ
Intelligence quotient. *See* intelligence tests.

itinerant teacher
A teacher who provides educational or therapeutic services to children with disabilities individually or in groups across multiple environments. Itinerant

teachers do not have their own classrooms but may serve as consultants and co-teachers to other teachers. *See also* mobile therapist.
Devender R. Banda

ITP
See individualized transition plan.

IVIG
Intravenous immunoglobulin. *See* immunologic therapy.

IWRP
Individualized written rehabilitation plan. *See* individualized plan for employment (IPE).

Jj

joint attention

Attending simultaneously with another individual to an event or object, with each partner understanding that the other is sharing the same focus. Joint attention emerges as an important milestone from approximately 9 to 12 months old (Carpenter, Nagell, & Tomasello, 1998). Research has shown that in their use of gestures to request something they want (*protoimperative* gestures), children with autism perform similarly to children with typical development or with other developmental disabilities when these groups are of similar mental ability (Baron-Cohen, 1989). The children with autism, however, show dramatically less use of communication for the purpose of sharing attention simply for pleasure or interest (*protodeclarative* communication). Unlike children with other developmental disabilities, many children with autism show limited improvement in joint attention skills with age (Leekam, Baron-Cohen, Perrett, Milders, & Brown, 1997). *See also* eye gaze, protodeclarative, protoimperative, social gaze.

Hannah Schertz

kinesthetic sense

The conscious awareness and perception of the active movement of one's own body and position in space, such as knowing where to place one's feet when ascending stairs. The kinesthetic sense is related to the function of the vestibular system, which enables reception and response to movement stimuli and enables balance. It is not unusual for children with autism and other pervasive developmental disorders (PDDs) to display clumsy motor planning and movement; these children may trip, accidentally break dishes, spill beverages, and so forth.

Proprioception, the sense of touch, relates to and is important for the kinesthetic sense. Proprioception, kinesthetic sense, and vestibular function are interrelated and interdependent for smooth, effective motor behavior. *See also* praxis, proprioception, sensory processing, vestibular.
Denise Lynn Schilling

lactose intolerance

See diet therapy, food intolerance.

Landau-Kleffner syndrome

A particular type of epilepsy syndrome specific to individuals with autism. Children with this disorder lose language skills, often around age 2–3 years, and may appear more distant or confused. It is debated whether this disorder is a manifestation of autism or a separate disorder that resembles autism (see Tuchman, 1997; Tuchman & Rapin, 1999). Although antiseizure medications have been used in children with autism and seizures, improvement in behavior or development has not usually been evidenced, nor has progress in development been fostered. Landau-Kleffner syndrome, however, may represent an exception to this observation. Corticosteroid treatment in children with this disorder has been shown to lead to improvements in language skills and alertness. *See also* epilepsy, seizures.
Jeanette C. Ramer

LEA

See local educational agency.

leaky gut syndromes

Several intestinal disorders related to increased permeability of the intestinal wall in which substances are thought to leak through the walls into the bloodstream and cross the blood–brain barrier. In theory, these substances then act as neurotransmitters and may create confused sensory input. Causes of leaky gut syndromes include use of certain anti-inflammatory drugs, presence of parasites, presence of toxins, intestinal infections, and allergens. Children with autism frequently have bowel problems, and some professionals, including advocates of special diets, link leaky gut problems

not only to bowel problems but also to behaviors associated with autism. *See also* antigluten therapy, diet therapy, food intolerance.
John T. Neisworth & Pamela S. Wolfe

learned helplessness

Term coined by Seligman (Hiroto & Seligman, 1975) to describe the phenomenon in which an individual may have the necessary skills to accomplish a task but does not use these skills and appears to be helpless. The helplessness is due to a learning history wherein the person has received reinforcement for giving up, for not persisting, or for not being self-sufficient. For example, an individual who has been taught to tie his shoes may not attempt the task, saying that he cannot complete the task, and then someone may usually do it for him. Getting things done by others, instead of by oneself, teaches the person to be reliant on others, that is, to be helpless. *See also* reinforcement.
John T. Neisworth & Pamela S. Wolfe

learning styles

Individual preferences in approaches to learning. These preferences could be based on an individual's preferred sensory modality and include *visual* (learning best by seeing, i.e., needing to see something in order to remember it), *auditory* (learning by listening), and *kinesthetic* learning styles (learning by doing). Learning styles may also be based on the depth of learning and include *surface* (involving rote memory and aiming for reproduction of what has been studied) and *deep learning* (involving a real understanding of what has been studied). Differences in learning styles may also stem from learning context, such as teaching methods. Thus, some students may learn best while doing projects, others by drills, and yet others through discussion. It is important to note that each learning style has its own strengths and weaknesses and that none of the styles is better than another. To some extent, different contexts trigger the use of different styles by the same individual; however, an individual tends to use some styles more often than others (Ferrari & Sternberg, 1998). The identification of students' learning styles is essential for individualized approaches to teaching. The most common learning style of individuals diagnosed with autism spectrum disorders (ASDs) is the *visual learning style*. Individuals diagnosed with ASDs are also *detail-focused learners*. Because of their extreme focus on details, children diagnosed with ASDs may require extra help in getting the *big picture*. In the workplace, however, this orientation is advantageous in jobs that require focus on details and precision. *See also* cognitive processes, sensory processing.
Ljiljana Vuletic

least restrictive environment (LRE)

Derived from English law and the doctrine of minimum government intrusion, a legal term specifically defined under the regulations for the Individuals with Disabilities Education Act (IDEA) and its amendments. Under these regulations, the LRE mandate means

(1) That to the maximum extent appropriate, children with disabilities, including children in public or private institutions or other care facilities, are educated with children who are nondisabled; and

(2) That special classes, separate schooling or other removal of children with disabilities from the regular educational environment occurs only if the nature or severity of the disability is such that education in regular classes with the use of supplementary aids and services cannot be achieved satisfactorily. (Assistance to States, 2003, § 300.550[b])

The important elements of LRE that can be distilled from the law are placement with peers without disabilities to the maximum extent appropriate for the individual; provision of supplemental services such as teacher assistants, communication devices, and behavioral support to allow the student to succeed in the general education environment; a continuum of placement options ranging from full-time placement in the general education setting to full-time placement in a special education setting; and placement based on the individualized education program (IEP). *See also* due process, inclusion, individualized education program (IEP), Individuals with Disabilities Education Act (IDEA), mainstreaming.
James K. McAfee

least-to-most prompting

See prompt hierarchy.

levels of assistance

Criteria for unassisted or assisted performance often used in assessment and/or scales. Levels of assistance may range on a continuum from low to high, minimum to maximum, or never to always. Levels of assistance may also be defined in response prompt systems that include verbal prompting, modeling, and physical assistance. *See also* assessment, modeling, prompt hierarchy.
John T. Neisworth & Pamela S. Wolfe

life skills support

Type of classroom or environment that typically includes the provision of functional curricula or the skills needed in everyday life. Life skills might include self-care (e.g., selecting appropriate clothing for the season), functional academics (e.g., reading a bus schedule), or community living (e.g., buying groceries). *See also* functional goals.
John T. Neisworth & Pamela S. Wolfe

light-technology device

See low-technology device.

limbic system

Interrelated brain structures (including the amygdala and hippocampus) that are evidently associated with regulation of aggression, emotions, and sensory input and with aspects of learning and memory. Damage or atypical development of limbic system components relates to often-reported characteristics of autism such as compulsive behavior, difficulty with novelty, social avoidance, and unusual responsivity to stimuli. Most of the information concerning limbic system damage is based on animal research in which parts of the brain are removed or injured. Postmortem research on the brains of individuals with autism has shown increased density and abnormal branching of neurons within limbic components. Abnormal size or density of neurons is linked to early (most likely prenatal) developmental impairment. (It should be noted that surgical damage to the limbic structures of adult animals does not produce similar outcomes.) Speculative evidence based on neuroimaging research suggests that other parts of the brain that relate to the limbic system may be important to aspects of functioning pertinent to autism, including difficulties with face recognition, reading the emotional expression of others, perspective sharing, and other dimensions of "social intelligence." Caution is needed in interpreting and extrapolating limbic research, which is preliminary but ongoing. *See also* amygdala, neuroimaging, theory of mind (ToM).
John T. Neisworth & Pamela S. Wolfe

local educational agency (LEA)

A school district or service unit that provides instruction under the auspices of a state educational agency (SEA) such as a state department of education; the local public education, tax-supported agency. *See also* state educational agency (SEA).
John T. Neisworth & Pamela S. Wolfe

locomotion

Movement of one's self from one place to another. Locomotion may be accomplished in multiple ways (e.g., walking, crawling, using a wheelchair). *See also* gross motor skills.

John T. Neisworth & Pamela S. Wolfe

Lovaas approach

Behavioral language intervention that uses discrete trial training and other procedures based on principles of applied behavior analysis (ABA). Lovaas and colleagues developed and prescribed formats for their discrete trial training, and the Lovaas approach is often referred to as *discrete trial training, Discrete Trial Training,* or *DTT.* The Lovaas approach is one among an array of methods based on ABA techniques to foster skill acquisition and behavior change. It should also be noted that the use of discrete trial instruction is not unique to the Lovaas approach and that such instruction— referred to in this book as *discrete trial training* (all lowercase)—is recognized as useful in teaching material to diverse learners. Lovaas-type discrete trials are referred to in this book as *Discrete Trial Training* (upper- and lowercase) or *DTT.*

The Lovaas approach breaks skills down into discrete trials, or small, measurable steps, that are presented in a massed and rapid sequence. Lovaas procedures (see Lovaas et al., 1981) are based on behavior (operant) principles. Often skills are taught to mastery one to one with a therapist, a parent, and/or a teacher. The short, discrete trials have a distinct beginning, middle, and end and are separated by brief intertrial pauses (5 seconds or less). Each trial consists of an instruction (discriminative stimulus or S^D), response, and feedback. Instructions are given in simple language. Prompts, given only when required, can be physical, verbal, or visual. Feedback in the trial is given immediately for a correct or incorrect response (e.g., if a child correctly responds to "Give me a ball," the teacher says, "That's good. It's a ball"; if a child does not respond or is incorrect, the teacher says, "Let's try again"). Trials are repeated in sequence until the child acquires the targeted skill.

The major application of the Lovaas approach has been with children with autism. Intervention begins between ages 2 and 4 years in a child's home and is recommended for approximately 40 hours per week. Steps of the initial approach to developing a child's language include increasing the frequency of vocalizations; teaching the child to vocalize within a few seconds of instruction; teaching sound imitation; teaching word imitation; and imitating volume, pitch, and speed. (Prior to this instruction, it is often necessary to teach eye contact, compliance, and other prerequisite behaviors.) When certain words are mastered, the child can move on to object and action labeling. One-to-one instruction is gradually expanded to large-group instruction.

Lovaas' initial research was based on results of a 15-year study, the Young Autism Project. Results indicated that 47% of the experimental group scored in the average range on standardized tests and adaptive scales (Lovaas, 1987). The findings have been criticized as having methodological flaws (Gresham & MacMillan, 1997). The Lovaas approach has since been empirically validated (New York State Department of Health, Early Intervention Program, 1999a) and is widely advocated and sought by parents who seek early and intensive therapy. The approach, however, has been faulted for lack of generalization of skills outside of training contexts, dependence on prompts, and missed social opportunities. The approach involves many hours of professional and parent participation and is considered by some as too demanding; advocates defend the time requirements as needed to deliver effective treatment. Criticisms of the method (e.g., generalization problems, developmentally inappropriate demands) are being addressed in more current practices through thinning reinforcement, fading prompts, and embedding mastered skills in natural activities and settings.

Use of the method requires appropriate training in conducting trials, establishing rapport with the child, delivering reinforcers, evaluating child progress, and adjusting pace and procedures. Training in the Lovaas approach is available from therapists who are specially trained. *See also* applied behavior analysis (ABA), discrete trial training, massed practice. *John T. Neisworth, Pamela S. Wolfe, & Devender R. Banda*

low registration

Also called *poor registration*. A pattern of sensory processing characterized by high sensory thresholds and a passive self-regulation strategy. People who have a low registration pattern of sensory processing notice sensory stimuli much less than others (Dunn, 1997a, 2001). People who have low registration patterns seem uninterested, self-absorbed, and sometimes dull in affect. They do not notice what is going on around them and miss cues that might guide their behaviors. Some studies suggest that people with disabilities such as autism and schizophrenia are significantly more likely to experience low registration (Dunn, 1997a). Interventions are directed at increasing the intensity of sensory input to improve the chances for noticing and responding to environmental demands. *See also* hyporesponsiveness. *Winnie Dunn*

low-technology device
Also called *light-technology device*. An "item, piece of equipment, or product system...used to increase, maintain, or improve the functional capacities of a child with a disability" (Individuals with Disabilities Education Act [IDEA] Amendments of 1997, PL 105-17, § 1401[1]) that does not include mechanical parts. Low-technology devices include devices for communication (e.g., picture communication board) or for daily living (e.g., spoon with a large handle for easier gripping). Low-technology devices are contrasted with high-technology devices, which are electronic or mechanical (Turnbull, Turnbull, Shank, & Smith, 2004). *See also* assistive technology (AT) device, augmentative and alternative communication (AAC), communication board, high-technology device.
John T. Neisworth & Pamela S. Wolfe

LRE
See least restrictive environment.

MA

See mental age.

magnesium therapy

See vitamin B$_6$ and magnesium therapy.

magnetic resonance imaging (MRI)

A neuroimaging technique that employs magnetic fields, rather than X-rays, to provide images. The computer-generated images are based on the normal variation in water content within the brain and cerebral blood vessels. MRI scanning uses a powerful magnetic coil that detects small variations in energy generated by the hydrogen molecules in water when polarized by the magnet. This pattern is read by a computer and used to generate a picture of the brain and its structure. It is particularly suited to assessment of brain anatomy because it can characterize gray and white matter pattern and subtle structural abnormalities, in addition to providing accurate pictures of major brain anatomy. Functional MRI (fMRI), a newer technique, is able to image the parts of the brain and pathways that are active in an awake individual while he or she is performing specific tasks. MRI scanning does not require use of radiation and is not painful, conveying an advantage over positron emission tomography (PET), which requires administration of small doses of a radioactive tracer.

Studies in individuals with autism using MRI technology have confirmed increased brain volume in 20%–40% of young children with autism (Cody, Pelphrey, & Piven, 2002). The enlargement is generalized and involves both gray and white matter. Increased brain size is not typically evident in children with autism after about the age of 8 years (Cody et al., 2002). The amygdala, a region in the medial temporal lobe, has been noted through MRI to be consistently larger in children with autism, with a correlation between the degree of increase compared with typically developing

age peers and severity of symptoms of autism. *See also* amygdala, functional magnetic resonance imaging (fMRI), head circumference, hippocampus, positron emission tomography (PET).
Jeanette C. Ramer

mainstreaming

The practice of enrolling and providing educational services to children with disabilities in general education classrooms alongside students without identified disabilities. The practice is an application of the philosophical principles of normalization and inclusion to the education of students with disabilities. Although the term *mainstreaming* predates the term *inclusion,* the latter term is used more often now to describe enrollment of children with disabilities in general education. In the United States, the least restrictive environment (LRE) provision of the Individuals with Disabilities Education Act (IDEA) Amendments of 1997 (PL 105-17) provides the legal rationale for inclusion. In inclusion, the teacher and children with disabilities in the general education environment receive the necessary support for an appropriate educational experience that meets the individual educational needs of the child. Inclusion for students with autism is a controversial issue in that there is concern that the educational needs for these students may not be met in a general education environment (Mesibov & Shea, 1996). However, models for inclusion for children with autism and evidence of their effectiveness have been published (Harrower & Dunlap, 2001; Kamps, Leonard, Potucek, & Garrison-Harrell, 1995). *See also* inclusion, Individuals with Disabilities Education Act (IDEA), least restrictive environment (LRE), normalization.
Samuel L. Odom

maintenance

Retention of learned skills. Procedures for skill maintenance typically involve similar procedures as those used for teaching generalization of skills. Maintaining behavioral increases often includes gradually delaying reinforcement and fading the structure of the instruction (Baer, 1999). Procedures for maintaining behavioral reductions include strengthening functional alternatives to the undesirable behavior; using functional, naturally occurring reinforcers; having the treatment and maintenance conditions closely resemble one another; using intermittent reinforcement and reinforcement delay; employing natural consequences; fading therapist control; teaching self-control; and developing peer support. *See also* fading, generalization, reinforcement.
Kimberly A. Schreck & Richard M. Foxx

maladaptive behavior

A behavior practiced by an individual that causes difficulties in developmental progress, socialization, and/or success in specific environments (e.g., classroom, work setting). Maladaptive behavior is, in general, self-defeating and viewed as socially unacceptable. Such behavior may be vocal (e.g., screaming, echolalia) or motoric (e.g., reckless running, hitting oneself or others). More intense autism may be characterized by the presence of some extremes of maladaptive behavior, such as serious self-injurious behavior (SIB). Specific tests and checklists are available that assess the presence and extent of maladaptive behavior (a number of preschool instruments are useful to early interventionists); these materials can be used to identify maladaptive behaviors for reduction and replacement with adaptive behaviors (see Appendix A). Functional behavior assessment (FBA) has been especially helpful in discovering the functions that maladaptive behaviors may serve for an individual and in providing information for teaching acceptable alternative behaviors. Primary treatments for maladaptive behavior in autism and other pervasive developmental disorders (PDDs) include applied behavior analysis (ABA) and medication. Psychotherapy and counseling may also be used, especially with typically developing older children and adults who exhibit specific maladaptive behaviors (e.g., excessive fears, extreme shyness, trouble controlling anger). *See also* adaptive behavior, echolalia, functional behavior assessment (FBA), self-injurious behavior (SIB).
John T. Neisworth & Pamela S. Wolfe

mand

See verbal behavior (VB).

mand fluency training

Also called *mand model*. (A *mand* is a word or gesture that functions to obtain something.) Training that involves reinforcing appropriate attempts to communicate requests. Use of words, pictures, sign language, or augmentative and alternative communication (AAC) to request items or activities is reinforced. Discrete trials may be used to shape specific response topography (e.g., making the request "Say 'cookie,'" while shaping muscular movements of hands or mouth), but incidental teaching provides greater opportunities for naturally occurring reinforcement. *See also* fluency, incidental teaching, reinforcement, verbal behavior (VB).
Thomas P. Kitchen

mania

Uncontrollable emotions and extreme enthusiasm. The *Diagnostic and Statistical Manual of Mental Disorders, Fourth Edition, Text Revision (DSM-IV-TR;* American Psychiatric Association, 2000), describes a manic episode as a period enduring at least 1 week in which there is an abnormal mental or emotional state characterized by a heightened, unreserved, or bad-tempered mood. Symptoms of the mood disturbance may involve racing thoughts, hyperactivity, a sense of exaggerated self-importance, a decreased need for sleep, accelerated or incoherent speech, abusive language, and excessive participation in self-gratifying behaviors that could possibly lead to negative consequences (e.g., gambling, sexual indiscretions). Manic episodes are often severe enough to lead to decreased social and occupational performance and to require hospitalization. Manic episodes exist at one extreme on a continuum followed by hypomania through normal mood to depression on the opposite end. Manic episodes, however, can alternate with depression in a condition known as *bipolar disorder*. Although behavioral excesses displayed by children and adolescents with autism might be viewed as manic, research indicates low rates of mania in these individuals (Ghaziuddin, Tsai, & Ghaziuddin (1992). *See also* bipolar disorder, depression, mood-stabilizing medications.
Sharise Wilson

massed practice

The intensive practice of a skill or behavior over a short period of time. A common example of massed practice is cramming for an exam. Distributed practice is typically better than massed practice for building fluency and retention (Dempster, 1989). *See also* distributed practice, fluency, naturalistic interventions.
Charles A. Hughes

MAWA

See mutually acceptable written agreement.

MDE

See multidisciplinary evaluation.

MDT

Multidisciplinary team. *See* team models.

mean length of utterance (MLU)

An average number of meaningful sounds or words (morphemes) or words only used per sentence or unit of thought (utterance). MLU is most often calculated using morphemes rather than words only. A morpheme is the smallest grammatical unit of meaning and may be a word (e.g., *a, the, elephant*) or a word part (e.g., *re-, un-, spect, -ing*). An utterance is a sentence or a unit of language that is separated by a change in the voice or a pause that indicates a new thought. Increases in MLU correspond to specific periods of language development in young children (Brown, 1973). MLU is viewed as an estimate of language complexity (Owens, 1992). When computing MLU for a child, it is typical to collect a 50- to 100-word utterance sample to analyze the child's overall speech production. Once the sample is collected, it is transcribed and each utterance is analyzed by morphemes. The total number of morphemes is divided by the total number of utterances to compute the child's MLU. *See also* expressive language, prosody.
Jennifer Harris Tepe

mental age (MA)

A construct used in assessment of cognitive functioning expressed in years and months (e.g., MA = 4,8 or 4 years, 8 months). The referent for estimating MA is the average performance in standardized tests of children of typical development; a *typical* child who has a chronological age (CA) of 4 years would have an MA of 4. A child who has a CA of 4 years but who is assessed as functioning like a 3-year-old intellectually would be described as having an MA of 3 years. The MA construct is generally no longer used in intellectual assessment, having been replaced with percentile and standard deviation (*SD*). *See also* chronological age (CA), intelligence tests.
John T. Neisworth & Pamela S. Wolfe

mental health counselor

A professional specializing in the diagnosis and treatment of mental and/or emotional disorders as well as counseling and other interventions meant to prevent mental and emotional disorders. Unlike psychiatrists (and, in some states in some limited cases, psychologists), mental health counselors cannot prescribe medications.
Lynn Atanasoff

mental retardation (MR)

Overall impairments in intellectual functioning and/or adaptive skills. Most commonly, MR is defined as a disability characterized by significant limi-

tations both in intellectual functioning and adaptive behavior as expressed in conceptual, social, and practical adaptive skills that originates before age 18 (American Association on Mental Retardation, 2002). Intellectual functioning is measured by standard intelligence tests, the diagnostic criteria for MR being approximately two standard deviations ($SD = 15$ points) below the mean (100). When taking into consideration measurement of error, the cut-off score for MR is approximately an IQ of 65–75. Intellectual functioning is subdivided by the American Psychiatric Association (2000) into four degrees of severity: mild (an IQ of 50–55 to about 70), moderate (35–40 to 50–55), severe (20–25 to 35–40), and profound (20–25 and below). When a clinician is gathering evidence for the criterion of impairments in adaptive functioning, both adaptive behavior scales as well as other reliable independent sources are to be used. Since the 1960s, the concept of mental retardation has under gone substantial changes involving terminology, IQ cut-off levels, and the role of adaptive behavior. *See also* adaptive behavior; *Diagnostic and Statistical Manual of Mental Disorders, Fourth Edition, Text Revision (DSM-IV-TR)*.
Lise Roll-Pettersson

mercury

A metallic element (chemical symbol: Hg) that has no known required biological function. Exposure to mercury in infancy or early childhood, particularly to the organic mercury that in the vaccination preservative thimerosal, is hypothesized to cause or contribute to autism (Bernard, Enayati, Redwood, Roger, & Binstock, 2001). Several lines of evidence support this hypothesis:

- Mercury is a known neurotoxin and is particularly toxic to the developing central nervous system (CNS) when in an organic form.
- A bolus exposure to mercury (i.e., occurring all at once, such as with a vaccination) is far more toxic than the same amount of mercury exposure over time.
- All biologic and behavioral signs of autism have been reproduced experimentally in animals and accidentally in humans following mercury exposure.
- Autism was first described in the early 1940s after mercury-containing vaccinations became available in the late 1930s.
- The increases of autism has paralleled the increase in mercury-containing vaccination exposure.
- The 4:1 male–female ratio of autism is similar to the gender ratio observed in low-level mercury intoxication.

- The selective, regional brain abnormalities found in autism also occur with mercury exposure (e.g., the amygdala, an area of the brain that controls eye contact, is dysfunctional in autism and damaged by mercury). Since infant and child vaccination mercury exposure exceeds both individual exposure and cumulative government safety guidelines, the U.S. Food and Drug Administration and the American Academy of Pediatrics have recommended that routine pediatric vaccines no longer contain mercury-based preservatives. Because of this, the incidence of newly diagnosed autism within the next decade will convincingly test the hypothesis that mercury exposure in vaccinations is a major cause of autism. *See also* heavy metals, thimerosal, toxicology.
Robert A. Da Prato

metallothionein

A specific type of protein that maintains proper levels of metals in the circulatory system and also across the blood–brain barrier in the central nervous system (CNS). A higher copper–zinc ratio has been found for individuals with autism spectrum disorders (ASDs) (Walsh, as cited in Kidd, 2002). Walsh argued that a copper–zinc imbalance affects 99% of the individuals with autism and its variants. An elevated copper–zinc ratio has a variety of implications for brain functioning and for ASDs. Surplus levels of copper damage the brain. Also, typically low levels of zinc produce neurological difficulties (Takeda, 2003).
J. Michael Pickle

methodology

See experimental design.

mitigated echolalia

See echolalia.

milieu teaching

An approach to teaching that uses the child's natural environment as the teaching situation. This approach is in contrast to decontextualized teaching, in which skills are taught in controlled or contrived settings (e.g., at a desk, a table, or a booth). *See also* embedded skills, naturalistic interventions.
Dana J. Stevens

mindblindness

Difficulty in sensing and appropriately reacting to the beliefs, desires, emotions, and intentions of others. It is suggested that individuals with autism spectrum disorders (ASDs) lack a theory of mind (ToM), which is sometimes referred to as *mindblindness* (e.g., Baron-Cohen, 1995). Mindblindness is proposed as being responsible for the social and communication impairments that define autism spectrum disorder (ASD) (Tager-Flusberg, 1999). *See also* amygdala, false-belief paradigm, theory of mind (ToM).
Johanna F. Lantz

MLU

See mean length of utterance.

mobile therapist

A professional who works with children in the home, at school, and in community settings to provide consistency of intervention. Occupational, physical, speech-language, and other therapists may travel from setting to setting (and from district to district) to provide therapy services. For example, a speech-language pathologist (SLP) may work on expressive and receptive language skills with a child with autism in the school, home, and local neighborhood. *See also* itinerant teacher, occupational therapist (OT), physical therapist (PT), speech-language pathologist (SLP).
Linda Crane Mitchell

mobile work crew model

Usually three to eight workers with significant disabilities who have one or two supervisors. This differs from an enclave or sheltered workshop because the mobile work crew travels throughout the community doing several different contract services. *See also* sheltered workshop, supported employment program.
Lynn Atanasoff

modeling

See imitation.

mood disorder

See bipolar disorder, depression, mania.

mood-stabilizing medications

Medications that have classically been used to decrease extreme mood swings associated with bipolar disorder. Mood-stabilizing medications are used to treat cyclic behavioral deterioration and overreactivity in children with autism. The medications can assist in moderating the rapidly evolving anger outbursts that characterize the behavior of some of these individuals. Many of the medications in this group are also used to treat seizures. The most commonly used medications in this group are sodium valproate (e.g., Depacon, Depakene, Depakote) and lithium (e.g., Eskalith, Lithobid) (Mitchell & Malhi, 2002). *See also* bipolar disorder, mania, psychopharmacology.
Jeanette C. Ramer

morbidity

A disease, a disorder, or an illness. *Co-morbidity* refers to the presence of a disease, disorder, or illness in addition to the primary diagnosis; for example, mental retardation is often co-morbid with autism. *See also* co-occurring.
John T. Neisworth & Pamela S. Wolfe

most-to-least prompting

See prompt hierarchy.

motivating operation

See establishing operations (EO).

motor imitation

Mimicry of the actions of others that requires movement of one or more body parts. Motor imitation typically appears in early child development and is considered an early pivotal skill on which other critical developmental skills are based (i.e., motor, communication, social). Individuals with autism exhibit impairments in motor imitation tasks (e.g., imitating a gesture) compared with object imitation tasks (e.g., copying a diagram). Motor imitation difficulty is proposed to be related to the overall developmental delays in autism. *See also* imitation, modeling.
Latha V. Soorya

motor planning

See praxis.

movie talk

Recitation of dialogue, passages, words, or a phrase from movies and television repeatedly or intermittently throughout the day. Movie talk is thought to be a form of delayed echolalia. Recitation of scripts from movies may serve to self-stimulate or calm the individual or to communicate with others. *See also* echolalia.
Britta Saltonstall

MR

See mental retardation.

MRI

See magnetic resonance imaging. *See also* functional magnetic resonance imaging (fMRI).

MSDD

See multisystem developmental disorder.

multidisciplinary evaluation (MDE)

An evaluation of a child to determine strengths, needs, and eligibility for special education services. If a child is deemed to be eligible for special education services, he or she also has an MDE periodically thereafter. The evaluation team is usually composed of a parent or guardian and a variety of professionals from different backgrounds. Commonly included professionals are special educators, psychologists, physical therapists (PTs), speech-language pathologists (SLPs), and occupational therapists (OTs); other professionals can be included if necessary (e.g., the general educator if the child will be placed in the general education classroom). The evaluation may include formal testing, observations, play-based assessments, checklists, and parental interviews and must be completed within 45 days of the parent's or guardian's referring the child or signing a permission form for the child to be evaluated. Evaluation can be completed in one of two ways: each professional and the child's parents observing and assessing the child individually at different places and times or (less commonly) simultaneous assessment, in which all of the professionals and the family are gathered at the same place and same time to test, observe, and record information about the child. At the conclusion of the MDE, one team member collects all of

the information and assembles a completed evaluation report to be shared with all team members. *See also* diagnosis, evaluation report, team models.
Susan Wuchenich Parker

multidisciplinary team (MDT)
See team models.

multisystem developmental disorder (MSDD)
As described in the *Diagnostic Classification of Mental Health Disorders of Infancy and Early Childhood (DC: 0-3;* ZERO TO THREE's Diagnostic Classification Task Force, 1994), MSDD refers to the language, social, and affective difficulties of children who may be labeled as having autism or another pervasive developmental disorder (PDD) using the *Diagnostic and Statistical Manual of Mental Disorders, Fourth Edition, Text Revision (DSM-IV-TR;* American Psychiatric Association, 2000). MSDD refers to the functional problems of a child and is not a psychiatric pathology classification. The Developmental, Individual-Difference, Relationship-Based (DIR) model is designed to address MSDD. The *DC: 0-3* classification system is considered by some as an alternative to other classification systems and as more appropriate for very young children. *See also* Developmental, Individual-Difference, Relationship-Based (DIR) model; *Diagnostic Classification of Mental Health Disorders of Infancy and Early Childhood (DC: 0-3).*
John T. Neisworth & Pamela S. Wolfe

music therapy
An approach based on a conceptual model that uses music to accomplish therapeutic goals. The process involves the use of music to develop expressive behaviors in individuals to facilitate positive changes in physical, cognitive, communication, social, or emotional development. Music therapy strategies are predicated on the belief that music can decrease stress, provide a distraction from pain, serve as a focus of attention, and develop positive interpersonal relationships. Music therapy has been used with individuals with a variety of disabilities, including autism and mental retardation (MR). Music therapists are board certified by the American Music Therapy Association. Due to the lack of evidence regarding the efficacy of music therapy as an effective intervention for use with individuals with autism, it has not been recommended as a treatment (New York State Department of Health, Early Intervention Program, 1999a).
Linda Crane Mitchell

mutually acceptable written agreement (MAWA)

Statement that details certain arrangements and funding between separate state agencies. MAWAs are especially pertinent when students with disabilities make the transition from early intervention (EI) services (birth to 3 years) to school-age special education services. *See also* early intervention (EI), Individuals with Disabilities Education Act (IDEA).
John T. Neisworth & Pamela S. Wolfe

natural environment

An everyday setting in the home or community that includes routines and activities typical for individuals and their families, such as mealtime, interacting, and shopping. Natural environments do not include places individuals go because they have disabilities or medical concerns, such as a clinic, a hospital, a professional office, or a special classroom. Each family has its unique set of natural environments. For individuals with autism spectrum disorders (ASDs) and who are easily distractible, typical routines and settings may sometimes appear to be inappropriate learning environments; however, by using structured learning situations in these familiar settings, an individual with autism and his or her family may have increased opportunities to learn targeted skills and reduce issues related to generalization from contrived settings to natural environments (Connecticut Birth to Three Natural Environments Task Force, 1999). *See also* embedded skills, milieu teaching, naturalistic interventions.
Janice H. Belgredan

natural language paradigm (NLP)

A model for language acquisition that uses behavioral strategies within child-centered, natural environments (Koegel, O'Dell, & Koegel, 1987). Teachers follow a child's lead and employ a mand-model strategy (e.g., teach names for things and activities chosen by the child). Use of the child's interest and natural settings relates language with play and other social activities. Guided use of new and diverse communicative initiations enhances generalization, as does use of natural contexts.
John T. Neisworth & Pamela S. Wolfe

naturalistic interventions

Techniques and/or strategies that occur in a natural environment (e.g., classroom, home, community), rather than in a decontextualized setting, and that

are designed to teach specific functional behaviors or skills (i.e., relevant for the settings in which they are learned). Specific intervention approaches often described as naturalistic are activity-based intervention (Losardo & Bricker, 1994; Pretti-Frontczak & Bricker, 2004), incidental teaching (McGee, Krantz, & McClannahan, 1985), milieu and enhanced milieu training (use of structured, prepared circumstances to increase learning opportunities) (Hancock & Kaiser, 2002; Warren & Bambara, 1989), natural language paradigm (use of natural routines and ongoing situations for learning and practice of language as opposed to pull-out language training in contrived arrangements) (Koegel, O'Dell, & Koegel, 1987), and some applications of prompt delay (Charlop & Trasowech, 1991). The advantage of naturalistic interventions is that they capitalize on an individual's interest, sometimes allow choice, and do not depend on the individual's ability to generalize skills learned in a separate, contrived training context (e.g., discrete trial setting). *See also* incidental teaching, milieu teaching, natural language paradigm (NLP), pivotal response training, routine-based instruction.
Samuel L. Odom

negative punishment
See punishment.

negative reinforcement
See reinforcement.

negative reinforcer
See reinforcer.

neuroimaging
A group of procedures that employ radiological techniques for assessing the structures and functions of the brain. Many of the procedures are emerging and are preliminary in their applications (e.g., magnetic resonance spectroscopy [MRS], magnetoencephalography [MEG]) but have great promise in helping to explore what parts of the brain are involved in various dimensions of human activity, such as emotion and memory and dysfunctions in these areas. *See also* functional magnetic resonance imaging (fMRI), magnetic resonance imaging (MRI), positive emission tomography (PET), single photon emission computed tomography (SPECT).
John T. Neisworth & Pamela S. Wolfe

neurologist

A board-certified physician who specializes in the assessment, diagnosis, and treatment of nervous system disorders, including diseases of the brain, spinal cord, nerves, and muscles. Neurologists work along with physical therapists (PTs), occupational therapists (OTs), and speech-language pathologists (SLPs) to treat neurological or muscle problems. Current thinking is that autism and other pervasive developmental disorders (PDDs) involve neurological differences that account for the syndrome. See also neurology, neuropsychology.
Devender R. Banda

neurology

Study of the nervous system of the body, including the brain and spinal cord as well as peripheral nerves. A neurological assessment involves examination and evaluation of cranial nerves, reflexes, motor/cerebellar functioning, sensory functioning, general mental alertness, and speech. New neuroimaging techniques allow examination of parts of the brain thought to be implicated in autism. A convergence of findings based on new technologies as well as research accumulated over several decades points to a neurological basis for autism and other pervasive developmental disorders (PDDs) (Tuchman, 2000). See also functional magnetic resonance imaging (fMRI), head circumference, magnetic resonance imaging (MRI), neurologist, positron emission tomography (PET).
John T. Neisworth & Pamela S. Wolfe

neuromotor

Pertaining to the co-functioning of nerves and muscles important to coordinated movement. Physical and occupational therapists (PTs and OTs) work with the neuromotor difficulties and physical awkwardness often associated with autism and other pervasive developmental disorders (PDDs). See also neurologist, neurology, neuropsychology.
John T. Neisworth & Pamela S. Wolfe

neuropsychology

Study of relationships between the brain and behavior (Kolb & Whishaw, 1996). Neuropsychological research has produced cognitive profiles presumably associated with specific disorders. A neuropsychological evaluation is intended to examine an individual's cognitive abilities, including sensory functioning, attention, visuospatial ability, language, memory, and execu-

tive functions. These evaluations are thought to be useful in the diagnosis of certain childhood disorders such as congenital brain abnormalities, attention-deficit/hyperactivity disorder (ADHD), specific learning disability, and autism. Neuropsychological evaluations can also be helpful in assessing the functioning of an individual who has experienced a traumatic brain injury, a cerebrovascular accident such as a stroke, or a serious brain disease (e.g., meningitis). In addition, evaluations are sometimes conducted before and after medical treatments that may affect memory and cognition, such as certain types of radiation treatments and brain surgery. *See also* neurologist, neurology, neuromotor.
Laura Arnstein

neurotoxic
Referring to the effects of substances (e.g., lead, certain chemical compounds) that destroy or damage neural tissue. Neurotoxins can be generated as by-products of metabolism, such through incomplete metabolism of sugar (as in diabetes).
John T. Neisworth & Pamela S. Wolfe

neurotransmitter
Chemical substance (e.g., acetylcholine, dopamine) that carries impulses along nerve cells (neurons). Neurotransmitters are involved in regulating physiological and anatomical functioning and may be implicated in the basis and expression of the characteristics of autism. Neurotransmitters can be active centrally (i.e., brain function) and peripherally (e.g., intestinal function).
John T. Neisworth & Pamela S. Wolfe

NLP
See natural language paradigm.

NNP procedures
No-no-prompt procedures. *See* error correction.

No Child Left Behind Act of 2001 (PL 107-110)
Public Law detailing the education reform by President George W. Bush. Central to the act is increased accountability for states, school districts, and schools; choice for parents regarding whether to send their children to low-performing schools; flexibility in allocating federal education monies; and

an emphasis on reading. The act calls for states to use standardized testing at the end of each school year to determine individual and school district progress. The legislation has raised issues related to alternative testing (alternate assessment) for individuals with disabilities. *See also* standardized tests. *John T. Neisworth & Pamela S. Wolfe*

no-no-prompt (NNP) procedures
See error correction.

NOREP
See notice of recommended educational placement.

normalization
Term coined by Nijre (1969) and Wolfensberger (1972) to describe the process of ensuring that conditions and patterns of life for individuals with disorders are similar to or the same as those made available to individuals without disabilities. The principle of normalization has been used to guide human services and educational services delivery (e.g., inclusion, mainstreaming). The normalization movement includes efforts to remove physical barriers so that individuals with disabilities can move about as do individuals without disabilities, to make modifications to instructional materials, to put in place classroom adaptations, and to foster change in social expectations and attitudes. *See also* adaptive skills, inclusion, mainstreaming. *John T. Neisworth & Pamela S. Wolfe*

norm-referenced assessment
Form of assessment in which an individual's performance is compared against the performance of others in a normative group (usually typical age peers). Norm-referenced tests differ from criterion-referenced tests that are designed to identify what a student can achieve on a predetermined set of educational goals, concepts, or skills. When a norm-referenced test is developed, a representative group or national sample representing a large and diverse selection of students is given the test before it is presented to the public. The scores these students receive are considered to be *norms*. The norms are the average performances of many students of various ages, grades, and demographic profiles. The scores of all students taking the test after it is made available to educators are compared with the scores of the original or norm group. Norm-referenced tests typically are used to determine eligibility for

early intervention or special education and classify (diagnose) students. In contrast, criterion-referenced tests are useful in helping teachers identify and plan instruction for students who need help in specific areas (although criterion-referenced measures also can be used with norm-referenced tests to gather more information about a student). *See also* assessment, criterion-referenced assessment, curriculum-based assessment (CBA), diagnosis.
Sue H. Krul

notice of recommended educational placement (NOREP)

A state form summarizing recommendations for a child who qualifies for special education services when services are to begin for the first time or whenever a change is made in the services (e.g., when the child no longer qualifies for services) or when the mutually acceptable written agreement (MAWA) does not specify changes requested (by the parents or anyone else). Also provided on the NOREP form are the reason that the action was proposed or refused; a description of any other options that were considered; the reasons that these options were rejected; a list of evaluation procedures, test records, or reports that were used as a basis for the proposed action or refused action; and any other factors relevant to the proposal or refusal. The last part of the NOREP form includes the educational placement recommended (including the type of service, type of support, and location) and the parents' signature of approval or disapproval. If parents disapprove of the recommended placement, they may indicate on the form that they would like an informal meeting, mediation, a prehearing conference, or a due process hearing. A copy of the procedural safeguards is included with the NOREP to provide information on these options. If the parents disapprove of the NOREP, they are also asked to give a reason for their disapproval. *See also* Individuals with Disabilities Education Act (IDEA), mutually acceptable written agreement (MAWA), procedural safeguards.
Donna Meloy

nutritional supplement

See diet therapy, vitamin B$_6$ and magnesium therapy, vitamin therapy.

objective

Intended outcomes stated in terms of behaviors or products that can be assessed. Typically, the term *objectives* refers to behavioral objectives, that is specific skills that parents and professionals state as instructional and/or therapeutic targets. Shorter-term objectives that relate to annual goals in individualized education programs (IEPs) should have three components: the circumstances or materials related to the expected skill, the skill itself, and the criterion for judging mastery. For example, a social objective might be, "When asked a question about a story that the teacher has just read, Billy will offer an answer or say that he does not know 100% of the time." *John T. Neisworth & Pamela S. Wolfe*

obsessive-compulsive disorder (OCD)

Recurrent obsessions and/or compulsions that are time consuming and that cause an individual marked distress and/or significant impairment in social and occupational functioning (American Psychiatric Association [APA], 2000). Obsessions are persistent thoughts, ideas, or impulses. The most common forms of obsessions in children are fear of germs, fear of harm to self or others, and excessive scrutiny of one's thoughts and actions (March, Leonard, & Swedo, 1995). Compulsions are repetitive behaviors and rituals that are performed to reduce anxiety and distress, not for pleasure or gratification (APA, 2000). Stereotypic behaviors (e.g., hand flapping, body rocking), which are more common in autism spectrum disorders (ASDs), and self-injurious behavior (SIB) may be compulsions if performed to reduce anxiety or distress rather than gratification or pleasure. The most common forms of compulsions in children are washing and cleaning, checking, counting, repeating, and touching (March et al., 1995). Obsessive-compulsive symptomatology is more common in individuals with ASDs than in the general population (Green, Gilchrist, Burton, & Cox, 2000). Individuals with autism may exhibit symptoms of OCD without meeting formal diagnostic criteria for OCD. *See also* anxiety, stereotypic behavior.
Scott Bellini

occupational therapist (OT)

A professional trained to assess and assist a person to learn and use purposeful activities. *Occupation* is defined as work, play, and self-help involving perceptual and/or fine motor skills. OTs may also address an individual's sensory processing, attending, arousal, and sensorimotor development. OTs enter the field with a bachelor's, master's, or doctoral degree and must pass a national examination to earn certification. Academic coursework includes study of psychology, orthopedics, anatomy, neurology, and psychiatry. The majority of states in the United States regulate occupational therapy practice. *See also* fine motor skills, occupational therapy (OT), physical therapist (PT).

E. (Rocky) Landers

occupational therapy (OT)

A health profession that supports a person's occupational performance within a specific environment. Occupational performance is viewed in terms of work, play, and self-help. Treatment consists of purposeful activities to promote higher function that may address sensorimotor, neuromuscular, perceptual, developmental, and/or psychosocial areas as they relate to carrying out activities of daily living (self-help skills); leisure; and perceptual, fine motor, and oral-motor skills. Also addressed in occupational therapy are the need for, training in, and use of adaptive equipment, as well as support of family members and caregivers. *See also* fine motor skills, occupational therapist (OT), physical therapy (PT).

E. (Rocky) Landers

OCD

See obsessive-compulsive disorder.

omission training

Differential reinforcement of other behavior (DRO). *See* differential reinforcement.

operant conditioning

Learning that occurs through consequences. The process of building, weakening, or otherwise altering behavior through the consequences or outcomes of behavior. *Operants* (a term coined by B.F. Skinner) are behaviors that operate on physical or social environments and are changed by their effects (functions or outcomes). Operant conditioning is the central approach used in applied behavior analysis (ABA).

For example, a child may receive a favorite snack (consequence) after cleaning his room. Given that the snack is a reinforcer, the child will probably engage in room cleaning behavior more often in the future. Likewise, a behavior that results in an aversive consequence will be weakened and less likely to occur in the future. Many factors are involved in operant learning (e.g., immediacy and consistency of consequences, competing reinforcers). Consequences can be natural, that is, the outcome of an activity itself (e.g., building a tower of blocks) or contrived (e.g., receiving a reward for cleaning a room). It is generally agreed that rewards that are natural are preferred if they are effective; often, contrived reinforcers must be used initially to build a behavior that can then be further built and maintained by its natural consequences. Language training may begin with contrived rewards, but when the child can makes his or her needs known and have his or her requests satisfied, then the child's requests have their natural rewards. *See also* applied behavior analysis (ABA), consequence, punishment, reinforcer, reinforcement.
David L. Lee

oral sensitivity

Rejection of certain food textures and liquid consistencies, choking, and/or gagging on foods and liquids, chewing of nonfood items, teeth grinding (bruxism), and drooling. Some children with autism demonstrate oral sensitivity. *See also* hyperresponsiveness, hyporesponsiveness.
Lynn Adams

oral-motor skills

Voluntary movements of the oral cavity (mouth) including tongue, lip, and jaw. Oral-motor skills include biting, chewing, kissing, or smiling. Oral-motor skills (often specifically taught by occupational therapists [OTs]) are different from motor speech skills (used in speech production). Improvement in oral-motor skills does not necessarily lead to improvement in motor speech skills. *See also* occupational therapist (OT); occupational therapy (OT).
John T. Neisworth & Pamela S. Wolfe

OT

See occupational therapist, occupational therapy.

overcorrection

A behavior reduction procedure that involves having a learner engage in a behavior repeatedly as a consequence for exhibiting an inappropriate behavior. Overcorrection (a form of punishment) takes one of two forms: positive practice or restitution. The appropriate form to use as an intervention is determined by the extent to which the environment is disrupted by the specific inappropriate behavior and the feasibility of correcting the disruption. In positive practice, the individual must repeatedly demonstrate a positive alternative behavior. For example, if a student repeatedly leaves his seat and wanders around the room, he may be required to remain in his seat during a subsequent break and must practice stating the classroom rule, "I will get permission to leave my assigned area." In restitutional overcorrection, the individual must restore the environment to an enhanced state (e.g., if intentionally spilling milk, the individual must wipe up the milk on the table, mop the floor, and clean the sink). Overcorrection procedures can be used when inappropriate behaviors are repeated or are intentional; these procedures are not suitable to use when behaviors are accidental or are not repeated. Overcorrection procedures have been demonstrated to be effective in reducing some inappropriate behaviors, but there are concerns regarding the use of physical guidance and the focus on inappropriate behaviors. *See also* punishment.
Kathy Ruhl

overfocused attention

See overselectivity.

overresponsiveness

See hyperresponsiveness.

overselectivity

Also called *overfocused attention*. Fixation of attention to an object or task and tuning out of surrounding stimuli. This tunnel vision can become so intense that individuals with autism are often suspected of having hearing impairments due to failure to react to competing stimuli. Overselectivity may occur because individuals with autism are uncomfortable with or are overaroused by wide ranges of stimuli or because they may overfocus their attention on minute stimuli, thereby decreasing their arousal (Kinsbourne, 1991). The theory of overfocused attention was first developed with children with attention-deficit/hyperactivity disorder (ADHD) and later extended to children with pervasive developmental disorders (PDDs). An overfocused child may engage in stereotypic behaviors. *See also* hyperresponsiveness, hyporesponsiveness, stereotypic behavior.

Celine A. Saulnier

Pp

patterning
See Doman/Delacato approach.

Pavlovian conditioning
See respondent conditioning.

PBS
See positive behavior support.

PDD
See pervasive developmental disorder.

PDD-NOS
See pervasive developmental disorder-not otherwise specified.

PECS
See Picture Exchange Communication System.

pedantic speech
Speech that is marked by the avoidance of slang words or other informal speech. It is characterized by the use of technical, precise, bookish language. Pedantic speech often is identified as a communication difference displayed by individuals with autism spectrum disorders (ASDs), especially Asperger syndrome (AS). (The label "Little Professor" is sometimes used to refer to a child whose language seems pedantic for his or her age.) *See also* prosody.
John T. Neisworth & Pamela S. Wolfe

peer-mediated intervention
Intervention or instruction delivered by a peer to an individual with autism (Odom & Strain, 1984). The intervention may be designed to promote social,

communication, academic, and other skills. Peers are usually taught specific behaviors and instructions to direct to an individual with autism. A peer may have to reach a criterion during training before providing the intervention, may receive prompts from the teacher, and/or may receive a reward or reinforcement for participating as a peer mediator. Peer-mediated interventions have been used primarily with preschool and elementary-age children with autism, and they are well supported by single-subject design research (Odom & Strain, 2002). *See also* social skills training.

Samuel L. Odom

peptide

Two or more amino acids joined together. There are 20 kinds of amino acids that may bond in peptide chains; a protein is made up of peptide sequences. Some propose that certain diets (e.g., gluten free, casein free) should be prescribed for individuals with autism. Gluten, found in wheat, and casein, found in dairy products, are proteins. Some theorize that individuals with autism have a metabolic difference that results in gluten and caseins being broken into opioids (peptides produced by one's own body and also found in opiate drugs, e.g., morphine). These opioids enter the digestive system and affect the brain, either causing or exacerbating the difficulties associated with autism (e.g., sensory reactions, cognitive functioning). Currently, evidence for the theory and efficacy of the gluten- and casein-free diets is based on parent and professional report and surveys; controlled double-blind studies are not yet available. *See also* amino acids, antigluten therapy, casein, diet therapy.

John T. Neisworth & Pamela S. Wolfe

percentile

A score expressed as a percentage that indicates the position of that score relative to scores achieved by others on the same test. A raw score that is at the 87th percentile is one that is higher than 86% of other scores. Standardized, norm-referenced tests typically supply tables showing raw scores and corresponding percentiles.

John T. Neisworth & Pamela S. Wolfe

performance objective

See behavioral objective.

perseveration

Repetition of the same activity without apparent advantage (e.g., singing the same song over and over, asking the same question incessantly, spinning

a coin repeatedly). Perseverative behavior and speech are characteristic of individuals with autism. *See also* atypical behavior, stereotypic behavior.
John T. Neisworth & Pamela S. Wolfe

person-first language

Language referring to an individual with a disability in which the person is put before the disability (e.g., *children who have autism* rather than *autistic children*) and, preferably, before the supports or needs of the person (e.g., *child with mobility needs* rather than *physically disabled child*). Person-first language also avoids group nouns (e.g., *the mentally retarded*). Use of person-first language is in keeping with self-advocacy for individuals with disabilities and is professionally preferred unless contrary to the desires of the person or parents. *See also* self-advocacy.
John T. Neisworth & Pamela S. Wolfe

pervasive developmental disorder (PDD)

A general designation for a group or a spectrum of specific disorders characterized by pervasive (i.e., reaching across multiple contexts and domains) and significant impairments in the development of social and communication functioning and in the development of normal patterns of behaviors or a range of interests. The disorders include autism, Rett disorder, childhood disintegrative disorder (CDD), Asperger syndrome (AS), and pervasive developmental disorder-not otherwise specified (PDD-NOS). PDD-NOS, sometimes referred to as *atypical autism,* is a catch-all label designated for individuals demonstrating levels of impairment that do not meet the criteria for other disorders within the PDD spectrum. PDD, therefore, is not itself a disorder but an umbrella term to describe any disorder within this spectrum of disorders. Because the term *pervasive developmental disorder* is confusing and often misunderstood, the educational system and some related fields have adopted the term *autism spectrum disorder* (ASD) as an alternative to the PDD label. *See also Diagnostic and Statistical Manual of Mental Disorders, Fourth Edition, Text Revision (DSM-IV-TR);* pervasive developmental disorder-not otherwise specified (PDD-NOS).
Richard J. Cowan & Keith Allen

pervasive developmental disorder-not otherwise specified (PDD-NOS)

A diagnosis used when a child displays fewer criteria than are required for a diagnosis of autism but does evidence autism-like problems that constitute

developmental risk. PDD-NOS can be considered as *subthreshold autism* (Mesibov, 1997) and is often used when a child is too young for a more definitive diagnosis. Children diagnosed as having PDD-NOS often evidence higher language and cognitive skills than children with an autism diagnosis. *See also Diagnostic and Statistical Manual of Mental Disorders, Fourth Edition, Text Revision (DSM-IV-TR);* pervasive developmental disorder (PDD).
John T. Neisworth & Pamela S. Wolfe

PET
See positron emission tomography.

pharmacology
The science of drugs; the characteristics of and reactions to drugs and their therapeutic value. Drugs employed in the treatment of autism and other pervasive developmental disorders (PDDs) are often used in conjunction with behavior therapies and other interventions. Such drugs can be classified as antianxiety medications, anticonvulsants, antidepressants, antipsychotics, beta-blockers, opiate blockers, sedatives, and stimulants. *See also* antianxiety medications, antidepressant medications, antipsychotic medications, psychoactive medications, psychobiology, psychopharmacology, stimulant medications.
John T. Neisworth & Pamela S. Wolfe

phenothiazines
See antipsychotic medications.

phenotype
The expressed physical characteristics (e.g., anatomical, physiological) of an individual resulting from that person's heredity and environment. Phenotype and genotype may not be the same. For example, two people may both have brown hair (same phenotype for hair color), but one person may have two genes for brown hair, whereas the other person may have one gene for brown hair and one gene for blond hair. *See also* genotype.
John T. Neisworth & Pamela S. Wolfe

phobias
Intense fears, often viewed as excessive and unreasonable. To be formally diagnosed as having a phobia, a person must react with fear and anxiety (e.g.,

increased heart rate, breathing, and sweating; thoughts and/or statements reflecting fear; behavioral attempts to avoid or leave the situation) when he or she is in—or anticipates being in—a feared situation. Among the most common *specific phobias* are fears of certain animals (e.g., snakes, dogs, cats); natural environments (e.g., high places, storms, water); situations (e.g., flying in airplanes, riding in elevators, being in crowded or enclosed places); and blood, injections, and bodily injury (American Psychiatric Association, 2000). Some children and individuals with autism and other autism spectrum disorders (ASDs) may have strong reactions to loud noises and people in costume. A major class of phobias that is separately distinguished is that of *social phobia* (often referred to as *social anxiety disorder*). In an individual with an ASD, it must be noted whether the person does, indeed, have an apparent interest in interacting with other people before a social phobia is diagnosed; absence of social interest would not permit a diagnosis of social phobia. In individuals with challenging behavior, it may appear that the function of their behavior is to escape from demands, when in fact it may be to escape or avoid the feared situation. This latter distinction is critical as the two alternative interpretations call for different intervention strategies. Phobias are among the problems most successfully treated by behavior therapy. Such therapy may include any or a combination of the following: contingency management (to reduce avoidance and reward the individual for successfully remaining in the presence of the feared object or situation), systematic desensitization (using relaxation or a distracting activity while gradually exposing the person to the feared situation), prolonged exposure (e.g., flooding or implosion, which is *not* recommended for children or adults with autism and related disorders), modeling (in which a model, e.g., a trusted teacher, demonstrates successfully remaining in the feared situation), and self-control (a range of relaxation, imagery, and cognitive strategies). *See also* anxiety, behavior therapy, desensitization, modeling, social phobia.
Joseph R. Scotti

physical therapist (PT)

Also called *physiotherapist.* Professional who works in conjunction with physicians and educators to provide services to clients with impairments, functional limitations, disabilities, or changes in physical function and health status as the result of injury, disease, or other causes. PTs provide prevention and wellness services and collaborate with other health professionals to consult, educate, and engage in research. PTs are graduates of a college or university accredited physical therapy program and licensed in the state(s)

in which they practice. Individuals with autism who have gross motor difficulties may require PT services. *See also* gross motor, occupational therapist (OT), physical therapy (PT).
Denise Lynn Schilling

physical therapy (PT)

Also called *physiotherapy*. Health care discipline dedicated to diagnosis and management of movement dysfunction; enhancement of physical and functional abilities; and restoration, maintenance, and promotion of optimal physical function, optimal fitness and wellness, and optimal quality of life as it relates to movement and health. In addition, PT is involved in the prevention of the onset and symptoms and progression of impairments, functional limitations, and disabilities that may result from diseases, disorders, conditions, or injuries. PT may include the use of physical agents or treatment methods, therapeutic exercise, manual procedures, neuromuscular reeducation, respiratory hygiene, and gait training. Physical therapy is sometimes provided to children with autism to reduce motor awkwardness and to improve gross motor skills and motor planning. Physical therapy also includes use of various sensory-based treatments that are sometimes employed with children with autism. *See also* gross motor, occupational therapy (OT), physical therapist (PT).
Denise Lynn Schilling

physiotherapist

See physical therapist (PT).

physiotherapy

See physical therapy (PT).

pica

Ingestion of inedible materials such as paint, dirt, feces, and hair. The behavior can have harmful effects, including poisoning and intestinal obstruction or perforation. According to the *Diagnostic and Statistical Manual of Mental Disorders, Fourth Edition, Text Revision* (*DSM-IV-TR;* American Psychiatric Association, 2000), for a diagnosis of pica, the behavior must occur for at least 1 month and must not be part of a culturally sanctioned practice. The behavior occurs in many populations, most often with individuals having severe mental retardation, including children who also have autism (Hardan

& Sahl, 1997). In some cases the behavior may occur in individuals with certain nutrient deficiencies (e.g., iron deficiency, zinc deficiency). Therefore, a medical examination should be conducted; functional behavior assessment (FBA) is also recommended. *See also Diagnostic and Statistical Manual of Mental Disorders, Fourth Edition, Text Revision (DSM-IV-TR); functional behavior assessment (FBA).*
Laura Arnstein

Picture Exchange Communication System (PECS)

A system often used by individuals with autism involving the use of picture symbols to initiate communication through the exchange of symbols with partners (Bondy & Frost, 1994). Training consists of six phases: exchange, distance and persistence, discrimination, building sentences, responding, and commenting. PECS can be an effective form of communication and, in some cases, fosters increases in verbal language for individuals (Schwartz, Garfinkle, & Bauer, 1998). Research further supports PECS for improving emerging speech and decreasing problem behaviors in children with autism (Charlop-Christy, Carpenter, Le, LeBlanc, & Kellet, 2002). PECS communication books require maintenance and the continual addition of new picture symbols as the individual's language repertoire increases. PECS can be considered a useful tool that eventually may be phased out in favor of more typical forms of communicating, depending on the child's capabilities (Frost & Bondy, 1994). *See also* visual schedule, visual strategies.
Devender R. Banda

pivotal response training

An approach based on teaching fundamental behaviors that then permit the child to acquire many other behaviors. The selection of key or pivotal behaviors is in contrast to teaching a series of separate skills. Learning pivotal behaviors (e.g., functional communication) produces collateral improvement in other areas, such as marked reduction in disruptive behavior (Carr & Durand, 1985). Likewise, teaching central skills such as social reciprocity and responsivity to multiple cues has been reported as highly effective for facilitating language development (Camarata, in press; Koegel, O'Dell, & Dunlap, 1988). Self-management is clearly a pivotal behavior that makes possible rapid learning of innumerable skills across contexts and time. Guidelines for teaching self-management are available (Koegel, Koegel, & Parks, 1995). Joint attention (a major problem in autism and other pervasive developmental disorders [PDDs]) recently has attracted more intensive research and intervention due

to its recognition as a pivotal behavior (Adamson & Russell, 1999; Mundy & Stella, 2000; Whalen & Schreibman, 2003). Pivotal behavior training employs basic behavior principles and procedures (e.g., reinforcement, shaping, discrimination). The training is typically conducted in a child's natural settings with parent–professional consultation and often involves parents as teachers. Problems associated with limited generalization (use of learned skills outside the training context) are avoided. *See also* applied behavior analysis (ABA), generalization, joint attention.
John T. Neisworth & Pamela S. Wolfe

PL
See Public Law; *see also specific laws.*

PL 91-230
See Education of the Handicapped Act (EHA) of 1970.

PL 93-112
See Rehabilitation Act of 1973.

PL 94-142
Education for All Handicapped Children Act of 1975. *See* Individuals with Disabilities Education Act (IDEA).

PL 99-457
Education of the Handicapped Act (EHA) Amendments of 1986. *See* Education of the Handicapped Act (EHA) of 1970 (PL 91-230).

PL 101-336
See Americans with Disabilities Act (ADA) of 1990.

PL 101-476
See Individuals with Disabilities Education Act (IDEA).

PL 105-17
Individuals with Disabilities Education Act (IDEA) Amendments of 1997. *See* Individuals with Disabilities Education Act (IDEA).

PL 105-220

Rehabilitation Act Amendments of 1998. *See* Rehabilitation Act of 1973 (PL 93-112).

PL 107-110

See No Child Left Behind Act of 2001.

placebo

A kind of control treatment that is used in experimental study. Placebos can be an inactive substance (e.g., a sugar pill in a medical drug trial) or a pseudo-treatment (e.g., equivalent interaction with a behavior therapist but not exposure to specific therapy). Placebos are used so that participants in research cannot determine whether they have received the independent variable under study. For example, in a study to determine whether a new drug is effective, the researchers would divide participants into two groups. Both groups would receive a pill. One group would receive a pill with the active medication; the second group would receive a placebo that looks the same but that does not contain the active medication. Use of a placebo can lessen potential observer bias. However, the best control situation is a double-blind technique in which neither the experimenter nor subject knows when the placebo or active treatment is in place (this is not typically feasible in behavior interventions). *See also* bias, clinical trial, control condition, double blind, experimental design.
John T. Neisworth & Pamela S. Wolfe

poor registration

See low registration.

positive behavior support (PBS)

Process of problem solving and using effective strategies to support student learning. PBS provides preventative interventions to students at the individual, classroom, and schoolwide level. Functional behavior assessment (FBA) is often part of PBS and used to determine the function of challenging behaviors and build a support plan. PBS is a proactive model for behavior management. *See also* emotional support, functional behavior assessment (FBA), functions of behavior.
Dana J. Stevens

positive practice
See overcorrection.

positive punishment
See punishment.

positive reinforcement
See reinforcement.

positive reinforcer
See reinforcer.

positron emission tomography (PET)
A neuroimaging technique that permits the study of biochemical brain processes. In particular, it provides information of the oxidative metabolism and blood flow of the brain (Horwitz & Rumsey, as cited in Bauman & Kemper, 1994). PET scans can map localized brain metabolism because it is assumed that during a particular cognitive function, the regions of the brain participating in that function become more active and increase their rates of oxidative metabolism. PET scans are useful because otherwise, for a person with anatomic abnormalities that are characteristic of a certain disorder, it may not be possible to tell which regions of the brain are affected. PET scans sometimes enable the neurobiologic basis for a disorder to be uncovered. During a PET scan, and the patient must remain still in the scanner for a specified time. PET involves the use of radiological compounds; when using PET with a child, the dosage of radiation must be lowered, which reduces the sensitivity of the method. *See also* neuroimaging.
Jean M. Wood

posttraumatic stress disorder (PTSD)
PTSD is a psychiatric disorder classified in the *Diagnostic and Statistical Manual of Mental Disorders, Fourth Edition, Text Revision* (*DSM-IV-TR;* American Psychiatric Association, 2000) in the category of anxiety disorders. The precursor to onset of this disorder is normally a specific highly traumatic event or series of events that caused the person to experience intense fear, helplessness, or horror. Three specific sets of symptoms must be present in order for PTSD to be diagnosed: persistent reexperiencing of the event through flashbacks, distressing dreams, and/or play reenactments; avoidance of reminders of the traumatic event or numbing oneself to the effects of such

reminders (e.g., avoidance of physical stimuli, attempting to cut off emotion, use of alcohol or drugs to numb one's feelings); and an increased level of vigilance or awareness to the environment or oneself. PTSD symptoms do not necessarily occur immediately following the traumatic event but persist for at least 30 days after onset (Sue, Sue, & Sue, 2000). *See also* antianxiety medications, anxiety, depression.
Teresa Babula

pragmatics

A set of rules concerned with the way language is used rather than the way it is formed; language use in a communicative context, specifically, conversations. Rules governing conversations include turn taking, topic initiation, maintenance and closing, repair strategies when communication breaks down, eye contact, and the physical proximity of speaker and listener. Pragmatics is generally accepted to be the foundation for language acquisition. Pragmatic language is a major area of impairment for children with autism and is the subject of research and focused instruction. *See also* communication disorder, functions of communication, verbal behavior (VB).
Lynn Adams

praxis

An individual's planning, organizing, and carrying out of a newly acquired, nonhabitual motor action. For example, when students are learning a new motor action (e.g., writing their name, climbing through a tunnel), they plan how to begin, then the sequence of action is typically automatically formulated. When motor praxis problems occur, motor performance is compromised. Common actions such as putting on a coat, participating in sports (and imitating others), or exploring an unfamiliar playground climber would be very challenging to a child with motor praxis problems. Children with autism may have difficulty making and imitating specific sounds or facial movements; this difficulty may indicate oral-motor praxis problems. Praxis and motor planning can be evaluated informally by observation of a child's ability to carry out novel tasks, to imitate, and to sequence movements. *See also* gross motor, oral-motor skills.
E. (Rocky) Landers

precision teaching (PT)

An empirically validated teaching technology (originally developed by O.R. Lindsley, 1971, 1990) focusing on the development and measurement of skill fluency. Fluency is measured in terms of accuracy and rate of behavior. Performance is measured via plotting on a chart that can be applied to any behavior. A typical application of PT is to teach expressive labeling. A goal of a number of responses per minute is set. When presented with an array of objects and an initial cue to begin, the learner labels as many of the objects as possible within a predetermined counting time. The learner's responses per minute and the number of errors that occurred within that period are recorded. These data are recorded as dots on a chart that contains similar data from previous days (often on a semilogarithmic chart, in which frequency data are compressed on a logarithmic scale to permit graphing of increasing numbers). The angle of the line that results from connecting the dots indicates how quickly the individual is acquiring the skill. PT involves systematic phases for developing and delivering instruction and for promoting generalization, which is especially pertinent for children with autism. *See also* fluency. *Thomas P. Kitchen*

predictive validity
See validity.

Premack principle
Sometimes referred to as *Grandma's law,* the Premack principle (Premack, 1965) directs one to do what one should before one does what one wants (e.g., *Eat your peas, then your ice cream; Do your homework, then watch TV*). When faced with two chores (e.g., ironing and vacuuming, with vacuuming the preferred activity), the individual should engage in the less preferred then the more preferred activity (ironing followed by vacuuming). People skilled at self-management employ the Premack principle to complete their work and thus get their lower probability behaviors accomplished and reinforced. In clinical and educational settings, therapists can require individuals to engage in less desired before more desired behavior to help them build weak but desirable capabilities. *See also* contingency, contingency contracting, reinforcement. *John T. Neisworth & Pamela S. Wolfe*

prepubertal schizophrenia
See childhood-onset schizophrenia (COS).

present level of performance
Statements concerning current competencies in all areas applicable to educational functioning or life skills (part of the individualized education program, or IEP). It describes the strengths and unique needs of the child from

information collected through observations, assessments, and interviews. *See also* individualized education program (IEP).
Devender R. Banda

presymbolic thought

A style of cognitive development in which individuals think in concrete terms and do not think representationally. In Piaget's theory of cognitive development, the end of the sensorimotor stage (at about 2 years of age in typically developing children) is marked by the development of what is called symbolic thought. *See also* symbolic thought.
Maryjo M. Oster

prevalence

The *total* number of active cases of a specific disease or disorder in a population (usually in a specific country). Prevalence is frequently expressed as a percentage of the current population (and should not confused with incidence, which is the number of *new* cases). Prevalence of autism in large countries cannot be assessed directly through screening the entire population and instead must be estimated. Because the diagnostic criteria for autism have changed over time, comparisons across time are difficult to interpret. Prevalence of autism spectrum disorders (ASDs) is several times higher than autism. Estimates of prevalence in the United States vary, with 1.5 million estimated by the Autism Society of America (n.d.) for ASDs. In 2001, the U.S. Department of Education estimate for individuals 6 through 21 receiving special education services was about 80,000. *See also* incidence.
Raymond G. Romanczyk

probe

A procedure for assessing the status of a behavior, or a sampling of a child's work or behavior. Probes are often used to quickly appraise the extent of generalization in language training. Probes are useful in applied research and evaluations of ongoing instruction and/or therapy. Probes can be used to appraise a child's reading rate and comprehension, can be repeated over sessions, and are fairly accurate as compared with more time-consuming methods. *See also* assessment, curriculum-based assessment (CBA).
John T. Neisworth & Pamela S. Wolfe

probiotics

See antiyeast therapy.

procedural safeguards

Strategies used to ensure that client rights are protected during treatments and/or interventions. Safeguards may include review of plans by individuals outside an agency or school, provision of informed consent, and evaluation of procedures such as criteria for determining effective treatment (Axelrod, Spreat, Berry, & Moyer, 1993). *See also* best practice guidelines.
John T. Neisworth & Pamela S. Wolfe

prompt dependence

The continued use of prompts for accomplishing a behavior. Children with autism may become dependent on prompts used during therapy and instruction. Prompts should be faded from instruction as children acquire the targeted behavior to avoid prompt dependence. *See also* discrete trial training, fading, Lovaas approach, prompting.
Devender R. Banda

prompt hierarchy

Systematic use of sequential levels of prompts to teach a new skill. Prompts are based on the nature of the task and the student (Cuvo & Davis, 1998). There are two types of hierarchies: decreasing prompt hierarchy and increasing prompt hierarchy. A decreasing prompt hierarchy, or *most-to-least prompting* (Anderson, Taras, & Cannon, 1996), begins with the most intrusive level of prompting (often full physical guidance) and gradually reduces the amount of assistance given to the student as learning progresses. This strategy is often used when a student is learning an unfamiliar skill. For example, while teaching a child to use a spoon, the teacher might initially place his or her hand completely over the student's hand and help with holding and guiding the spoon (full physical guidance). Prompting would later be faded to a model in which the teacher demonstrates scooping while the student holds the spoon. This assistance then would be faded to a verbal prompt. Until the student is independently using the spoon, reinforcement is given at each level of prompting regardless of the level of assistance needed. An increasing prompt hierarchy, also called *least-to-most prompting* (Anderson et al., 1996) or the *system of least prompts* (Alberto & Troutman, 1990; Cuvo & Davis, 1998), begins by giving the student the opportunity to perform the skill independently, then gradually increases the level of prompting given until the student responds appropriately. This strategy is used to increase spontaneity (Anderson et al., 1996) and to promote maintenance of a previously learned skill. An example of an increasing prompt hierarchy would be

teaching a student to request a snack. Initially, the teacher would simply set up the snack and pause to give the student the opportunity to initiate the request. The teacher could then give a statement that is an indirect model of the name of the snack food (e.g., "Today for snack we have cookies and pretzels"). If the student does not respond, the teacher may ask a question (e.g., "What do you want?"). If the student still does not respond, the teacher could give a choice verbally (e.g., "Do you want cookies or pretzels?"), or by showing the pictures of the cookies and the pretzels. If there is still no response, the teacher could give a direct model (e.g., "Say, 'I want pretzels'"). *See also* fading, graduated guidance, prompting.
Marcia K. Laus

prompting

Actions by a teacher, trainer, or caregiver that accompany an instruction and make the desired response more likely to occur. Prompting is designed to increase the rate of correct responding by providing cues for the expected behavior. Prompts may be subtle (e.g., looking at a box of tissues to encourage a student to blow his nose) to intrusive (e.g., physically guiding a child through an activity). Common prompts include verbal prompts ("What do you do next?"), visual prompts (a list of the classroom rules), physical prompts (tapping an individual's hand that is holding a pencil when asked to begin a worksheet). Individuals with autism may become dependent on prompts and may be unable to correctly respond to instruction without a prompt. To reduce prompt dependency, prompts must be gradually removed or faded. *See also* fading, graduated guidance, prompt hierarchy.
Rachel L. Loftin

pronoun errors

Reversal of pronouns during language production, often characteristic of children with autism. Pronoun errors are found in children's normal language development up to age 5 (e.g., "Me want to eat"). Reasons for pronoun errors are disputed and may be related to echolalia. *See also* communication disorder, echolalia.
Lynn Adams

proprioception

Awareness of the sensation of movement and the position of one's own body in relation to people and objects. The function of proprioception is to increase body awareness, motor control, and motor planning. Effective proprioception permits smooth movements for walking; climbing; running; and movement through different positions, such as standing to lying down, and are often a part of assessments by physical therapists. When provided appropriately, proprioceptive activities can be used to decrease anxiety and increase alertness. Individuals with autism may overrely on proprioception and underrely on vision (Masterton & Biederman, 1983).

Proprioception and vestibular processing are thought to possibly contribute jointly to the perception of active movement and the development of body scheme and postural control. These systems, in conjunction with vision, provide awareness and coordination of head movements in space; coordination of the eyes, head, and body; and stabilization of the eyes in space with head movements.

In the past proprioception was thought to be the unconscious sense of movement, whereas kinesthesia was thought to be the conscious sense. In more recent times, the difference between proprioception and kinesthesia has not been as well defined by researchers. It is thought that although there is still a difference between conscious and unconscious movements, these two systems should be classified under one—proprioception. See also kinesthetic sense, sensory integration (SI), vestibular.
Jane Singletary

prosody

The pitch, loudness, tempo, rhythm, resonance, phrasing, and stress of an individual's speech; the melody of speech, important in conveying information beyond the meanings of the words themselves in discourse. Children with autism display unusual prosodic characteristics (often speaking in a monotone or a sing-song voice). Nonverbal children with autism often make unusually pitched sounds (Baltaxe & Simmons, 1985; Schreibman, Kohlenberg, & Britten, 1986). Children with autism may also have poor comprehension of others' prosody. See also expressive language, speech-language pathologist (SLP).
Elizabeth A. Kelley

protodeclarative

Pertaining to early vocalizations or nonverbal language used by an individual to get another person to look at or listen to something. Use of protodeclarative communication is part of joint attention skills. Lack of protodeclarative (not to be confused with protoimperative) pointing is a major marker of autism in children under age 3. See also eye gaze, joint attention, protoimperative, social gaze.
John T. Neisworth & Pamela S. Wolfe

protoimperative

Pertaining to early vocalizations or nonverbal language used by an individual to get another person to obtain what is wanted; requests. *See also* eye gaze, protodeclarative, social gaze.
John T. Neisworth & Pamela S. Wolfe

proximal development

See zone of proximal development (ZPD).

pseudoscience

False science; inquiry that appears to use scientific methods and makes every effort to give that impression. This so-called research, however, is actually based on ineffective, unscientific methods. Parents as well as some professionals often try a particular intervention because it appears to be based on scientific research. Markers of a pseudoscientific approach include the following:

- Use of some aspect of science as evidence (but with studies that are poorly designed and uncontrolled and that have unreliable or unreplicable results)
- Reliance on anecdotes or testimonials (e.g., a magazine advertisement that shows a parent explaining how a particular dietary intervention "cured" her child with autism does not mean that the intervention actually works)
- Avoidance of disproof (instead of confronting evidence or reports of contradictions to pseudoscientific interventions, advocates sidestep the problem by rearranging the theory a bit or by adding elements to the theory)
- Reduction of complex phenomena to overly simplistic concepts (e.g., the causes of autism are likely to be many and quite dependent on individual differences between children; however, pseudoscientific investigators might try to promote a vitamin intervention by explaining autism as a simple deficiency in a particular vitamin)

See also best practice guidelines, empiricism, experimental design.
Christopher Jones

psychiatrist

A medical doctor (M.D.) or doctor of osteopathic medicine (D.O.) who specializes in the diagnosis and treatment of problems of thinking, emotion, and behavior. Although other professionals may also provide mental health care (and order and conduct psychological, developmental, achievement

testing, and so forth), in the vast majority of states only the psychiatrist can order medical tests (e.g., lab tests, radiology) and prescribe medication. Training to be a psychiatrist requires an undergraduate degree; 4 years of medical school; and at least 4 years of approved residency training in medicine, neurology, and general psychiatry with adults, as well as some experience with children. After training in general psychiatry, psychiatrists may undergo further training and subspecialize in areas such as child and adolescent psychiatry, geriatric psychiatry, forensic psychiatry, or addiction psychiatry. *See also* psychoactive medications, psychopharmacology.
Lisa Jamnback

psychoactive medications

Medications prescribed to treat mental, emotional, and behavioral problems; they affect the central nervous system (CNS), correcting chemical imbalances of neurotransmitters in the brain. The main types of chemicals that are affected include serotonin, norepinephrine, dopamine, acetylcholine, histamine, gamma-aminobutyric acid, and glutamate; serotonin and dopamine are thought to be especially pertinent to behavior characteristic of autism. Common types of psychoactive medications for individuals with autism include antidepressants, mood stabilizers, antipsychotics, stimulants, sedatives, and antianxiety medications. *See also* antianxiety medications, antidepressant medications, antipsychotic medications, mood disorder, moodstabilizing medications, psychopharmacology, sedative medication, serotonin, stimulant medications.
Lisa Jamnback

psychobiology

An umbrella term for disciplines focused on brain–behavior relationships, including psychopharmacology, neuropathology, electrophysiology, and brain imaging. Psychobiology also uses cognitive neuroscience and classical neuropsychology to specify how the behaviors of individuals with autism differ from those of typically developing individuals; these efforts are sometimes termed *behavioral phenotyping*. The most frequently replicated biological finding in autism is enlarged head and brain size (head circumference). Most imaging studies relating to brain enlargement have not analyzed regional abnormalities. A comprehensive magnetic resonance imaging (MRI) morphometric study by Herbert et al. (2003) revealed widespread brain enlargement in autism; however, specific regions do not appear to be markedly disproportionately large or small. *See also* genetics, head circumference, heredity, twin studies in autism.
Curtis K. Deutsch

psychologist

A professional who engages in the study of the human mind and behavior. Use of the title (certification) or practice of psychology (licensure) may be restricted by state law and typically requires a graduate degree. Psychologists may provide services related to either groups or individuals and may specialize in a number of areas such as clinical, counseling, educational, industrial-organizational, social, developmental, and experimental psychology. Psychologists in applied fields (e.g., clinical, counseling, school) may provide mental health services in hospitals, clinics, schools, or private settings; in most states, psychologists may not prescribe medications or order medical tests. Industrial-organizational psychologists apply psychological principles to the workplace. Other psychologists study the physical, cognitive, emotional, social, or developmental aspects of humans. *See also* behavior plan, functional behavior assessment (FBA), intelligence tests.
Marley W. Watkins

psychometrics

1. The study and measurement of psychological characteristics such as intelligence, personality, stress, and adjustment. 2. The qualities of a test, such as reliability and validity. Psychometric procedures involve statistical manipulations of score data to develop test scales, checklists, multiple-choice questions that meet standards of reliability and validity. The resulting psychometric materials may then be standardized, norm-referenced, and used for purposes of screening, eligibility determination, and progress evaluation. *See also* norm-referenced assessment, reliability, standardization, validity.
John T. Neisworth & Pamela S. Wolfe

psychopharmacology

The study of the effects of medications on thinking, emotions, and behavior, as well as side effects, drug interactions, contraindications, and other issues that relate to safe and effective use of psychoactive medications. Pharmacotherapy with psychoactive medications is often part of a more comprehensive treatment plan, which may also involve applied behavior analysis (ABA) or other types of interventions. *See also* bipolar disorder, depression, mania, psychiatrist, psychoactive medications, serotonin.
Lisa Jamnback

psychosocial

Pertaining to psychological development concerned with relating to others as well as coping with or adjusting to social situations and expectations.

Psychosocial development is a core domain for assessment and intervention for all children within the autism spectrum. *See also* core deficits, social cognition, social competence, social impairment, social skills.
John T. Neisworth & Pamela S. Wolfe

PT
See physical therapist, physical therapy; *see also* precision teaching.

PTSD
See posttraumatic stress disorder.

Public Law (PL)
A mandate enacted by the U.S. Congress. Public Laws are identified first according to the number of the session of Congress that passed the law, then the sequence in which the law was passed within that session. For example, PL 94-142 refers to the 142nd law passed by the 94th Congress (a new session of Congress has convened every 2 years since 1789; thus, the 94th Congress convened in 1975–1976). *See also specific PLs.*
John T. Neisworth & Pamela S. Wolfe

punishment
An operant procedure in which the future probability of the occurrence of a behavior or a response is reduced. Punishment in which a behavior is followed by an unpleasant event is defined as Type I or positive punishment (referred to as *positive* because the aversive event is added after a behavior); examples of positive punishment include requiring a child to clean all of the desks in the room as a punishment for marking his or her own desk or requiring a child to walk properly down the hall several times for running in the hall. Punishment involving the removal or withdrawal of positive reinforcement is defined as Type II or negative punishment. Type II punishment is more commonly used than Type I (Foxx, 1982). A punishment procedure must always include positive reinforcement for alternative, appropriate behaviors. *See also* overcorrection, response cost, time-out.
Richard M. Foxx & Kimberly A. Schreck

pyridoxine
Vitamin B_6. *See* vitamin B_6 and magnesium therapy.

reactive attachment
disorder of infancy or early childhood
See attachment disorder.

receptive language
The comprehension of the language of others. Receptive language generally precedes expressive language or language production (i.e., the child understands language before he or she uses language). *See also* expressive language, verbal behavior (VB).
Lynn Adams

reciprocal communication/interaction
Communicative behavior that is appropriate and demonstrated based upon the communication of another person, often an area of weakness for individuals with autism (e.g., a person with autism may not respond to a typical greeting such as "Hello"). Reciprocal interaction often serves to prolong a communication exchange. For example, if a person says, "I love pizza," a second individual may respond that he or she likes hamburgers as well as pizza. Reciprocity is typically directly taught rather than expected of children with autism and other pervasive developmental disorders (PDDs) and is an important component of instructional programming. *See also* communication disorder, social skills training.
Thomas P. Kitchen

refrigerator mother
A designation coined by Bettelheim (1967) for a mother who did not relate or bond with her baby. The distancing or cold relations and rejection of the child were proposed as a central cause of autism. The theory held that the infant misread a mother's feelings or assessed her negative feelings and withdrew from her and the world. The mother would then become frustrated and

respond with anger, causing the child anxiety (Bettelheim, 1967). This approach, of course, put a burden on the mother, who might have sought or been advised to seek treatment for herself or for repairing her relationship with her child. This designation, strongly based in Freudian psychology, is no longer accepted as an explanation of the etiology of autism. *See also* etiology.
Natalie Brunnhuber

regression

A loss of established skills and return to more primitive/immature skills. Childhood disintegrative disorder (CDD) and Rett disorder are characterized by marked regression in which a period of typical development for the first 12–16 months of life is followed by loss of skills prior to 24 months of age in domains such as communication, social, cognitive, and/or self-help. Regression may occur quickly over a period of days or more slowly. Skills may be regained, although few individuals recover fully. As many as half of children with reported regression actually showed prior delays in skills (Werner & Munson, 2001). *See also* childhood disintegrative disorder (CDD), Rett disorder.
Karen Toth

Rehabilitation Act of 1973 (PL 93-112)

PL 93-112 mandated the services provided in the federal–state Vocational Rehabilitation Services Program (Parker & Szymanski, 1998). It has been revised or amended regularly, most recently as the Rehabilitation Act Amendments of 1998 (PL 105-220). The 1973 version of the law focused on individuals with severe disabilities, consumer involvement, program evaluation and accountability, support for research, and civil rights for individuals with disabilities (Rubin & Roessler, 1995). Section 504 of PL 93-112 addressed discriminatory practices in housing, health care, education, and employment. Some students who are not eligible for special education and related services under the Individuals with Disabilities Education Act (IDEA) and its amendments may receive some services under the auspices of Section 504. *See also* Individuals with Disabilities Education Act (IDEA).
Lynn Atanasoff

rehabilitation engineer

A professional who applies engineering principles to the design, modification, customization, and/or fabrication of assistive technology for individuals with disabilities. *See also* assistive technology (AT).
Lynn Atanasoff

reinforcement

Presentation or removal of a stimulus following a behavior that increases the future probability of that behavior. Reinforcement is classified as positive and negative. *Positive reinforcement* is the occurrence of a stimulus following a behavior resulting in the increase of that behavior (e.g., free time provided after working on math problems is a positive reinforcer if it increases the time the student spends on the problems). *Negative reinforcement* is the removal of a stimulus following a behavior, resulting in the increase of that behavior (e.g., if a student is excused from math class when she says that she has a headache, she may increase the number of times she says she has a headache). Escape and avoidance behavior is maintained by negative reinforcement. Negative reinforcement is often confused with punishment; punishment, however, refers to the presentation or addition of an aversive event after a behavior. *See also* operant conditioning, punishment, reinforcer.

A. Celeste Roberts & Craig H. Kennedy

reinforcer

A key component of operant conditioning, a reinforcer is a consequence that follows a behavior and increases the likelihood or probability of that behavior occurring. Reinforcers are divided into two distinct categories: positive and negative. Positive reinforcers increase the frequency of a behavior when presented to the individual and are often referred to as *rewards*. Rewards, however, are only reinforcers if their effect on behavior is to increase it. Examples include food, praise, social approval, or anything the person would work to get. Negative reinforcers also increase behavior, but do so as a result of their removal contingent on behavior. Examples include the removal of pain, task demands, social disapproval, or anything the individual would work to avoid (e.g., a child's tantrums may be negatively reinforced if the tantrums succeed in permitting the child to escape from task demands).

Reinforcers can be primary or secondary. Primary reinforcers are unlearned, common to all people, and relate to access to things that fulfill basic needs such as food, water, or sexual stimulation. Secondary reinforcers increase behavior through an association with primary reinforcers; that is, they are learned (e.g., a mother's face, voice, and words become reinforcing to a baby through their initial pairing with feeding and contact). Money and tokens are secondary (generalized) reinforcers because they can be exchanged for other reinforcers.

It is important to note that a behavior followed by either a positive or negative reinforcer results in an increased probability of the behavior occurring in the future. *See also* operant conditioning, punishment, reinforcement.

John T. Neisworth & Pamela S. Wolfe

related services

Professionally delivered therapies or assistance that are part of the educational or developmental program for a child with a disability and that are required to assist the child to benefit from special education, including "transportation and...developmental, corrective, and other supportive services" (Individuals with Disabilities Education Act Amendments [IDEA] of 1997, PL 105-17, § 602 [22]). Related services can include several related professional services, including audiology, counseling, physical therapy (PT), occupational therapy (OT), psychology, and speech-language pathology. Medical related services are limited to diagnosis and evaluation. The provision of the related services is specified in the individualized education program (IEP) or individualized family service plan (IFSP). The services are considered *related* services in relation to the core educational program.
John T. Neisworth & Pamela S. Wolfe

reliability

The degree of agreement between observers or repeated measures of the same events. In psychometrically based standardized tests (e.g., intelligence tests, tests of development), a high correlation between tests results is expected across at least two independent testers (interrater reliability) or at least two administrations of the test by the same tester (test–retest reliability). The reliability, for example, of two scales for measuring weight can be assessed by determining the degree to which they agree. In behavioral research, reliability is assessed by examining the level of interobserver agreement. When two or more observers agree in their ratings or frequency counts (e.g., 90% agreement or higher), their reports are said to be *reliable.* Reliability does not necessarily ensure high validity of a measure (two measures may agree but may not be measuring what is intended). Quality measurement materials and procedures include reports of their reliabilities. *See also* observation, standardized tests, validity.
John T. Neisworth & Pamela S. Wolfe

required relaxation

An overcorrection procedure that requires an agitated individual to remain quiet and relaxed until all signs of agitation are absent for a predetermined amount of time (Foxx & Bechtel, 1983). *Required relaxation* is synonymous with *quiet training* or *relaxation training.* (Required relaxation should not

be confused with time-out, which involves placing a person who is displaying unwanted behavior in a setting containing much less reinforcement). *See also* graduated guidance, overcorrection, time-out.
Richard M. Foxx & Kimberly A. Schreck

respite care

Patient care provided in the home or institution intermittently in order to provide temporary relief to the caregiver. Family members of children with autism frequently need respite care, which is often provided through formal (e.g., from a paid service provider) and informal (e.g., from friends or volunteers) social support. *See also* service coordinator.
John T. Neisworth & Pamela S. Wolfe

respondent conditioning

Sometimes referred to as classical conditioning or Pavlovian conditioning, respondent conditioning is a process whereby a neutral stimulus is presented with an unlearned or unconditioned stimulus. After a number of pairings, the neutral stimulus becomes conditioned and can elicit the unconditioned response by itself. It is associated with Pavlov's (1927) observation that dogs salivated upon seeing a lab assistant who fed them. Pavlov rang a bell (a neutral stimulus that did not initially cause salivation) before presenting food (an unconditioned stimulus) to the dogs. After several pairings, the sound of the bell alone elicited salivation. It should be noted that in respondent conditioning, no new behavior is learned, but existing behaviors (usually reflexive) become associated with new stimuli. Most applied behavior analytic intervention is based on operant, rather than respondent, conditioning. Some forms of behavior therapy (e.g., desensitization) employ respondent principles. *See also* desensitization, operant conditioning, phobias.
Charles A. Hughes

response cost

Loss of reinforcers, contingent upon inappropriate behavior, which subsequently decreases the probability of the inappropriate behavior. Response cost is a negative punishment procedure. Some examples of response cost include the loss of tokens for being out of one's seat, docking of allowance money for breaking curfew, and reduction of television-watching time for not completing assigned chores. *See also* punishment, token economy.
Maria G. Valdovinos & Craig H. Kennedy

response latency

The amount of time that passes between the presentation of a discriminative stimulus (instruction) and performance of the desired behavior (response). Decreased response latency is indicative of more fluent behavior, which directly relates to increased utility of the behavior or skill. Increased response latency is likewise indicative of less fluent responding, which directly relates to less functional application of the behavior or skill. Instructional programs for children with autism may use mastery criteria that fall short of the fluency needed for use of skills in natural settings; fluency training can bring skills to a needed level of speed. *See also* fluency.
Thomas P. Kitchen

restitution

See overcorrection.

restricted interest

Preoccupation with a limited range of activities and objectives. Often, there is an insistence on sameness and inflexible routines. Along with stereotypic behavior, the presence of restricted interests is a major criterion for a diagnosis of autistic disorder (American Psychiatric Association, 2000). *See also* core deficits, perseveration, stereotypic behavior.
John T. Neisworth & Pamela S. Wolfe

retrospective infant video analysis

The study of early home (or other) videotapes to evaluate initial symptoms of autism. Through observation of home video clips that show infant behavior in interactional settings, researchers compare the behavior of infants who subsequently showed typical development with the behavior of infants who received a later diagnosis of autism. Research has found subtle behavioral differences within the first year of life between children with and without later diagnoses of autism; however, the behavioral differences become more evident after the children's first birthday (Werner, Dawson, Osterling, & Dinno, 2000). *See also* diagnosis.
Hannah Schertz

Rett disorder

Also called *Rett syndrome.* A progressive and degenerative pervasive developmental disorder (PDD) characterized by the occurrence of multiple devel-

opmental impairments following a time of normal functioning after birth. Until approximately 5 months of age, head circumference and growth are normal, as are motor skills and social interactions. Between 5 months and 2 years, head growth slows in children with Rett disorder. There is also a loss of previously acquired purposeful hand movements and a development of stereotypic hand movements, most commonly hand wringing or movements that resemble hand washing. In addition, other repetitive movements may occur, such as licking or biting one's fingers, tapping, or slapping oneself. Furthermore, all language skills (i.e., receptive and expressive skills) are lost. Several years after onset, interest in the social environment decreases significantly and levels off at developmental levels equivalent to 6–12 months of age. The eventual development of some social skills, however, is possible. Finally, poor muscle coordination in gait or trunk movements is present. Adults living with Rett disorder continue to function at cognitive, social, and adaptive levels equivalent to developmental levels acquired during the first year of life. Rett disorder has been reported only in females and, although prevalence data are limited, some reports suggest six to seven cases of Rett disorder per 100,000 girls. The disorder is much less common than autism. Although preliminary data suggest a genetic mutation to be the cause of Rett disorder, it is generally accepted that the cause is unknown. Some researchers have stated that the progressive course of deterioration is similar to that of an inborn metabolic disorder (American Psychiatric Association, 2000; Kaplan & Sadock, 1998). Although Rett disorder and childhood disintegrative disorder (CDD) both involve developmental regression, the losses with CDD come much later (typically between 3 and 10 years of age) than in Rett disorder, after typical development and no notable earlier markers. *See also* autism, Asperger syndrome (AS), childhood disintegrative disorder (CDD), receptive language.
Theresa A. Gibbons

reward
A positive reinforcer. *See* reinforcer.

role release
The sharing of a professional function with others to enable team collaboration and communication. Interdisciplinary teamwork requires members to avoid independent and sometimes disparate contributions and to work toward crossing professional boundaries for assessment and program delivery. The

importance of role release is heightened in the treatment of an individual with autism, which often requires multiple professionals (e.g., physician, behavior analyst, speech-language pathologist [SLP], occupational therapist [OT], physical therapist [PT], special educator). *See also* team models.
John T. Neisworth & Pamela S. Wolfe

routine-based instruction
See embedded skills, naturalistic interventions.

rumination
Spitting up of food or liquid that then escapes from the mouth or is rechewed and reswallowed. Chronic rumination appears to be related to low-interest environments and may be a form of self-stimulation. Applied behavior analysis (ABA) is a treatment of choice. Rumination is not a frequent problem with children but may be evident with children who have more intense special needs. *See also* stereotypic behavior.
John T. Neisworth & Pamela S. Wolfe

Ss

savant syndrome

A rare condition in which individuals with various developmental disabilities, especially autism spectrum disorders (ASDs), have areas of ability that are in contrast with their overall functioning level. People with savant skills were formerly referred to as *idiot savants* or *idiots savant*. The striking skills displayed by these individuals are typically restricted to a narrow range of talent domains, such as mathematical skill, musical proficiency, and calendrical calculation (prediction of days of the week for dates in the past or future). Studies reveal that approximately 1 in 10 individuals with ASDs have savant skills at either a splinter skill, talented, or prodigious level (Rimland & Fein, 1988). *See also* hyperlexia, splinter skills.

Gregory L. Wallace

SCERTS™ model

A multidisciplinary model encompassing social communication, emotional regulation, and transactional supports developed over 25 years of research and clinical and educational practice by a team of professionals to enhance communication and socioemotional abilities (Prizant, Wetherby, Rubin, & Laurent, 2003). *The SCERTS™ Model Manual* (Prizant, Wetherby, Rubin, Laurent, & Rydell, in press) will be available in the near future (from Paul H. Brookes Publishing Co.). The model is based on the premise that although children with autism spectrum disorders (ASDs) share similar developmental challenges, especially in the areas of socioemotional reciprocity, communication, cognition, and sensorimotor development, considerable heterogeneity exists within this group of individuals. The model can serve to provide a framework for considering a child's current developmental level, learning about the child's strengths and weaknesses, and examining the fit of a specific treatment approach within the culture and lifestyle of an individual family. Rather than follow a prescribed curriculum, the SCERTS™ Model recognizes the importance of developing an individualized curriculum when creating treatment goals.

Devender R. Banda

schedule of reinforcement

Terms under which reinforcers are delivered. Schedules include continuous (reinforcement is delivered after every instance of a targeted behavior), intermittent (some instances of targeted responses are reinforced and others are not), and extinction (reinforcement is not delivered after a targeted behavior). Ratio intermittent schedules are generally based on the number of responses required before a response is reinforced (ratio of responses to reinforcers), whereas with interval intermittent schedules, reinforcement availability depends on passage of time. The four intermittent schedules most often discussed are fixed ratio (FR), variable ratio (VR), fixed interval (FI), and variable interval (VI) schedules. Schedules of reinforcement are altered during intervention, typically going from continuous schedules to establish a skill to leaner, intermittent schedules for skill maintenance. *See also* fluency, maintenance, reinforcement.
David L. Lee

schizophrenia

A serious, major mental disorder in the way a person perceives and relates to reality. A person with schizophrenia does not accurately separate real from imagined events. There are four subtypes: paranoid schizophrenia (characterized by delusions of persecution), disorganized schizophrenia (with unpredictable behavior; incoherent, jumbled speech; and often flat affect), catatonic schizophrenia (in which the individual exhibits little motion and assumes and maintains odd postures), and undifferentiated schizophrenia (in which symptoms do not clearly meet requirements for the other three subtypes). (It is a misconception that schizophrenia is a form of multiple personality disorder, which is a separate, unrelated disorder). In the past, autism was misdiagnosed as an early onset of schizophrenia. Autism is no longer considered related to schizophrenia. *See also* childhood-onset schizophrenia.
John T. Neisworth & Pamela S. Wolfe

screening

Quick procedure to identify individuals who may be at risk for a disability or a developmental or medical problem or who require more detailed assessment for diagnosis and for determination of eligibility for services and intervention. Screening usually is conducted through checklists, brief observations, and/or tests. Often, parents or others who know the child well complete parts of the screener, especially those items requiring knowledge of the child that the professional would not likely have (e.g., "Does your child typically sleep as would be expected?"). An example of a screening procedure is a routine health checkup in a school. Sometimes clinical checklists (see Appendix A) are used to detect autism. Screening results suggesting the presence of autism should lead to a full assessment.

Screening results may overidentify (yielding false positives) or underidentify (yielding false negatives). Adequate screening materials should be effective in detecting problems that are verified as problems through more thorough assessment. Three measures of screener quality are interrater reliability, sensitivity, and specificity. *Interrater reliability* is the degree of correspondence between two or more raters who use the same scale with the same child; it is often computed as a percentage of agreements divided by disagreements. *Sensitivity* is the degree (expressed as a percentage) to which a test identifies problems (e.g., syndromes, dysfunctions, delays) that are, indeed, verified by subsequent assessment. For example, assume a screening identified 5 of 100 children as possibly having autism. If later detailed assessment identified all 5 of these children as having autism, the screening measure would have a sensitivity of 100% (no false negatives). If the screener identified 4 children, it would have a sensitivity of 80% (20% false negatives). *Specificity* is the degree to which the test identifies typical status as, indeed, typical. Using the same example, if the screening test correctly identified all 95 of the children with typical development as developing typically, that test would have a specificity of 100%; if the screener only identified 85 of these 95 children, that test would have a specificity of about 90%. Most screening instruments tend to overidentify in order to avoid not detecting true cases. *See also* assessment, diagnosis, reliability.
John T. Neisworth & Pamela S. Wolfe

S^D

Discriminative stimulus; *see* Lovaas approach, response latency.

SD

See standard deviation.

SEA

See state educational agency.

secretin

A hormone secreted when the stomach empties that stimulates the pancreas, stomach, and liver functions needed for digestion. Secretin is used to test

for digestive problems. Interest in secretin arose from anecdotal reports about improvement of the symptoms of autism in children who had received secretin injections for digestive system testing (Lloyd, 2002). A preliminary report (Horvath et al., 1998) noted that after secretin injections, there was significant improvement in gastrointestinal symptoms in children with autism as well as improvement in the children's behavior, including improved eye contact, alertness, and expansion of expressive language. While improved gastrointestinal function can relate to improved general disposition, this should not be mistaken for amelioration of autism per se. Research indicates that secretin has no greater effect than placebo treatments (National Institutes of Health, 2001; Owley et al., 2001). *See also* hormone therapy, leaky gut syndromes.
Lisa Jamnback

Section 504
See Rehabilitation Act of 1973 (PL 93-112).

sedative medication
A drug used to calm an individual that induces sleep or tiredness by reducing brain activity. Sedatives may be used to quell hyperreactivity or excessive excitability (e.g., panic attacks) when deemed necessary by a physician. Sedatives may sometimes be prescribed to children with pervasive developmental disorders (PDDs) who have problems in regulation (e.g., hyperexcitability, sleep problems).
John T. Neisworth & Pamela S. Wolfe

seizures
Electrical disturbances within the brain that result in neurological abnormalities. The type of abnormality manifested depends on the area(s) of the brain affected by the seizure. Seizures can manifest as staring only, as subtle repetitive movements, as nystagmus (repeated back-and-forth eye movements), as change in consciousness, or unexpected falls. Some types of seizure are evident only at night or in the transition from sleep to wake. The electrical discharges associated with seizures can be recorded by electroencephalogram (EEG), a noninvasive test that records brain waves. It is important to remember that between seizures, the brain's electrical activity is often normal; therefore, a normal EEG does not completely eliminate the possibility that the individual has seizures. Children with autism are rec-

ognized to have a higher risk of seizures of several kinds. It is estimated that seizure disorders (epilepsy) are present in 4%–62% of children and adolescents with autism (7% in the general population of the same age) (Giovanardi Rossi, Posar, & Parmeggiani, 2000; Volkmar & Nelson, 1990). Approximately one third of people with autism evidence epilepsy by adulthood (Gillberg, 1991); seizures are more prevalent at more severe levels of autism. *See also* electroencephalogram (EEG), epilepsy, functional magnetic resonance imaging (fMRI).
Jeanette C. Ramer

self-advocacy

The practice of people, especially those who may be at a disadvantage, voicing their own opinions and speaking for themselves. These individuals control their own daily affairs instead of having others assume responsibility for them. Self-advocacy allows people with disabilities to know their rights and responsibilities, defend them, and form educated decisions concerning their lives. *See also* advocate.
Kasey Marie Kotz

self-contained classroom

Type of classroom environment in which individuals with disabilities are grouped with other individuals with disabilities for instruction. Self-contained classrooms are distinguished from environments in which individuals with exceptionalities are included in general education classrooms. Although trends toward inclusion are increasing, research indicates that less than one third of students with autism spend the majority of their educational day in a general education environment (U.S. Department of Education, 2001). *See also* inclusion, least restrictive environment (LRE), service delivery model.
John T. Neisworth & Pamela S. Wolfe

self-help skills

A domain area for instructional programming that may include functional skills such as hygiene care, grooming, eating, toileting, and/or dressing. *Activities of daily living (ADLs),* a term used by physical and occupational therapists (PTs and OTs) is a synonymous term. *See also* activities of daily living (ADLs), daily living skills, fine motor skills, occupational therapy (OT).
E. (Rocky) Landers

self-injurious behavior (SIB)

Any behavior that is self-inflicted and results in physical injury. Many individuals with severe autism exhibit SIB (Schall, 2002). Examples include biting one's hands or arms, scratching or hitting the face, eye gouging, ingesting nonedible materials (i.e., pica), and head banging. These behaviors may be somewhat mild in nature or life threatening. Assessment for the treatment of SIB should involve several modalities, including functional, psychometric, and clinical diagnostic assessments (Schroeder, Tessel, Loupe, & Stodgell, 1997). Steps in the functional assessment include an assessment of risk and protection from harm, an assessment of an adaptive repertoire, identification of reinforcers, and a functional analysis of behavior (Iwata, Zarcone, Vollmer, & Smith, 1994). Although behavior-reducing strategies such as punishment, avoidance conditioning, contingent restraint, and time-out have been employed, the current trend is toward positive behavior interventions. Effective treatment has been primarily in the area of behavior management, utilizing such strategies as reinforcement and stimulus-based treatments (Schroeder et al., 1997). *See also* atypical behavior, functional behavior assessment (FBA), pica, positive behavior support (PBS), stereotypic behavior.
Theresa A. Gibbons

self-management interventions

Interventions in which individuals are taught to manage their behavior. Interventions may include one or more of the four general types of self-management categories: self-monitoring, self-assessment, self-instruction, and self-reinforcement. For individuals with autism spectrum disorders (ASDs), self-monitoring is typically included in a self-management treatment program. Self-monitoring involves teaching the individual to record the occurrence or absence of the target behavior. Many children with ASDs do not appear to develop self-regulation or self-management skills on their own, and these must be taught directly. *See also* pivotal response training, self-regulation.
Rachel L. Loftin

self-regulation

The ability to reach a balanced state of arousal, alertness, and comfort. The state has to be maintained, and the level of arousal has to change appropriately for different situations. With a typical nervous system, an individual can maintain a sense of calm while sustaining an adequate level of alertness.

With adequate self-regulation, the individual can pay attention, concentrate, and complete tasks appropriately for the situation. Some individuals are typically well self-regulated, doing activities automatically to sustain attention while appearing organized, whereas it can be difficult for some individuals to make the transition from active situations requiring high arousal to activities requiring relaxation and a state of low arousal or vice versa. Proponents of sensory-based treatments propose that people with autism may engage in reassuring, familiar patterns of movement (e.g., rocking) or may do repetitive acts (e.g., flicking fingers in front of their eyes, verbally repeating certain phrases) in order to feel organized and calm. Programs and therapies are available to help individuals improve their self-regulation by first observing and identifying their needs and abilities to balance different states of arousal. Then, appropriate sensorimotor techniques (e.g., providing a balanced sensory diet) are used as strategies to modify the level of arousal and the subsequent behaviors (Miller-Kuhaneck, 2001). *See also* sensory diet, sensory integration (SI), sensory processing.
E. (Rocky) Landers

self-stimulatory behavior
See stereotypic behavior.

sensation avoiding
A pattern of sensory processing characterized by low sensory thresholds and an active self-regulation strategy. People who are sensation avoidant are bothered by input more than others. Children who show sensation-avoiding patterns often are rule bound, ritual driven, uncooperative, and engage in behaviors to limit their sensory input. Individuals with disabilities such as autism and schizophrenia are significantly more likely to engage in a high amount of sensation avoiding patterns (Dunn, 1997a, 2001). *See also* hyperresponsiveness, sensory sensitivity.
Winnie Dunn

sensation seeking
One of four quadrants in Dunn's (2001) model. Refers to the desire for and seeking of pleasure from sensation (active responding strategies) regardless of high or low thresholds. Individuals who are sensation seekers are more likely to have high thresholds. Individuals within this quadrant have a need for extreme input and generally add stimuli to their actions (e.g., fidgeting,

doodling). *See also* sensation avoiding, sensory integration (SI), sensory processing dysfunction.
Denise Lynn Schilling

sensorimotor

Pertaining to purposeful motor behavior produced and coordinated through the senses (e.g., sight, hearing, touch, smell, balance). Physical and occupational therapists (PTs and OTs) typically work with individuals who have problems with sensorimotor skills, such as eye–hand coordination and motor planning. Children with autism can benefit from assistance in sensorimotor development.
John T. Neisworth & Pamela S. Wolfe

sensory diet

Components and activities related to sensory integration (SI) theory, recommended to provide organizing sensory experiences. Teachers and therapists can select a balance of sensory activities appropriate to the individual's assessed needs. *See also* sensory history, sensory integration (SI), sensory sensitivity.
E. (Rocky) Landers

sensory history

A questionnaire or interview format for obtaining information about an individual's experiences with sensory input during everyday life. Some sensory histories are informal and have been designed by therapists in their individual practice settings, while other sensory histories have been formalized and standardized so that professionals can compare a person's responses with those of a peer group. Occupational therapists (OTs) and other professionals use sensory histories in their assessment plans because there is evidence that people with various disabilities have significantly different patterns of sensory processing when compared with their peers. There is some initial evidence that information about an individual's sensory processing pattern can be useful in the intervention process (Dunn & Westman, 1997). *See also* occupational therapist (OT), sensory diet, sensory sensitivity.
Winnie Dunn

sensory integration (SI)

Ability to organize sensory information. Ayres (1972) described a neurological process in which individuals organize sensation internally (from one's

own body) and externally (from the environment) in order to be efficient in an environment. Senses emphasized in SI include proprioceptive, tactile, and vestibular. When a person perceives information from all of the senses and information about gravity and movement but cannot put all of the information together to make appropriate movement and behavioral responses, then a problem in the integration of sensory information exists. Although SI is a central nervous system (CNS) process, it can also be used as a frame of reference for specialized treatment with individuals with motor planning, perceptual-motor, or modulation problems. *See also* proprioception, sensory diet, sensory processing dysfunction, sensory sensitivity, tactile, vestibular.
E. (Rocky) Landers

sensory integration (SI) therapy

A treatment for autism based on SI theory, an innate neurological process that integrates and interprets sensory stimulation from the environment. SI therapy purports to assist in the organization and processing of the senses. Individuals with autism may have either heightened (hypersensitive) or lessened (hyposensitive) perceptions of kinesthetic/tactile, auditory, or visual sensory input. This therapy does not usually involve the development of specific skills but instead consists of sensory process training, exposing students to various levels of sensory input and eliminating distracting or irritating sensory input. Empirical evidence supporting the use of SI therapy is scant, with no reports of controlled trials, and SI therapy currently is not a recommended practice (New York State Department of Health, Early Intervention Program, 1999a). SI therapy, however, may reduce the child's aversion to being touched and provides the benefits of physical exercise. *See also* sensory integration (SI), sensory processing dysfunction, sensory sensitivity.
Theresa A. Gibbons

sensory processing

Term related to the ability of the central nervous system (CNS) to receive and interpret stimuli. Sensory processing begins in specialized nerve cells (called *sensory receptors*) found in sense organs such as the eyes, ears, tongue, and nose and the rest of the body (i.e., in the skin, muscles, and joints). These cells detect specific sensory stimuli (e.g., light, sound) and transform them into electrical signals. These signals are then carried by the sensory nerve fibers to the CNS for their final evaluation, which can be either conscious or unconscious (Goldstein, 2001). There are seven main sensory systems, each with its own sets of neural connections and specialized to process

specific stimuli. The *visual system* enables us to see, the *auditory system* allows us to hear, the *gustatory system* is concerned with taste, and the *olfactory system* involves smell. The *somatosensory system* provides information about the body and includes three submodalities that make possible the sensitivity to touch (also called *tactile* sensitivity), pain, and temperature. The *vestibular system* provides information about the position and the movement of the head in relation to gravity (e.g., about a tilted head), while the *proprioceptive system* supplies information about the position and the movement of the body in space (e.g., sitting with a straight back, raising one's arm). Individuals diagnosed with autism spectrum disorders (ASDs), children in particular, have been found to have inadequate sensory processing, including over- and undersensitivity in almost all sensory domains and to have difficulties interpreting sensory information coming from different sense modalities at the same time. *See also* sensation seeking, sensory diet, sensory integration (SI), sensory processing dysfunction, sensory sensitivity.
Ljiljana Vuletic

sensory processing dysfunction

The inadequate processing of sensory information in one or more sensory modalities (i.e., visual, auditory, gustatory, olfactory, somatosensory, vestibular, and proprioceptive) that is not based in the sense organ per se. These difficulties include hypo- and hypersensitivity and multisensory integration difficulties (i.e., having difficulties organizing and interpreting information coming simultaneously from different sensory modalities) (Bogdashina, 2001). Sensory processing dysfunction is claimed by some to be responsible for unusual behaviors such as hand flapping; finger waving; responding to touch with rubbing, scratching, or withdrawal; excessive spinning or rocking; unusual reactions when injured; and smelling of objects. These and other unusual behaviors have been grouped into two categories: *sensation avoiding* (avoiding situations in which one might be exposed to certain stimuli; e.g., avoiding crowded and noisy places or certain kinds of food) and *sensation seeking* (placing oneself in a situation in which one would be exposed to certain kinds of stimuli; e.g., hand flapping, finger waving, spinning, rocking). Sensory processing dysfunction is often associated with developmental disorders including autism spectrum disorders (ASDs); however, sensory processing dysfunction is not included in the diagnostic criteria for autism. Related terms sometimes used interchangeably include *sensory processing abnormalities, sensory processing difficulties, sensory processing problems, sensory integration dysfunction,* and *sensory defensiveness.*

Behavioral indicators of sensory processing dysfunction can be

- *Visual* (e.g., having poor eye contact, excessive blinking or rubbing of eyes)
- *Auditory* (e.g., screaming and/or covering ears on hearing sounds of the vacuum cleaner or fire alarm, making strange or loud noises, giving the impression of not hearing without having a diagnosis of hearing loss)
- *Gustatory* (e.g., eating a very limited number of food items, displaying cravings for spicy foods)
- *Olfactory* (e.g., smelling objects often, displaying strong likes and dislikes regarding odors)
- *Tactile* (e.g., displaying negative facial expressions when touched, withdrawing from touch, complaining about tags in clothing, avoiding having one's hands dirty, avoiding walking barefooted, having arms or legs bare and touching everything)
- *Sensitivity to pain* (e.g., not showing usual reactions when injured, biting or pinching oneself, banging one's head)
- *Vestibular* (e.g., engaging in excessive spinning or rocking, being able to spin for a long time without becoming dizzy)
- *Proprioceptive* (e.g., walking on toes, playing too roughly, pushing other children)
- *Sensitivity to temperature* (e.g., not noticing if foods or objects are too hot or too cold)

Physiological indicators of sensory processing dysfunction include delayed, absent, increased, or decreased *event-related potentials* and *galvanic skin responses* (electrical changes in the brain and skin in response to stimuli, respectively); slower habituation to repeatedly presented stimuli (i.e., giving progressive less attention or reaction; no longer reacting to an event); and increased or decreased heart and breathing rate. *See also* hyperresponsiveness, hyporesponsiveness, sensory processing dysfunction, sensory sensitivity. *Ljiljana Vuletic*

sensory sensitivity

Individual differences in the reaction to sensory stimuli. There are two broad categories of sensory sensitivity: *hyper-* and *hyposensitivity. Hypersensitivity* involves an unusually low threshold (i.e., stimuli of low or ordinary levels of intensity are experienced as extremely intense). *Hyposensitivity* involves an unusually high threshold (i.e., stimuli of normal levels of intensity do not reach an individual's threshold and, therefore, do not get noticed). Individuals with autism spectrum disorders (ASDs) usually have unusual sensitivities to different kinds of sensory stimuli, most commonly auditory and tactile hypersensitivities. Auditory hypersensitivity usually manifests as a hyperreactivity to unexpected sounds (e.g., telephone ringing, dog barking) or continuous loud sounds (e.g., from electric tools and appliances such as vacuum cleaners and hair dryers). Children with this type of sensitivity may often be seen covering their ears with their hands. Hypersensitivity to touch (also referred to as *tactile defensiveness*) includes high sensitivity to certain kinds of touch (e.g., light stroking) or touch to a particular part of the body (usually the head, arms, and hands). Children with this kind of sensitivity may avoid washing, combing, and cutting their hair; wearing certain kinds of clothes; handling materials such as playdough and finger-paint; and hugging and other kinds of social touch. Individuals with ASDs are also often *hyposensitive* to some types of sensory stimuli (usually to pain, movement, and temperature) and may not show any reaction to painful stimuli that most people would find unbearable, may not get dizzy when spinning for a long time, may consume food that other people would consider too hot, or may wear summer clothes in winter and winter clothes in summer. It is important to note that somebody can be hypersensitive to sensory stimuli in one modality (e.g., auditory) but hyposensitive in another (e.g., visual) or can even be both hyper- and hyposensitive within the same modality (e.g., a child may not mind hearing the telephone ring but may intensely dislike hearing the dishwasher), depending on the kind of stimuli, emotional state, or previous experience (Williamson, Anzalone, & Hanft, 2000). Even though sensory sensitivity often gradually decreases during late childhood, it sometimes continues into adulthood. Sensory sensitivities may interfere with the development and everyday life of individuals with ASDs. Exposure to (or the anticipation of) some sensory stimuli may reduce the ability to concentrate or may cause anxiety or panic attacks, stereotypic behavior, tantrums, or aggressive outbursts (Myles, Cook, Miller, Rinner, & Robbins, 2000). Sensory-based interventions, such as sensory integration (SI) therapy and auditory integration therapy (AIT), may be helpful in reducing sensory sensitivities, although current research evidence is equivocal. In order to determine the appropriate sensory-based intervention, proponents recommend that a comprehensive assessment of sensory processing be conducted first. *See also* auditory integration therapy (AIT), sensory diet, sensory integration (SI), sensory processing dysfunction.

Ljiljana Vuletic

sensory stimuli

Things and/or events in the internal or external environment of an organism that can generate a behavior and/or physiological response. Sounds,

sights, odors, vibrations, pain, and temperature can cause an overt behavior (e.g., smiling, shouting, jumping) and/or a measurable change in heart rate, respiration, blood pressure, and other physiological functions. In order to be detected, stimuli have to reach a certain level of intensity. The lowest detectable intensity is referred to as an absolute threshold. Someone who is very sensitive to a particular kind of sensory stimuli is said to have a low threshold, whereas someone who has a low sensitivity has a high threshold (Goldstein, 2001). *See also* sensory sensitivity.
Ljiljana Vuletic

sensory threshold
See sensory stimuli. *See also* sensation avoiding, sensation seeking.

serotonin
A hormone that is a neurotransmitter that is found naturally in the brain, blood, and gut of humans and other mammals. Serotonin affects mood and behavior (including regulation of sleep, eating, and arousal) but also has activity in other areas that are particularly pertinent to autism, such as regulating contractions of blood vessels and pain tolerance. Serotonin has stimulated much neurochemical research in autism (Bauman & Kemper, 1994). Medications used to improve mood and behavior often influence the amount of serotonin available to exert its action as a neurotransmitter. Some medications affecting serotonin include antidepressants and antipsychotics; medication affecting serotonin is sometimes used as part of the treatment for pervasive developmental disorders (PDDs) (Namerow, Thomas, Bostic, Prince, & Mounteaux, 2003). *See also* antidepressant medications, antipsychotic medications, hormone therapy, psychoactive medications, psychobiology, psychopharmacology.
Lisa Jamnback

service coordinator
Also called *case manager.* Paid employee who helps individuals with disabilities and families deal with the complexities of the health care system, including medical, insurance, government, and corporate agencies. The service coordinator can be part of the service system, such as a mental health or mental retardation professional, and can be part of the child's individualized family service plan (IFSP) or individualized education program (IEP) team. The coordinator organizes various services, arranges appointments, and may be the parents' single point of contact. *See also* advocate, team models.
Jean M. Wood

service delivery model

Context in which intervention services are offered. Typically models are based on a continuum. For example, in early intervention, services can be offered at hospitals, at centers, or in the home. In education, service delivery models can include instruction in general education classes, self-contained classes, home schooling, and distance learning. In education, children with autism are served in a range of service delivery models, from self-contained to inclusive environments. Furthermore, individuals with autism can learn skills in natural community-based settings (e.g., practicing speech and social skills at a restaurant) that increase generalization of the skills. *See also* home-based services, inclusion, least restrictive environment (LRE), mainstreaming, self-contained classroom.

John T. Neisworth & Pamela S. Wolfe

setting events

Circumstances that influence the rate, intensity, or duration of behavior by affecting the reinforcing or punishing value of established stimulus events (see Carr et al., 1994; Durand, 1990). A person's behavior changes as a result of setting events not directly related to the immediate situation. For example, any parent is familiar with the scenario in which a child who typically may be somewhat enthusiastic or only slightly reluctant to complete a simple household chore has an unexpected tantrum when asked to complete that same chore on a day when he or she is sick, is somewhat hungry, or has not slept well the night before. Nothing has changed about the task (the level of demand and the reinforcement for completion), but the conditions under which it is being requested have changed. Such conditions, or setting events, fall into three broad categories: biological (or physiological), social, and physical circumstances (see Durand, 1990). Biological circumstances include illness, hunger, fatigue, pain, seizure activity, medication effects and interactions, and exposure to allergens. Social circumstances refer to the particular people who are present or absent and how people are interacting with each other within the immediate situation or in recent situations (e.g., parental arguing earlier that day, recent or past abuse or neglect). Physical circumstances include the features of the environment (e.g., room temperature and humidity, noise level, number of people present, size of available space, lighting, comfort of furniture, unpleasant or noxious odors). Setting events are not in themselves the immediate causes of behavior, whether challenging or desirable. Rather, they influence the probability that someone who is already more likely to engage in a certain behavior will do so, regardless of the function of that behavior. Thus, a boy with a history of escaping

or avoiding task demands via aggressive behavior may be more likely to engage in aggression following a demand when he had not slept well the night before, his usual teacher is not present, and the room is crowded and overheated. Evaluation of the setting from informal problem solving to highly structured functional analyses may point to specific and broader individual or ecological changes needed to structure the setting for effective learning and prevention of problems (see Meyer & Evans, 1989). *See also* antecedent, antecedent-behavior-consequence (ABC) analysis, consequence, establishing operation (EO), functions of behavior.
Joseph R. Scotti

shadowing
See graduated guidance.

shaping
Process of bringing behavior and action closer and closer to a desired performance. First, a target behavior is identified, then successive approximations are reinforced. For example, in shaping social proximity, children who do not enjoy being with peers may initially be rewarded for being in the same room with other children, then for engaging in parallel play, and then for playing a game with other children. *See also* applied behavior analysis (ABA), reinforcement.
Lise Roll-Pettersson

sheltered workshop
A workplace that provides an environment where individuals with physical or cognitive disabilities can acquire vocational experiences. Work behaviors and skills addressed in such a setting include job attitudes, work attendance, and/or production skills. Jobs are usually related to production, and workers are paid on a piece rate, often adjusted to the productivity of the individual in the workshop compared with an average producer in private industry. Sheltered workshops are not as prevalent as in the past but are important placements for individuals who are not ready for or suited for work in other settings. *See also* supported employment program.
Lynn Atanasoff

SI
See sensory integration. *See also* sensory integration therapy.

SIB
See self-injurious behavior.

Sibshops
Opportunities for brothers and sisters of children with special health and developmental needs to obtain peer support and education within recreational contexts (e.g., outdoor play, lunches, parties, dances) (Meyer & Vadasy, 1994). Sibshops are not therapy, group or otherwise, although their effect may be therapeutic for some children. There are more than 200 Sibshops across the United States and in eight other countries. *See also* respite care.
Donald J. Meyer

sign
An objective, verifiable marker or feature that may indicate a disease or disorder. Signs can be observed or detected through physical examination and/or laboratory tests. Syndromes are defined by combinations of signs. Autism has no recognized physical or genetic markers and is diagnosed by observed behavioral signs and reported symptoms, such as problems in eye contact, sleep disturbances, inability to self-calm, social avoidance, little or no language, and the presence of atypical characteristics (e.g., insistence on routine, stereotypic behavior, sensory reactivity). Early detection of autism and other pervasive developmental disorders (PDDs) uses checklists and rating scales based on recognized signs and reported symptoms (see Appendix A). *See also* early signs, symptom, syndrome.
John T. Neisworth & Pamela S. Wolfe

sign language
See American Sign Language (ASL), augmentative and alternative communication (AAC).

single subject
Pertaining to an experimental design in which there is no separate control group. The experimental group usually contains a small number of participants (e.g., two to five), although it may sometimes contain a larger group of individuals (e.g., a classroom of students). Analysis of data is done by visual inspection of baseline and intervention phases (versus statistical analysis of group designs). Designs can include multiple baselines across individuals, interventions, or settings. Baseline and interventions phases can be presented

in a number of ways (e.g., AB, ABA, ABBC, in which A = baseline, B = intervention 1, and C = intervention 2). Because baseline measurement is used, the experimental group serves as its own control group. Single-subject design typically involves direct observation over an extended period of time; the experimental approach contrasts with a case study, in which there is no systematic manipulation of variables. *See also* control condition, direct observation, empiricism.

John T. Neisworth & Pamela S. Wolfe

single photon emission computed tomography (SPECT)

Functional neuroimaging technique that allows doctors to assess brain function. SPECT is sometimes suggested as part of an overall health assessment for children who are suspected as being at risk for a disability or disorder, such as autism. A small amount of radioactive tracer is administered intravenously and travels through the bloodstream to the brain. Images are gathered by a special camera that is sensitive to the tracer. Sedation may be needed during the procedure for young children or uncooperative patients. SPECT studies are performed most often with the intent of mapping cerebral blood flow or brain glucose metabolism. *See also* functional magnetic resonance imaging (fMRI), positron emission tomography (PET).

Julie L. FitzGerald

SLP

See speech-language pathologist.

social anxiety disorder

See social phobia; *see also* phobias.

social cognition

The processes involved in the understanding, interpretation, and use of socially relevant information (including awareness, perception, reasoning, and judgment) necessary to function in the social world. Several developmental disorders, including autism, are characterized by impairments in social cognition (Travis & Sigman, 1998). Impairments are typically manifested through poor nonverbal and verbal communication, often marked by failure to take the other's point of view, impairments in the comprehension and use of pragmatic language, problems interpreting face information (including

facial identity and emotion), poor quality and quantity of social overtures, and subsequent difficulty developing and maintaining interpersonal relationships. *See also* core deficits, face recognition, theory of mind (ToM).
Jessica Lord

social communication

Use of speech, gestures, or other means to relate to others. A major aspect of social communication includes conversational skills, which involve turn-taking; reading facial cues to know when to restate a point or when to stop; knowing how and when to initiate, maintain, and terminate a discussion; and keeping appropriate social distances.

Methods of social communication training include direct instruction (specific materials are available), positive practice, role playing, video modeling, and use of social stories (Reamer, Brady, & Hawkins, 1998). Children with autism typically need special and focused instruction to develop social communication skills, which are considered important to making and keeping friends and for attaining comfort in social situations. *See also* video modeling, video self-modeling (VSM).
John T. Neisworth & Pamela S. Wolfe

social competence

Various skills, attitudes, and behaviors necessary to appropriately engage in social interactions; all responses that produce, maintain, or enhance positive effects for behaviors. Children with autism display impairments in social competence in the areas of eye contact, joint attention (i.e., sharing attention toward an object with another person), body language and position, and social play and interactions (American Psychiatric Association, 2000). *See also* core deficits, social cognition, social impairment, social skills.
Theresa A. Gibbons

social gaze

Communicative use of eye contact during social interactions for both expressive and receptive purposes. An important aspect of social gaze is looking at another person's eyes during a social interaction in order to infer emotion. Social gaze can also communicate information about third parties or objects, such as looking at a person's eyes and then looking at an object to direct attention to the object (i.e., joint attention). Abnormalities in social gaze are among the earliest detectable symptoms of autism; by 12 months, infants with autism tend to look less at other people's faces than typically develop-

ing infants or infants with developmental delay. Research suggests that problems with social gaze persist into adulthood and that adolescents and adults with autism exhibit abnormal patterns of visual attention when observing social interactions (e.g., focusing on speakers' mouths instead of their eyes) (Meyer & Minshew, 2002). *See also* eye gaze, joint attention, social competence, social impairment.
James McPartland

social impairment

Impairment in social skills, including difficulties initiating interactions, engaging in reciprocity, maintaining eye contact, showing empathy, and recognizing or understanding the perspective of others. Impairment in social functioning is a central feature of autism spectrum disorders (ASDs) (Szatmari, Bartolucci, Bremner, Bond, & Rich, 1989). Social skills training programs are often used to alleviate social impairment. In addition, individuals with ASDs have difficulty recognizing and comprehending facial expressions, gestures, and other forms of nonverbal communication. The majority of individuals with autism, but not all, have persistent social impairment. Some individuals with ASDs may have an interest in interacting with others but often lack the necessary skills to do so effectively. *See also* social cognition, social competence, social skills training, theory of mind (ToM).
Scott Bellini

social phobia

Excessive fear of scrutiny by others, leading to embarrassment or negative evaluation by others in either vocational or social situations. Individuals with social phobia typically experience anxiety prior to actual exposure to the feared situation. The most common anxiety disorder is social phobia (also called *social anxiety disorder*). Social phobia is a recognized and diagnosed disorder defined by the *Diagnostic and Statistical Manual of Mental Disorders, Fourth Edition, Text Revision (DSM-IV-TR;* American Psychiatric Association, 2000). Half of individuals with social phobia also have a related disorder (Rapee, 1995). Other disorders that frequently co-occur with social phobia include simple phobia, major depression, panic disorder, and substance abuse. It is suggested that relatives of individuals with autism may have higher rates of major depression and social phobia than do relatives of individuals with Down syndrome (Piven & Palmer, 1999). *See also* anxiety; desensitization; *Diagnostic and Statistical Manual of Mental Disorders, Fourth Edition, Text Revision (DSM-IV-TR);* phobias.
Jennifer M. Gillis

social play

Engagement in reciprocal social interaction in informal settings. Over time, children show the capacity to engage in a continuum of social play behaviors including onlooker (observing peers at play), parallel play (playing alongside peers at play), common focus (reciprocal exchanges around joint activities without a formal agenda), and common goal (cooperative play activity involving a formal agenda) (see Wolfberg, 2003). Children on the autism spectrum present distinct variations with respect to developing social play. The vast majority of these children show delay or differences in the development of joint attention, spontaneous imitation, and emotional responsiveness (Sigman & Ruskin, 1999). Without structure or support, children with autism tend to remain isolated and make fewer overt initiations to peers. There is strong evidence to suggest that with specialized intervention, children on the autism spectrum are capable of improving within the social dimension of play (for reviews, see Wolfberg, 1999, 2003). *See also* imagination, Integrated Play Groups (IPG) model, spontaneous play, symbolic play.
Pamela J. Wolfberg

social skills

Specific skills an individual uses to interact with others. The skills are *goal-oriented* in that learners use their social skills for a specific reason (e.g., to make friends) (Chadsey-Rusch, 1992). The specific skills used to accomplish the goal should be *socially acceptable* or valued by others (e.g., peers, parents, teachers) (Gresham, Sugai, & Horner, 2001). If the skills used are socially acceptable, they should elicit *positive or neutral responses* during social interactions, rather than negative responses (Chadsey-Rusch, 1992). Socially acceptable skills may be observable, overt behaviors (e.g., verbally asking someone to play), affective behaviors (e.g., displaying feelings such as happiness), or nonobservable cognitive behaviors (e.g., understanding how someone feels). Social skills are also *situation specific* in that social situations that vary, for example, according to physical setting or people in the setting call for different social skills to be displayed. For example, the types of social skills used in a library are different from the skills used at a party. Similarly, a person may use one set of social skills to talk to a friend and a different set to talk to a boss. In addition, social skills may vary depending on the *social task* that needs to be accomplished in the social situation. For example, different skills are used at a party to give a compliment, start a conversation, or ask for directions to the restroom. Social skills are among some of the

most complex behaviors to learn and some of the most important because they have great impact on quality of life. Due to often marked social impairment, social skills training is almost always an important aspect of working with children with autism or other pervasive developmental disorders (PDDs). *See also* joint attention, pragmatics, social cognition, social competence, social skills training.
Janis Chadsey

social skills training

The teaching of social skills. Generally, social skills training for individuals with disabilities can be grouped into three different intervention approaches: contextual, individual, and peer. *Contextual* training is used to make changes in the environment or social activity arrangements (e.g., making changes to the physical setting, materials, or activities might help to promote social interactions with others). *Individual* training is used to change the social skills of individuals with disabilities through instructions by an adult (e.g., a child is taught to say "Good morning"). *Peer* training is used to change the behavior of others (e.g., peers might be asked to play with students with disabilities, be a buddy, or form a social support network, or a combination of approaches can be used) (Haring & Breen, 1992). A combination of these three approaches can also be used. Social skills training is often a part of curricula for individuals with autism because of their social impairments. *See also* social cognition, social competence, social impairment, social skills.
Janis Chadsey

Social Stories™

Stories written by parents or professionals from the perspective of the child to teach social skills. A Social Story™ is defined by a specific format and guidelines and objectively describes a person, skill, event, concept, or social situation. The goal is to share relevant information including *where* and *when* a situation takes place, *who* is involved, *what* is occurring, and *why*. *See also* social competence, social skills training.
Carol Gray

social validity

The perceived worth of a procedure and/or its results (also sometimes referred to as *treatment* or *social utility*). A treatment may be effective (e.g., electric shock) to suppress self-injurious behavior (SIB) but may not be considered

socially valid. Treatment or educational outcomes may also be evaluated as effective (e.g., resulting in a higher score on a standardized language test) but with little perceived actual improvement as reported by friends and family. Treatment aspects such as the time, effort, expense, and disruption to the family may also play a part in the appraisal of whether a treatment is socially valid or worthwhile. Recommended practice is to appraise (through checklists, ratings, and interviews) the social worth of therapeutic and educational objectives, procedures, and outcomes (see Sandall, McLean, & Smith, in press). (Social validity, by definition, is subjective and should not be confused with the statistical concept *test validity.*) *See also* behavioral objectives, functional goals, functional outcomes.
John T. Neisworth & Pamela S. Wolfe

social worker
See clinical social worker.

somatosensory
Pertaining to the part of the nervous system that responds to stimuli from the skin surface. The receptors for somatosensory input are imbedded in the skin and therefore provide information about the surface of a person's body. Many types of receptors make up the somatosensory system, including receptors for light touch, pain, and temperature sensations. There are also receptors called *touch-pressure receptors,* which detect firm pressure on the surface of the skin (Dunn, 1997b). *See also* hyperresponsiveness, hyporesponsiveness, tactile, tactile defensiveness, touch pressure.
Winnie Dunn

special education
1. A professional field of study within education, with a concentration on procedures and materials for assessing special educational needs and designing and delivering individually tailored instruction. 2. Specially designed individual or group instruction that is intended to meet individual educational needs of a qualifying child with disabilities as written in the individualized education program (IEP). Adaptations may be made to content of material, methods of instruction, or delivery of instruction (Assistance to States, 2003, § 300.26). Special education enables a child with a disability to receive instruction in the least restrictive environment (LRE), which can be an inclusive classroom, a resource room where special educators work with children with disabilities for part of the day, or a dedicated setting where all children have disabilities. Special education instruction and ser-

vices are part of tax-supported public education and now include early childhood special education and early intervention (EI) services.

For children from birth to 3 years of age, the identification of specific disabilities may be deferred in favor of the more general designation of developmental delay. Children diagnosed with autism are eligible for special education and related services, which may (depending on state and local resources and policies) include some specialized therapies and interventions, such as behavior plans, applied behavior analytic interventions, speech and language services, and physical and/or occupational therapy treatments. Often, the funding of specialized *therapies* (as distinguished from special *instruction*) is not available through public education and must be secured from medical insurance, private insurance, or other sources. *See also* early intervention (EI), inclusion, Individuals with Disabilities Education Act (IDEA), least restrictive environment, mainstreaming.

Jennifer Harris Tepe, John T. Neisworth, & Pamela S. Wolfe

SPECT
See single photon emission computed tomography.

speech delay
A type of developmental delay in which verbal ability and language development emerge later than typical. Children who have cognitive impairments often have delays in oral communication compared with chronological age peers. Oral communication can be delayed or not evidenced at all; between 28% and 61% of children with autism do not develop functional speech (Scott, Clark, & Brady, 2000). Children with autism who experience speech delays typically receive services from a speech-language pathologist (SLP). *See also* communication disorder, expressive language, receptive language, speech-language pathologist (SLP).

Britta Alin Åkerman

speech-language pathologist (SLP)
Also called *speech-language therapist* or *speech therapist*. Professional holding a master's degree in the science of communication disorders. SLPs work with individuals with problems in speech production, language comprehension and production, cognitive processing, and feeding and swallowing. In the United States, the highest level of credential for the SLP is the Certificate of Clinical Competence in Speech-Language Pathology (CCC-SLP) offered by the American Speech-Language-Hearing Association (ASHA). To obtain

the CCC-SLP, a clinician must hold a master's degree, pass a national examination, and complete a supervised fellowship year. *See also* communication disorder, speech delay, speech-language pathology.
Lynn Adams

speech-language pathology

The study and treatment of disorders in language and communication development and speech. Common problems treated are stuttering, articulation disorders, and language delay. The study and use of augmentative and alternative communication (AAC) devices and systems is part of speech-language pathology. The communication problems that are characteristic of children with autism often demand the involvement of the speech-language pathologist (SLP). Many universities include graduate programs in speech-language pathology, often as part of a medical or health and human development college. *See also* augmentative and alternative communication (AAC), communication disorder, speech-language pathologist (SLP).
John T. Neisworth & Pamela S. Wolfe

splinter skills

Areas of ability that far exceed what the child can do in other skill areas. Children with such abilities are sometimes referred to as *savants.* Although most children have ability profiles that are uneven, the term *splinter skills* is usually reserved for skills that are markedly above the child's other abilities or above average. Most splinter skills in autism are in the areas of mathematical calculation (e.g., identifying prime numbers, multiplying large numbers); calendrical calculation (i.e., knowing the day of the week for random dates); art; music; balance and other motor skills; and memory for locations, facts, or events. There are no definitive explanations for these abilities; the simplest is that obsessive interests lead to continual practice and skill development (see Hermelin, 2001). *See also* restricted interest, savant syndrome.
Deborah Fein

spontaneous play

An individual's natural inclination to engage in self-generated, freely chosen, intrinsically motivating activity without external demands or rewards (Garvey, 1977; Smith & Vollstedt, 1985). Children with autism lack a predisposition to engage in spontaneous play with peers (Howlin, 1986; Dewey, Lord, & Magill, 1988; Wing & Attwood, 1987) and when given opportunities to play freely, tend to spend excessive amounts of time pur-

suing repetitive activities in isolation. Evidence suggests that with specialized intervention, children on the autism spectrum are capable of acquiring spontaneous play abilities (Wolfberg, 1999, 2003). *See also* imagination, Integrated Play Groups (IPG) model, social play, symbolic play.
Pamela J. Wolfberg

standard deviation (SD)

Measure that expresses how far a score departs from the average (mean score). When scores are distributed normally (a bell-shaped curve), 68% of scores fall within ±1 *SD*. Many if not most standardized measures are psychometrically constructed with a mean of 100 points and 1 *SD* equaling 15 points. Therefore, when a score is 1 or 2 *SD* beyond the mean, that score is discrepant. Eligibility for early intervention or special education services is often based on use of standardized tests with cut-off scores that are set at one or more *SD* below the mean. Approximately 75% of individuals diagnosed as having autism also have subaverage intelligence scores (typically 2 *SD* or 30 points below 100 points). *See also* early intervention (EI), eligibility, special education.
John T. Neisworth & Pamela S. Wolfe

standard score

A score that is a conversion of a raw score into a metric (standard score) that indicates where that score falls within a (usually normal) distribution of scores. Intelligence test manuals, for example, typically contain conversion tables that allow the examiner to enter the raw score achieved by an individual into the appropriate age-based table and to determine how that score compares with scores of other individuals in the standardization sample (normative group) for that test. Standard scores are useful because they permit raw score conversions on various tests to be compared. *T* scores, *z* scores, and deviation IQ scores are frequently reported standard scores used in education and psychology. *See also* norm-referenced assessment, standardization, standardization sample.
John T. Neisworth & Pamela S. Wolfe

standardization

Standardization allows testers to compare the performance of children with their performances at another time as well as with the performances of other children by formalizing test stimuli and the criteria for evaluating children's responses. Formalizing stimuli ensures that when any child is asked a test question, that question is asked in exactly the same manner, no matter who asks the question, no matter where that question is asked, and no matter who is asked that question. Formalizing the criteria for evaluating children's responses ensures that identical responses are evaluated in identical ways, no matter who is evaluating the responses, where and when those responses are evaluated, and whose response is being evaluated.

Standardization relates directly to test fairness and appropriateness. Specifically, test stimuli (including oral or written directions) are presumed to be in a child's behavioral repertoire and therefore are presumed to be outcome neutral for all children. For example, suppose a test item requires an examiner to ask aloud, "*Lad* goes with *lassie* just like *boy* goes with _____?" First, it is assumed that the examiner says the words without accent or speech impairment and can articulate the words clearly. Next, it is assumed that the child not only can hear the words but can also understand English. Then it is assumed that the child knows the words *lad, lassie, boy,* and *girl.* Finally, it is assumed that the required response is within the child's behavioral repertoire. For example, there are several ways in which a child could respond to the *lad–lassie* analogy. He or she could say the answer, write the answer, select the answer from an array of words, point to a picture, and so forth. He or she could answer *girl* or some variant of *girl* (e.g., *girlie, little sister, young female*).

If a child responds to a test question correctly, all assumptions have probably been met. If a child responds incorrectly, however, one does not know if the assumptions were not met or, if the assumptions were met, if the child was unable to see the relationship inherent between *lad* and *lassie* and apply it to *boy* and *girl.*

When formalizing test questions it is of utmost importance to use stimuli and evaluation criteria that are within the repertoires of students likely to be tested. Tests are biased when groups of test takers earn systematically lower scores because of the way in which questions are asked or evaluated. The fairness of test stimuli and evaluation criteria are especially relevant when assessing children with pervasive developmental disorders (PDDs), including autism. While children without disabilities may be able and willing to converse with an adult tester, some children with PDDs who know the answer to a test question may lack expressive language, may be unable to sustain attention, may be unable to direct attention, may be incapable of sitting at a table, may be unwilling to look at a tester or testing materials, and so forth.

When children cannot be tested fairly using the formalized testing stimuli and evaluation criteria, alterations are sometimes made in the formalized testing procedures. These alterations can themselves be formalized for an individual child, and comparisons of the child's performances over time can be made. The alterations, however, preclude normative comparisons. (One simply cannot know how the performance of the standardization sample would change with new stimuli or different scoring criteria.) *See also* norm-referenced assessment.

John Salvia

standardization sample

A large group of test takers (usually 100 or more) who are representative of a population of test takers. For example, a test might be standardized on 100 boys and 100 girls between 5 and 6 years of age. Those children would usually be selected in such a way as to be representative of all children between 5 and 6 years of age: from rich and poor families, of all races and ethnic groups, of parents who have different levels of education, from urban and rural residences, from all geographic regions, and so forth.

Tests with standardization samples provide test users with considerable additional information. These tests provide test users with a variety of derived scores. For example, a test taker's score can be compared with the scores of other similar test takers using percentiles and standard scores. Most tests with standardization samples provide additional interpretative information for derived scores; for example, a test taker with a score between the 10th and 25th percentiles might be interpreted as being at risk for disability. Most tests with standardization samples also provide information of the accuracy (i.e., reliability) of test scores. Thus, test users know the degree to which they can have faith in a test taker's test score. Finally, tests with standardization samples usually provide some evidence that the inferences that are based on test performance are valid and unbiased. *See also* assessment, percentile, reliability, standard score, standardized tests, validity.

John Salvia

standardized tests

Tests administered under structured conditions and given the same way each time. Some tests are developed with strict requirements: The same items are presented in a prespecified order and manner, the same words and materials are used, strict time limits are used during each administration, and the same objective scoring criteria are used to evaluate responses. Other tests may be developed using greater flexibility, permitting variations in presentation. Standardized tests exist to assess skills in many different areas,

including intelligence, academic skills, motor skills, speech-language skills, and behavioral functioning. The purpose of standardized procedures is to decrease the effects of examiner biases and idiosyncrasies and to decrease extraneous influences that may affect a student's test performance (Sattler, 2001). Standardized procedures may not be feasible with children who do not or cannot accommodate to the testing circumstances. Standardized assessment of children with autism is frequently not feasible due to behavior or inability to follow instructions. *See also* assessment, intelligence tests, norm-referenced assessment.
Catherine M. Marcell

state educational agency (SEA)

In the United States, the agency that has primary responsibility of providing free appropriate public education (FAPE) for all children. The SEA, typically a state department of education, is responsible for implementing special education programs and related services for children ages 3 through 21 years old according to state and federal guidelines. *See also* free appropriate public education (FAPE), Individuals with Disabilities Education Act (IDEA), local educational agency (LEA), mutually acceptable written agreement (MAWA).
Devender R. Banda

statistical significance

See treatment effectiveness.

stereotypic behavior

An action that is repeated over and over with little variability in form, sometimes at high rates (see, e.g., Newell, Incledon, Bodfish, & Sprague, 1999). Stereotypic behavior is often referred to as *self-stimulatory behavior*. Inherent in the term *self-stimulation* is the idea that the person is engaging in a behavior that is in some way related to his or her level of stimulation or arousal. Several proposed explanations exist (see Guess & Carr, 1991, for discussion): First, people engaged in self-stimulatory behavior are thought to be in *under*stimulating environments, with few sources of activity or sensory stimulation; these people are, in essence, bored. Second, people are thought to be *over*stimulated by their environment (including their internal state). As a result, these people engage in behaviors that reduce, or shut out, the excessive stimulation, thereby *reducing* their overall level of arousal.

The form (or topography) of the behaviors include hand waving or hand flapping, body rocking (while sitting or standing), twirling of string or other

objects, vocalizing (humming, grunting, words), tapping (of objects or the body), mouthing of hands or objects, hand washing movements, and rumination (repeatedly bringing food up from the stomach, chewing, and reswallowing it). At times, self-stimulatory behaviors assume a form that borders on self-injurious, such as repeated tapping or hand mouthing that can cause sores or calluses or intense body rocking that can distort certain muscle groups. The persistence of such behaviors can also significantly interfere with educational and habilitative programs. A theory-neutral term to describe these types of behaviors is *stereotypic*. It behooves the interventionist to determine the functions of these behaviors by conducting a functional analysis to help determine not only if the behaviors are due to over- or understimulation (and are thus automatically reinforced) but also if they may be related to the functions of escape from demands or to gain access to social attention or tangible items (all of which have been investigated in the literature) (Scotti, Ujcich, Weigle, Holland, & Kirk, 1996). *See also* functions of behavior, perseveration, self-injurious behavior (SIB), self-regulation.
Joseph R. Scotti

stimulant medications

Drugs for treatment of attention and activity disorders. Ordinarily refers to substances such as methylphenidate and dextroamphetamine-based therapeutic agents that are prescribed to treat symptoms of attention-deficit/hyperactivity disorder (ADHD) and narcolepsy. Brand names for various formulations of methylphenidate include Concerta, Metadate, Methylin, and Ritalin; brand names for dextroamphetamine-based medications include Adderall, Dexedrine, and DextroStat. These medications differ in their duration of action: from hours, in the case of Ritalin, to (usually) all day, in the case of Concerta.

Stimulants appear to work by enhancing the concentration of the neurotransmitter dopamine in selected pathways in the brain, thus improving the child's ability to properly attend and shift attention. These medications are effective for approximately 80% of children with ADHD. Side effects commonly include decreases in appetite, headache and/or stomachache, difficulty in falling asleep, and irritability. Tics (brief, involuntary jerky movements) are triggered by these medications in approximately 1 in 200 children (Handen, Johnson, & Lubetsky, 2000). Generally, tics subside when the medication is stopped, but, rarely, they can persist for months to years.

Children and adolescents with autism frequently display poor focus and hyperactivity; many could concurrently be diagnosed as having ADHD. However, the neurochemical underpinnings of autism seem to be somewhat

different than those of ADHD, as do some of the functional consequences. Individuals with autism commonly appear to be distracted by their own thoughts (internal distractibility) or obsessively fixated on one topic to the exclusion of everything else, while children with ADHD are more likely to be drawn off task by things in the environment around them (external distractibility). Likewise, the response to medication differs. Approximately 40% of children with autism respond positively to stimulants, usually with a modest reduction in hyperactivity and improvement in focus. Unfortunately, children with autism taking stimulants experience more intense side effects than children with ADHD taking stimulants, the most troublesome being irritability and worsening of stereotypic movements. Some children with autism or other pervasive developmental disorders (PDDs) benefit substantially from stimulant medications prescribed by their treating physicians, but families and school personnel need to monitor for side effects (Quintana et al., 1995). *See also* attention-deficit/hyperactivity disorder (ADHD), psychoactive medications, psychopharmacology.
Jeanette C. Ramer & Lisa Jamnback

stimulus

An environmental circumstance or change in the physical setting; a noticeable change in the environment. Stimuli are identified and manipulated in applied behavior analysis (ABA), an approach often used with success with individuals with autism or behavior disorders. Although the terms *stimulus* and *sensory stimulus* are essentially the same, a verbal request might be considered a stimulus by the behavior analyst, but this would not likely be considered a sensory stimulus in the way used by physical and occupational therapists (PTs and OTs) in reference to energy that is received by and that activates one of the senses. *See also* applied behavior analysis (ABA), operant conditioning, respondent conditioning, sensory stimuli.
John T. Neisworth & Pamela S. Wolfe

stimulus control

The influence exerted by stimuli that precede behaviors (antecedent stimuli). Antecedent stimuli come to occasion or *control* behavior when they reliably precede a behavior that is reinforced and they are not typically present when that behavior is not reinforced. A father may occasion certain behaviors of a child that the mother does not occasion, due to differences in who reinforces what behaviors. Likewise, words and objects exert stimulus control over verbal behavior because society reinforces the use of certain labels

only in the presence of appropriate printed words or objects. The sight of an orange, for example, occasions a child's behavior of saying "orange" because that verbal behavior has been reinforced when the orange is presented. Frequently, a child may have faulty stimulus control that requires intervention; for example, a child may scream at the sight of a particular therapist, perhaps due to inadvertent reinforcement of screaming in the presence of that therapist. Also, there may be numerous times when there is little or no stimulus control over appropriate behaviors, such as when a peer does not occasion cooperative play. Stimulus control is a central principle of and procedure in analyzing and improving all domains of behavior. Behavior analysts especially use stimulus control in helping children with autism or other pervasive developmental disorders (PDDs). *See also* antecedent, antecedent-behavior-consequence (ABC) analysis, discrimination, generalization.
John T. Neisworth & Pamela S. Wolfe

stimulus overselectivity

The focus on a sole aspect of an object or environment while ignoring other aspects (also referred to as *tunnel vision*). Many children with autism and/or mental retardation appear to be overselective, which results in limited learning (Dube & McIlvane, 1999; Lovaas, Koegel, & Schreibman, 1979). When a teacher shows a card for *dog,* a child with overselectivity may only look at the color of the card or at the letter *d* while ignoring other details. It is important for the teacher to point out relevant details of an object or environment to children with autism to enhance learning. *See also* discrimination, generalization, stimulus control.
Devender R. Banda

Structured Teaching

A systematic approach to teaching new skills and adapting the environment for individuals with autism. A body of research demonstrates that children with autism or other pervasive developmental disorders (PDDs) respond much more favorably to structured than to unstructured approaches. The specific term *Structured Teaching* is associated with the TEACCH (Treatment and Education of Autistic and related Communication-handicapped CHildren) system (Schopler, Mesibov, & Hearsey, 1995). The Structured Teaching approach builds upon the strengths and interests of the individual and enables the individual to function more independently in all settings with fewer behavior problems. Visual supports and cues are viewed as *prosthetics* that can be changed, faded, or blended into the daily environment. *See also* fading.
Steve Kroupa

subthreshold autism

See pervasive developmental disorder-not otherwise specified (PDD-NOS).

supported employment program

A program to assist individuals with significant disabilities to be success-ful in paid employment in integrated work settings. Quality indicators for supported employment include meaningful competitive employment in integrated work settings, choice, control, employment of individuals with severe disabilities, full inclusion, long-term supports, community and busi-ness supports, employment outcome monitoring, and employer satisfaction. A central component of supported employment is consumer control of the employment process. Support strategies in employment settings vary depending on the individual but can include use of a job coach, environ-mental modifications (e.g., breaking down a task in a task analysis), and peers and co-workers. *See also* task analysis.
Paul Wehman

symbolic play

Play that refers to acting, doing something, or pretending to be someone else with an intent that is representational. Also called *advanced pretend, advanced pretense, make-believe,* and *imaginary play,* symbolic play typically develops between 2 and 3 years of age (for reviews, see Wolfberg, 1999, 2003). Precursors to symbolic play include *manipulation play* (also known as *exploratory* or *sensorimotor play*), whereby babies act on and respond to the physical properties of objects but do not use them in conventional ways (e.g., banging, twisting, shaking), and *functional play* (also known as *simple pretend, simple pretense, reality-oriented play,* or *relational play*), whereby chil-dren display the appropriate use of an object or conventional association of two or more objects (e.g., rolling a toy car on a surface, placing a cup on a saucer) (Sigman & Ungerer, 1981). Relative to other forms of play, symbolic pretend play is least likely to spontaneously develop in children with autism. When these children do show capacities for pretending, there are noticeable differences in the quality of play (Baron-Cohen, 1987; Harris & Leevers, 2000). There is strong evidence to suggest that with specialized intervention, children on the autism spectrum are capable of improving within the symbolic dimension of play (for reviews, see Wolfberg, 1999, 2003). *See also* imagination, Integrated Play Groups (IPG) model, social play, spontaneous play.
John T. Neisworth & Pamela S. Wolfe

symbolic thought

The ability to mentally conceive of one thing in place of another. Children who have an inability to think symbolically are earlier in the sensorimotor stage than when such thinking is typically expected or are beyond this stage and, due to an irregularity of some sort, are incapable of thinking representationally. *See also* presymbolic thought.

Maryjo M. Oster

symptom

Reports or complaints of a patient (or the parent of a child) concerning perceived physical or mental health disorder, pain, or developmental dysfunction. Symptoms are subjective reports (unlike *signs,* which are objective markers observed by others) that often are the basis for referral for assessment and diagnostic tests. Early symptoms reported by parents of children with autism include concerns related to a child's ability to calm after being upset, to sleep, to eat, to make eye contact, and to develop early language/communication skills. Retrospective reports of parents (in which parents are asked to recall if their child did or did not do certain behaviors) suggest the presence of symptoms of autism within the first year of the child's life. It should be noted that because autism has no physical or clear genetic markers, symptom reports and objective observations (signs) often concern the same characteristics (e.g., sleep disturbances, lack of eye contact). *See also* early signs.

John T. Neisworth & Pamela S. Wolfe

syndrome

A group of signs and symptoms that occur together and characterize a particular dysfunction or disorder. Eligibility for special education services is typically based on diagnosis or identification of a recognized syndrome (autism, Down syndrome, fragile X syndrome) or developmental delay. *See also* diagnosis; *Diagnostic and Statistical Manual of Mental Disorders, Fourth Edition, Text Revision (DSM-IV-TR); The International Statistical Classification of Diseases and Related Health Problems, Tenth Revision (ICD-10).*

John T. Neisworth & Pamela S. Wolfe

system of least prompts

See prompt hierarchy.

tact
See verbal behavior (VB).

tactile
Pertaining to the body's sense of touch. Tactile receptors are located throughout the body and give information about pressure (light and deep), temperature, texture, pleasure, and pain. Some individuals with tactile defensiveness may avoid touching others or being touched, may refuse messy play or particular foods (due to temperatures or textures), may dislike particular clothing, and/or may avoid grooming or hygiene experiences. Other individuals may have completely opposite tactile responses and may seek touch (people and/or objects, including those with certain textures), may mouth objects (including inedibles), or may not notice if someone is touching them or if food is on their face. *See also* sensation avoiding, sensation seeking, sensory sensitivity, sensory stimuli, tactile defensiveness.
John T. Neisworth & Pamela S. Wolfe

tactile defensiveness
A hyperresponsiveness or hypersensitivity to touch stimuli, including textures of clothing, interpersonal touch, and temperature changes, resulting in extreme reactions, aggressiveness, or avoidance behaviors (Ayres, 1979). Tactile defensiveness has been widely observed anecdotally and clinically in autism, yet there have been few empirical studies in this area. The existing research suggests that tactile defensiveness may be better seen as part of a broader disorder of sensory modulation (Baranek & Berkson, 1994). *See also* sensation avoiding, tactile.
Celine A. Saulnier

talent
See giftedness.

TALK
See Training for Acquisition of Language for Kids.

target behavior
The desired outcome; the focus of change. Before a behavior change is implemented, the behavior target is identified and described in precise, countable, observable terms, with an explanation of what the person will do when the targets are attained. For example, a target behavior could be for a student to say "Hello" when greeted by a peer. The terms *target behavior* and *behavioral objective* are somewhat synonymous; *target behavior* is used more by behavior specialists, whereas *behavioral objective* is widely employed by special educators. *See also* behavioral objective.
Lise Roll-Pettersson

task analysis
The process of breaking more complex skills or skill sequences into smaller, more easily learned units. Educational and therapeutic goals can be analyzed to provide a series of teachable objectives. Recommended steps for carrying out a task analysis (McLean, Bailey, & Wolery, 1996) include

1.   Specify the anticipated goal (e.g., will appropriately greet people).
2.   Break the goal into smaller, specific behaviors (e.g., will make eye contact, smile, say "Hello," and so forth).
3.   Sequence the specific behaviors (e.g., first look at the person, then smile, then say "Hello").
4.   Specify prerequisite behaviors (e.g., can speak, can make eye contact, and so forth).

Behaviors not currently in the person's repertoire can be separately taught and then properly sequenced. Task analyses are used for designing single lessons as well as for planning program sequences. Skills in all developmental domains (motor, communication, socioemotional, adaptive) can be analyzed to assist the person, his or her parents, and professionals to acquire highly complex behaviors and chains of behaviors that might not be attained otherwise.
John T. Neisworth & Pamela S. Wolfe

TC
See total communication.

TEACCH (Treatment and Education of Autistic and related Communication-handicapped CHildren)

Intervention approach that includes service/research programs; collaborations with parents at the individual, local, state, and national levels; a decentralized organization of nine regional centers (each located near a branch of a state university system); more than 200 TEACCH-affiliated public school classrooms; a residential program; and a multidisciplinary training program. TEACCH classrooms are highly structured, with predictable routines that use visual strategies. Training and services are offered to individuals with autism and their families from early childhood to adulthood.
Eric Schopler

team models

Approaches for bringing together professionals or their findings to assess or work with clients or patients. Three major models have been recognized for some time: multi-, inter-, and transdisciplinary. A *multidisciplinary team* (MDT) consists of two or more professionals from several disciplines who work independently of each other. Information gathered from the separate members may result in reports that are contradictory or redundant. Professionals involved in assessment and/or intervention with individuals with autism can include the physician, psychologist, physical therapist (PT), occupational therapist (OT), special educator, speech-language pathologist (SLP), and the general educator. Parents are to be included on the team. The MDT is most often used within the medical profession but is not the preferred model in early intervention and special education. An *interdisciplinary team* involves the collaboration of at least two professionals (e.g., SLP and special educator) who closely share and discuss observations and findings, minimizing discrepancies and redundancies. In a *transdisciplinary team,* two or more professionals work collaboratively in assessment and/or intervention and are sufficiently schooled in each other's profession that they can engage in role release, (i.e., can carry out each other's basic duties in assessment and intervention). For example, the general education teacher is sufficiently trained to do basic assessment of language development. Transdisciplinary team members may also substitute for each other in carrying out basic instructional and therapeutic procedures. A fourth model, the *collaborative team model,* combines the essential qualities of the transdisciplinary and integrated therapy models, involving virtually full professional role release (Cloninger, 2004; Giangreco, Cloninger, Dennis, & Edelman, 2000; Rainforth, Giangreco, Smith, & York, 1995). *See also* role release.
John T. Neisworth & Pamela S. Wolfe

terminal behavior
See behavioral objective.

test–retest reliability
See reliability.

testimonial
A report of a person or someone who knows the person, typically regarding the perceived improvement of the person and effectiveness of a treatment. Testimonials are not acceptable scientific evidence. Personal reports of so-called cures or improvements may result from factors not reported, but the treatment may be given full credit for the beneficial effects. The subjectivity of reports severely limits the quality of information, as do issues of accurate recall and identification of plausible alternative factors responsible for the changes. *See also* case study, empiricism, experimental design, pseudoscience.
John T. Neisworth & Pamela S. Wolfe

theory of mind (ToM)
The process of attributing a mental state (e.g., a belief, a desire, an intention, an emotion) to another in order to predict or understand that person's behavior (sometimes referred to as mind reading) (Baron-Cohen, 1995). Taking another person's conceptual perspective requires a theory of mind, whereas taking another person's visual perspective may not. People with autism have been shown to have specific delays in the development of a theory of mind, relative to their mental age. (These delays are sometimes referred to as *mindblindness.*) *Theory of mind* is sometimes used interchangeably with the term *empathy,* but the latter involves the additional component of an appropriate affective reaction to another's mental state. Individuals with Asperger syndrome (AS) often report being able to logically work out another's mental state without feeling an empathic, affective reaction. This suggests they may be using atypical strategies to decode others' behavior and mental states. Joint attention, gaze detection, and other social skills shown by typically developing infants are delayed or deficient in children with pervasive developmental disorders (PDDs). Problems with perspective sharing or mindblindness are seen as central to the social and communicative symptoms of children with autism and other PDDs. *See also* eye gaze, false-belief paradigm, joint attention, mindblindness.
Simon Baron-Cohen

therapeutic support staff (TSS) worker

An employee with a bachelor's degree who is hired to implement a child's or adolescent's unique behavior plan on a one-to-one basis for a prescribed number of hours per week in home, school, or community settings. The TSS worker uses various behavioral interventions, such as behavior contracts, data collection, modeling, feedback, reinforcement, redirection, time-outs, and crisis intervention. Support is also provided to the child's family, other caregivers, and teachers in implementing the behavior plan at home and in school. The TSS worker is directly supervised by a behavior specialist consultant who is responsible for writing the child's behavior plan. TSS services are prescribed by a psychologist and typically are approved and funded through noneducational sources (e.g., medical insurance or assistance). TSS services are not available in every state. *See also* applied behavior analysis (ABA), behavior plan, modeling, reinforcement, time-out.
Catherine R. Meier

thimerosal

A mercury-containing preservative used in vaccines that now has been removed from all vaccines because of a possible connection with autism. Proponents of this connection point out that the rate of occurrence of autism has risen in parallel to the increasing number of vaccines administered to young children. There is no consensus in the scientific community about either the purported rising incidence of autism or the relationship of autism to vaccines (Madsen et al., 2002). In 2004, the Institute on Medicine released a report that "favors rejection of a causal relationship between the MMR [measles, mumps, and rubella] vaccine and autism…and between thimerosal-containing vaccines and autism" (p. 1). *See also* chelation, detoxification, mercury.
Jeannette C. Ramer

three-term contingency

See antecedent. *See also* antecedent-behavior-consequence (ABC) analysis.

tic

See Tourette disorder.

time-out

Formerly known as *time-out from reinforcement*. A punishment procedure that involves the removal or withdrawal of reinforcement for a specific time

contingent on a person's behavior (Foxx, 1982). Two major categories of time-out exist: exclusionary and nonexclusionary (Foxx, 1982). Exclusionary time-out procedures involve removal of a person from the environment in which reinforcement is available. Common implementations involve use of a separate time-out space created by a partition separating the person from the environment or removal to a hallway or stairwell. Nonexclusionary time-out procedures allow the person to remain in the environment where reinforcement is available to others; however, the person is not permitted to engage in reinforcing activities (e.g., no attention is given to the person, he or she has no access to toys). Common implementations of the nonexclusionary time-out procedure include withdrawal of specific reinforcers (e.g., taking away access to a preferred toy), having the individual sit in a corner of the room, or having the person wear a ribbon on the wrist that indicates that the person has access to reinforcers (when the ribbon is removed, the person is considered in time-out). An important component of the effective use of time-out is that the person have access to a period of reinforcing *time-in* for appropriate behavior. Positive reinforcement should be easily accessible when the person is not in a time-out period. If not, the contrast between the two phases is not significant enough to result in behavior change. *See also* punishment, reinforcement.
Kimberly A. Schreck & Richard M. Foxx

toe walking

Use of the toes rather than use of the whole foot in heel–toe action for walking. Also called *equinus gait.* Toddlers typically go through a period of toe walking. If toe walking becomes preferred and the established pattern of gait, it may signal developmental problems. Toe walking may be a marker of mild cerebral palsy but also is frequently seen in children with autism.
John T. Neisworth & Pamela S. Wolfe

token economy

Use of points, chips, play money, and so forth as rewards (reinforcers) that are earned. Tokens acquire their reinforcing properties because they can be exchanged for established reinforcers (items and activities that are already desirable). Expert use of a token economy with an individual or a group can produce great increases in desirable behavior, often displacing unwanted behavior. Tokens may be saved and exchanged for greater rewards and at later times, depending on the developmental level of the individual. *See also* reinforcer.
John T. Neisworth & Pamela S. Wolfe

ToM
See theory of mind.

total communication (TC)
The use of signs, speech, fingerspelling, and/or any other means of communication that conveys the intended message for individuals with speech or hearing difficulties. For example, manual signs and fingerspelling could be simultaneously combined with speech and speech reading, depending on the environment or message. *See also* American Sign Language (ASL), communication disorder.
Devender R. Banda

touch pressure
Measure of sensory input to the surface of the skin. Some touch receptors are activated with firm pressure on the skin; more of these receptors fire when the pressure is applied across a large surface. Touch pressure input is more organizing for the nervous system. Some individuals with autism have difficulties with oversensitivity to touch and sound. Touch pressure devices (e.g., a hug machine) and activities can be used to provide more organized input to increase attention and reduce anxiety. *See also* deep pressure proprioception touch technique, hug machine, hyperresponsiveness, hyporesponsiveness, somatosensory.
Winnie Dunn

touch therapy
A massage therapy that involves moderate pressure and stroking. The head, neck, torso, arms, hands, legs, and feet may be massaged. (Individuals are fully clothed, except socks and shoes are removed.) Proponents of touch therapy suggest that it will help children who are anxious and avoidant about being touched, such as children with autism, accommodate to touch. A controlled study has suggested possible benefits of touch therapy (Field et al., 1997), but further research is necessary before this method can be recommended.
John T. Neisworth & Pamela S. Wolfe

Tourette disorder
Originally referred to as *Gilles de la Tourette syndrome,* a disorder characterized by the presence of multiple motor and vocal tics. A tic is a repeated and sudden nonadaptive movement or vocalization (American Psychiatric Association [APA], 2000). Typically, individuals can suppress a tic for some time but

experience an irresistible urge to engage in the tic behavior. Motor tics can be simple (e.g., eye blinking, grimacing, coughing) or complex (e.g., jumping, touching, smelling objects or people). Similarly, vocal tics can also be simple (e.g., grunting, barking) or complex (e.g., repeating words and phrases). Complex verbal tics can include use of obscene words and phrases (known as *coprolalia*) and repetition of the last words of others (known as echolalia). According to the APA's (2000) criteria, Tourette disorder is characterized by the presence of multiple motor tics and one or more vocal tics that occur many times per day nearly every day (or intermittently) for more than a year. Tourette disorder has its onset before age 18. Motor tics such as eye blinking typically appear in early childhood between ages 3 and 8 years, and vocal tics typically follow several years later. In many cases, the disorder is most severe during the teenage years. Although the exact cause of the disorder is still unknown, there is strong evidence to suggest that genetic factors play an important role (Leckman, 2002). Many individuals with Tourette disorder have symptoms of obsessive-compulsive disorder (OCD) and attention-deficit/hyperactivity disorder (ADHD). Although Tourette disorder and autism are considered to be clearly distinct, the occurrence of several behaviors in both disorders, including stereotyped movements, echolalia, repetitive verbal behaviors, and self-injurious behavior (SIB), has led some researchers to speculate about overlapping neurological origins of the two disorders (Barnhill & Horrigan, 2002). There is, however, no clear evidence yet to suggest an association between the two disorders. Treatment of Tourette disorder involves education, behavioral intervention, and pharmacological treatment. *See also* attention-deficit/hyperactivity disorder (ADHD), echolalia, obsessive-compulsive disorder (OCD), self-injurious behavior (SIB), stereotypic behavior.
John T. Neisworth & Pamela S. Wolfe

toxicology

The study of poisons (e.g., heavy metals, plant alkaloids, protein toxins), their pathophysiology, clinical presentation, and treatment. A major tenet of toxicology, *the dose is the poison,* recognizes that there is a level of exposure to all poisons at which no detectable biologic or behavioral abnormalities occur. As exposure increases from this *zero effect level,* however, abnormalities can be detected that initially are highly idiosyncratic, depending on each organism's unique characteristics determined by genes, experiential factors, and current environmental contexts. At higher levels of poison exposure, larger percentages of the exposed population exhibit adverse effects and the variability in symptoms and signs of toxicity decreases. At extremely high levels of poison

exposure, all subjects display fairly similar biologic and behavioral illnesses. Several major hypotheses involve exposure to various toxins such as heavy metals and neurotoxic peptides as causal factors in autism. *See also* heavy metals, mercury, metallothionein, peptides.
Robert A. Da Prato

Training for Acquisition of Language for Kids (TALK)

A behavior analysis model for teaching speech and language to young children with autism and other developmental disorders or delays (Drash & Leibowitz, 1973). The program is highly structured, data based, employs behavioral procedures (especially reinforcement), and involves center- and home-based interventions. The long-term goal is acquisition of typical or near-typical language. Speech sounds, words, naming of objects and activities (tacting), requesting (manding), and imitation training are systematically built through modeling, prompting and fading, and shaping. Program entry at age 4 or younger and extensive parent involvement optimize results. Research reports of TALK effectiveness are impressive, showing great gains in IQ and expressive language (Drash & Tudor, 1989, 2004). *See also* fading, modeling, prompting, shaping.
John T. Neisworth & Pamela S. Wolfe

tranquilizers

See antianxiety medications.

transdisciplinary team

See team models.

transition

Process of change in settings, events, or stages in life. The term *transition* may also refer to change in activities and locations during a day (e.g., homeroom to resource room, circle time to playground). Typical transitions for individuals with autism may occur when moving from early intervention (EI; birth to 3 years) to preschool, from preschool to elementary school, from elementary to secondary school, and from secondary school to adult life. Periods of transition may cause stress for individuals with autism and their families. The Individuals with Disabilities Education Act (IDEA) Amendments of 1997 (PL 105-17) mandate formal transition planning at age 16 (and at age 14 for some students). Formal transition planning may include planning for residential, vocational, and community living and is included in a section

of the individualized education program (IEP) referred to as the individualized transition plan (ITP). The document notes adult service agency linkages and timelines. IDEA also requires transition planning for children with disabilities or developmental delays when they move from early intervention (EI) services to preschool. *See also* individualized education program (IEP), Individuals with Disabilities Education Act (IDEA).
Paul Wehman

transition cue

Visual, auditory, or physical prompts used to indicate a change in setting or activity. For example, a bell may ring to indicate a class change or an individual may be given a picture of the next activity. Because individuals with autism may be resistant to and fearful of change, transition cues may be useful in daily scheduling. *See also* Picture Exchange Communication System (PECS), visual schedule, visual strategies.
John T. Neisworth & Pamela S. Wolfe

treatment effectiveness

The utility or influence of an intervention. Two separate and different criteria exist for determining the presence of an effect. The first, *statistical significance,* establishes the probability that the observed effects are different from that which would be expected by chance. The second, *clinical significance,* provides an estimate of the value or magnitude of the effect with respect to producing meaningful change in quality of life for the individual receiving treatment (i.e., the social validity of the change). In the term *treatment effectiveness,* the word *effectiveness* refers to consistently reproducible, measurable effects. It does not necessarily imply that the effect is of a magnitude that will produce clinically relevant change. Many advocates of treatments for autism claim effectiveness but provide only testimonials (National Research Council, Division of Behavioral and Social Sciences and Education, Committee on Educational Interventions for Children with Autism, 2001); such reports cannot be considered as having met minimal criteria for determining effectiveness. *See also* single subject.
Raymond G. Romanczyk

Treatment and Education of Autistic and related Communication-handicapped CHildren

See TEACCH.

triad of impairments
See core deficits.

trial
An attempt at demonstrating a skill. Trials can be presented in a variety of ways, including mass and distributed. In mass trials, a stimulus is presented repeatedly in succession (e.g., writing a name repeatedly). In distributed trials, a stimulus is presented over time throughout the day (e.g., writing a name on a lunch ticket and on a worksheet, writing a name in the morning and in the evening). Distributed trials are often recommended to help children with autism spectrum disorders (ASDs) to aid in generalization. *See also* distributed practice, massed practice.
Thomas P. Kitchen

TSS worker
See therapeutic support staff worker.

tunnel vision
See stimulus overselectivity.

twin studies in autism
Research conducted with identical (monozygotic, or from one egg) and/or fraternal (dizygotic, or from two eggs) twins related to genetics and/or environment. Twin studies have shown evidence of a genetic influence on autism (in separate environments or in the same environment). According to some studies, twins run a higher risk of developing autism. Autism in identical twins is stated to be 12 times higher than in the general population, and the rate of autism in fraternal twins is 4 times that of the general population (Greenberg, Hodge, Sowinski, & Nicoll, 2001). *See also* genetic factors.
Britta Alin Åkerman

Type I punishment; Type II punishment
Positive and negative punishment, respectively. *See* punishment.

typical antipsychotic medications
See antipsychotic medications.

underresponsiveness
See hyporesponsiveness.

vaccines
See chelation, detoxification, mercury, metallothionein, thimerosal.

validity
Degree to which an instrument measures what it asserts that it measures. For example, an instrument designed to measure a construct such as self-esteem should consist of items that encompass elements of self-esteem. There are a number of types of validity, including face validity (subjective assessment of whether a test adequately addresses a construct/behavior), content validity (whether test items adequately sample a larger group of possible items and/or behaviors), concurrent validity (whether test correlates with other similar tests), construct validity (whether a test corresponds with a theoretical model of behavior), and predictive validity (whether a test can predict a construct or behavior over time). Reliability, the degree to which

a measure is consistent over time and/or between two different tools, is necessary (but not sufficient) for validity. *See also* assessment, reliability.
John T. Neisworth & Pamela S. Wolfe

verbal behavior (VB)

A term first introduced by B.F. Skinner (1938) for any behavior (vocal, written, gestural, and other) that achieves its reinforcement through the mediation of another person's behavior. Skinner chose the term *verbal behavior* instead of *speech,* which involves only vocal behavior, and instead of *language,* which refers "to the practices of a linguistic community rather than to the behavior of any one member" (Skinner, 1957, p. 2).

Early behavioral efforts to teach language to children with autism made considerable use of Skinner's general analysis of operant behavior in terms of stimulus, response, and reinforcement but almost no use of the six special verbal categories—echoic, mand, tact, intraverbal, textual, and audience relation—described in *Verbal Behavior* (Skinner, 1957). Since the 1990s, however, language programs for children with autism have increasingly employed Skinner's specific analysis as part of their behavior approach. Only the echoic, mand, and tact categories are described here.

Echoic behavior consists of repeating what is heard—vocal imitation—and is an essential type of VB for learning other types. The mand is VB with the response form (what is said, written, signed, and so forth) determined by what the speaker *wants* from the listener. In more technical terms, the mand is determined by a motivating (or establishing) operation. In common-sense terms, mands are requests, commands, and questions. Mands can also consist of selection of a stimulus, such as when a person requests something by pointing at or handing a picture of that object to another person. The reinforcement for a mand is specific to that mand (e.g., receiving what is requested, the listener's doing what is demanded, receiving an answer to the question asked). This makes the mand different from all other elementary verbal relations, which typically receive generalized reinforcement, such as praise or approval. The tact is VB with what is said (or written or signed) determined primarily by an object, action, relation, or property of an object and affecting the person through any sense mode (vision, hearing, smell, taste, touch). That is, the tact consists of naming or describing. As with all VB except the mand, the reinforcement for the tact is usually social approval or agreement.

When a child says "cookie" as a result of hearing someone else say cookie or in response to a teacher's request to say "cookie," the VB is echoic, and the usual reinforcement is approval (e.g., "Good"). Saying "cookie" as a request for one is a mand, and the usual reinforcement is receiving a cookie. Saying "cookie" perhaps in response to someone else's question "What's that?" is a tact, and typical reinforcement is "That's right."

Language training using Skinner's analysis, sometimes referred to as the *verbal behavior approach,* typically involves a detailed assessment of the learner's repertoire in terms of the six elementary verbal relations. It also involves an early emphasis on mand training on the grounds that the reinforcements for mands (receiving something wanted) may be more effective for the learner than the social approval that functions as reinforcement for the other kinds of VB (Skinner, 1957). And because mand training is not easily accomplished with the typical discrete trial procedures, early phases of VB may seem quite different from those procedures relying more on discrete trials, but this is only a matter of degree. Most current behavioral approaches involve some form of discrete trial (e.g., presenting a task, waiting for a response, reinforcing if correct, repeating or correcting in some way if incorrect) with respect to behaviors prerequisite to instruction, such as sitting still, attending to the teacher, motor imitation, and vocal imitation (echoic behavior), and, to some degree, with respect to more complex VB. *See also* analysis of verbal behavior (AVB), discrete trial training, establishing operation (EO), mand fluency training, operant conditioning.

Jack Michael

vestibular

Pertaining to the portion of the central nervous system (CNS) that responds to position of the head in relationship to gravity and movement (speeding up or slowing down). Receptors are located in the inner ear. Typically when an individual has vestibular problems, he or she avoids activities and items that have movement (e.g., a seesaw, swings). The rate of vestibular stimulation tends to produce different effects. Constant, slow rocking or swinging tends to be relaxing, while fast or interrupted jerking movements tend to be arousing. Vestibular processing contributes to the development of smooth coordination of body movements as well as to visual skills such as watching moving objects or looking at a far object and then looking at a near object. Some sensory-based treatments for autism address vestibular problems. *See also* kinesthetic sense, proprioception.

E. (Rocky) Landers

video modeling

Instructional technique in which an individual observes a videotape of a model engaging in a target behavior and subsequently attempts to imitate the behavior. Educators can watch the video with the learner and pause or replay the model to emphasize the critical dimensions of the task, language demands and behaviors required in the task, and cues related to appropriate task performance. Video modeling (i.e., showing behavior of someone else to be imitated by the learner) has been shown to be effective for individuals with autism, particularly in social skill development (Krantz, MacDuff, Wadstrom, & McClannahan, 1991). Video techniques may be especially effective for children with autism because of the evident utility of visual learning for these children. Video modeling differs from video self-modeling (VSM) in that VSM involves the learner as the model to be imitated. *See also* modeling, social skills training, video self-modeling (VSM). *Valerie J. Postal*

video self-modeling (VSM)

Videotaping of individuals that allows them to observe their own behavior. Individuals can view themselves as the model for behavior (Hosford, 1981). Videotaped models are useful in that the behavior can be viewed as often as needed and desired or as long as the symbolic model holds the learner's interest (e.g., attention). Like live models, virtual or videotaped models are more effective when they have similar characteristics to the learner (Bandura, 1986). When the model and the learner are the same, similarity is, of course, ensured. Whether VSM is more effective than other modeling techniques, whether it is effective for children, and which characteristics are most effective await further research. Video self-modeling has been shown to be effective with individuals with autism for teaching appropriate request behaviors, an important aspect of communication and social development (Buggey, 1995; Wert & Neisworth, 2003). *See also* modeling, video modeling. *Barbara Yingling Wert*

visual acuity

See acuity.

visual schedule

A visual strategy that presents a sequence of steps, events, activities, and/or routines in visual form. A visual schedule is static, thus allowing the individual to refer to the schedule one or more times during its use, enhancing the predictability of events or activities, and/or reassuring the individual which events have been completed. Visual schedules can be designed with pictures, icons (symbols), photographs, phrases, and/or sentences. *See also* Picture Exchange Communication System (PECS), transition cue, visual strategies.

Lynn A. Weeks Dell

visual strategies

A broader term used for a variety of visual tools and systems. Visual strategies can be used to augment information so that an individual with autism can better receive information (input). Visual strategies can also be used as tools to augment the individual's communication abilities so that the individual may express him- or herself more effectively and efficiently (output).

Visual input strategies are useful not only for preparing individuals with autism for changes in settings and routines (e.g., visual schedules representing the daily schedule, mini activity schedules, transition helpers) but also for assisting these individuals to learn concepts, clarify information, organize thoughts, make transitions in the environment, and/or to understand cues presented by teachers. Additional examples of visual input tools and systems include a visual listing of words and/or sentences used during communication exchanges between two individuals (a visual script) and visual aids representing categories to illustrate curricular concepts (graphic organizers).

Visual output strategies can also be developed for augmenting an individual's verbal/vocal communication skills. These augmentative communication visual strategies are used to augment and not replace functional expressive communication skills (speech). Used as communication tools, visual output strategies can be used to exchange information between the individual with autism and the communication partner.

Visual input and output strategies may be designed in a variety of forms: objects, photographs, symbolic representations (icons), simple line drawings, and/or printed words/sentences. It is critical to determine why the individual is using the particular visual system/tool designed. *See also* augmentative and alternative communication (AAC), Picture Exchange Communication System (PECS), transition cue, visual schedule.

Lynn A. Weeks Dell

visual-motor

Relating to the ability to coordinate one's eyes and hands for small-scale tasks, such as writing letters and drawing shapes. Visual-motor skills differ from *eye–hand coordination,* which is more basic, typically develops earlier, and relates to larger scale tasks such as throwing and catching. *Maryjo M. Oster*

vitamin B$_6$ and magnesium therapy

Vitamin B$_6$ and magnesium therapy was one of the earliest nutrient supplement therapies ever used for autism spectrum disorder (ASD). This combination treatment has both theoretical and experimental support. Vitamin B$_6$ (pyridoxine) and magnesium are pivotal nutrients involved in neuronal cellular energy production. Deficiencies of either can lead to disordered central nervous system (CNS) integration of all body processes (Grimaldi, 2002). Magnesium deficiency inhibits the production and tissue uptake of pyridoxal phosphate, the active form of vitamin B$_6$. A vitamin B$_6$ deficiency causes increased magnesium excretion. In animals and humans, experimental or accidental deficiencies of magnesium and B$_6$ cause many abnormalities associated with autism (e.g., neuromuscular hyperexcitability, muscle spasm, heightened sensitivity to touch and sound, inattention, abnormal movements). Since 1965 several dozen studies have demonstrated some improvement, occasionally dramatic, in approximately half of study participants using various regimens of vitamin B$_6$ and magnesium supplementation in individuals with autism (Pfeiffer, Norton, Nelson, & Shott, 1995; Rimland & Edelson, 2003). It is unlikely that vitamin B$_6$ and magnesium deficiencies are primary causes of autism. Many behavioral and physiologic abnormalities of autism can cause negative vitamin B$_6$ and magnesium balance (e.g., decreased intake due to restrictive self-selected diets and malabsorption, increased excretion secondary to chronic gastrointestinal abnormalities). Whether independent of or caused by the underlying pathophysiology of autism, vitamin B$_6$ and magnesium deficiencies may add adverse physiologic consequences to the autism spectrum, expanding its heterogeneous presentation. Because of low cost, relative safety, and some literature support, a therapeutic trial of these nutrients at appropriate dosages may be attempted to ameliorate symptoms of autism, although this treatment currently is not recommended (New York State Department of Health, Early Intervention Program, 1999a). *Robert A. Da Prato*

vitamin therapy

Use of specific vitamins (or increased amounts) with the intention of improving behavior or reducing symptoms. Vitamin therapy for autism and other pervasive developmental disorders (PDDs), employing primarily vitamin B_6 and magnesium, was first studied in Europe in the 1960s. Formulations containing multiple vitamins and minerals in addition to vitamin B_6 and magnesium have been developed. Side effects can include enhanced hyperactivity and irritability. Doses of vitamin B_6 over the long term can lead to the development of peripheral neuropathy, leading to tingling of hands and feet. Current research does not support the use of vitamin therapy for individuals with autism (New York State Department of Health, Early Intervention Program, 1999a). *See also* diet therapy, dimethylglycine (DMG), vitamin B_6 and magnesium therapy.
Jeanette C. Ramer

vocational evaluator

A professional who identifies what an individual does well, what he or she likes or is attracted to, and what he or she does well vocationally, with the end result of identifying employment goals and related services needed to meet these work-related goals. A vocational evaluator provides the evaluation service to identify the individual's vocational potential and works to document the individual's interests, values, temperaments, work-related behaviors, aptitudes, skills, physical capacities, learning style, and training needs. A vocational evaluator has some job tasks that are similar to those of a certified rehabilitation counselor (CRC); however, the vocational evaluator focuses primarily on assessment. *See also* certified rehabilitation counselor (CRC).
Lynn Atanasoff

vocational rehabilitation

See certified rehabilitation counselor (CRC), individualized written rehabilitation plan (IWRP), Rehabilitation Act of 1973 (PL 93-112).

VSM

See video self-modeling.

wait training

Teaching that delivery of a requested reinforcer will be delayed for gradually increasing periods of time. For example, an instructor may pair a verbal "Wait" cue with a visual card or tactile manipulative when a student requests an item or activity. The item or activity is then delivered after 1 second in exchange for the card. After success, the instructor gradually increases the amount of time between the initial request and the delivery of the reinforcer. Eventually, the use of the card may be faded, and the child's appropriate waiting behavior is occasioned by the word *wait*. *See also* reinforcer.
Thomas P. Kitchen

weak central coherence

A theoretical process to account for the tendency of individuals with autism to emphasize details over global meaning (a reverse of the typical developmental trend) (Frith, 1989). *Coherence* refers to pulling or putting things together, that is, making sense of parts as a whole. The theory of weak central coherence has been used to explain why individuals with autism spectrum disorders (ASDs) typically have an uneven cognitive profile with peak performance occurring in tasks requiring rote memory and visuospatial skills and why they may not "see the forest for the trees." *See also* hyperlexia, savant syndrome.
John T. Neisworth & Pamela S. Wolfe

Wilbarger protocol

See deep pressure proprioception touch technique.

wraparound services

See behavioral health rehabilitation (BHR) services.

Yy

yeast
See antiyeast therapy.

Zz

zero effect level
See toxicology.

zero inference strategy
A term (coined by Brown, Nietupski, & Hamre-Nietupski, 1976) that refers to teaching of skills, especially communication skills, in natural environments. Use of the strategy reduces problems of generalization. Teaching conversational and other language skills in the situations in which such skills are expected is useful for students with autism, who have difficulties generalizing.
John T. Neisworth & Pamela S. Wolfe

zero reject
The first principle of the Education for All Handicapped Children Act of 1975 (PL 94-142) and its amendments, which state that there can be no exclusion of students from free appropriate public education (FAPE), regardless of the severity or type of disability. Thus, children with autism and

other pervasive developmental disorders (PDDs) cannot be excluded from public education. This does not necessarily mean that all children must be educated in the general classroom (full inclusion), but FAPE services must be provided. *See also* eligibility, free appropriate public education (FAPE), inclusion, Individuals with Disabilities Education Act (IDEA).
John T. Neisworth & Pamela S. Wolfe

ZERO TO THREE diagnostic classification
See Diagnostic Classification of Mental Health Disorders of Infancy and Early Childhood (DC: 0-3).

zone of proximal development (ZPD)
A developmental model (based on Piaget's and Vytgotsky's theories) that stresses the advantages of first estimating the developmental level of the child without guidance (e.g., prompting, outside incentives), then the level with guidance; this difference is the ZPD. An application of this model is the selection of developmental activities and goals; the optimal objectives are almost within reach of the child but not too easy or difficult.
John T. Neisworth & Pamela S. Wolfe

References

Adamson, L.B., & Russell, C. (1999). Emotion regulation and emergence of joint attention. In P. Rochat (Ed.), *Early social cognition: Understanding others in the first months of life* (pp. 281–297). Mahwah, NJ: Lawrence Erlbaum Associates.

Aggleton, J.P. (Ed.). (2000). *The amygdala: A functional analysis* (2nd ed.). New York: Oxford University Press.

Alberto, P., & Troutman, A. (1990). *Applied behavior analysis for teachers* (pp. 304–317). New York: Macmillan.

American Academy of Pediatrics. (1982). The Doman-Delacato treatment of neurologically handicapped children. *Pediatrics, 70,* 810–812.

American Academy of Pediatrics. (1996). *The classification of child and adolescent mental diagnoses in primary care: Diagnostic and statistical manual for primary care (DSM-PC) child and adolescent version.* Elk Grove Village, IL: Author.

American Association on Mental Retardation. (2002). *Mental retardation: Definition, classification, and systems of supports* (10th ed.). Washington, DC: Author.

American Psychiatric Association (APA). (1952). *Diagnostic and statistical manual: Mental disorders.* Washington, DC: Author.

American Psychiatric Association (APA). (1968). *Diagnostic and statistical manual of mental disorders* (2nd ed.). Washington, DC: Author.

American Psychiatric Association (APA). (1980). *Diagnostic and statistical manual of mental disorders* (3rd ed.). Washington, DC: Author.

American Psychiatric Association (APA). (1987). *Diagnostic and statistical manual of mental disorders* (3rd ed., Rev.). Washington, DC: Author.

American Psychiatric Association (APA). (1994). *Diagnostic and statistical manual of mental disorders* (4th ed.). Washington, DC: Author.

American Psychiatric Association (APA). (2000). *Diagnostic and statistical manual of mental disorders* (4th ed., Text rev.). Washington, DC: Author.

Americans with Disabilities Act (ADA) of 1990, PL 101-336, 42 U.S.C. §§ 12101 *et seq.*

Anderson, K.N., Anderson, L.E., & Glanze, W.D. (Eds.). (1998). *Mosby's medical, nursing, & allied health dictionary* (5th ed.). St. Louis: Mosby-Year Book.

Anderson, S., Taras, M., & Cannon, B. (1996). Teaching new skills to young children with autism. In C. Maurice (Ed.), *Behavioral intervention for young children with autism: A manual for parents and professionals* (pp. 181–194). Austin, TX: PRO-ED.

Assistance to States for the Education of Children with Disabilities, 34 C.F.R. § 300 (2003).

Ausubel, D.P., & Youssef, M. (1965). The effect of spaced repetition on meaningful retention. *Journal of General Psychology, 73,* 147–150.

Autism Society of America. (n.d.). *What is autism?* Retrieved May 28, 2004, from http://www.autism-society.org/site/PageServer?pagename=whatisautism

Axelrod, S., Spreat, S., Berry, B., & Moyer, L. (1993). A decision-making model for selecting the optimal treatment procedure. In R. Van Houten & S. Axelrod (Eds.), *Behavior analysis and treatment* (pp. 183–202). New York: Kluwer Academic/Plenum.

Aylward, E.H., Minshew, N.J., Field, K., Sparks, B.F., & Singh, N. (2002). Effects of age on brain volume and head circumference in autism. *Neurology, 59,* 175–183.

Ayres, A.J. (1972). *Sensory integration and learning disorders.* Los Angeles: Western Psychological Services.

Ayres, A.J. (1979). *Sensory integration and the child.* Los Angeles: Western Psychological Services.

Baer, D.M. (Vol. Ed.). (1999). How to plan for generalization. In R.V. Hall & M.L. Hall (Series Eds.), *How to manage behavior series* (2nd ed.). Austin, TX: PRO-ED.

Baer, D.M., Wolf, M.M., & Risley, T.R. (1968). Some current dimensions of applied behavior analysis. *Journal of Applied Behavior Analysis, 1,* 91–97.

Baltaxe, C.A., & Simmons, J.Q. (1985). Prosodic development in normal and autistic children. In E. Schopler & G.B. Mesibov (Eds.), *Communication problems in autism* (pp. 95–125). New York: Kluwer Academic/Plenum.

Bandura, A. (1977). *Social learning theory.* Upper Saddle River, NJ: Pearson Prentice Hall.

Bandura, A. (1986). *Social foundations of thought and action: A social cognitive theory.* Upper Saddle River: Pearson Prentice Hall.

Baranek, G.T., & Berkson, G. (1994). Tactile defensiveness in children with developmental disabilities: Responsiveness and habituation. *Journal of Autism and Developmental Disorders, 24,* 457–471.

Barnhill, J., & Horrigan, J.P. (2002). Tourette's syndrome and autism: A search for common ground. *Mental Health Aspects of Developmental Disabilities, 5,* 7–15.

Baron-Cohen, S. (1987). Autism and symbolic play. *British Journal of Developmental Psychology, 5*(2), 139–148.

Baron-Cohen, S. (1989). Perceptual role taking and protodeclarative pointing in autism. *British Journal of Developmental Psychology, 7,* 113–127.

Baron-Cohen, S. (1995). *Mindblindness: An essay on autism and theory of mind.* Cambridge, MA: MIT Press.

Bauman, M.L., & Kemper, T.L. (Eds.). (1994). *The neurobiology of autism.* Baltimore: The Johns Hopkins University Press.

Bellugi, U., Birhle, A., Neville, H., Jernigan, T., & Doherty, S. (1992). Language, cognition, and brain organization in a neurodevelopmental disorder. In M. Gunnar & C. Nelson (Eds.), *Developmental behavioral neuroscience* (pp. 201–232). Mahwah, NJ: Lawrence Erlbaum Associates.

Berkell, D., Malgeri, S., & Streit, M.K. (1996). Auditory integration training for individuals with autism. *Education and Training in Mental Retardation and Developmental Disabilities, 66–70.*

Bernard, S., Enayati, A., Redwood, L., Roger, H., & Binstock, T. (2001). Autism: A novel form of mercury poisoning. *Medical Hypotheses, 56,* 462–471.

Bernstein, D., & Tiegerman-Farber, E. (2002). *Language and communication disorders in children* (5th ed.). Boston: Allyn & Bacon.

Bettelheim, B. (1967). *The empty fortress: Infantile autism and the birth of the self.* New York: The Free Press.

Bijou, S.W., Peterson, R.F., & Ault, M.H. (1968). A method to integrate descriptive and experimental field studies at the level of data and empirical concepts. *Journal of Applied Behavior Analysis, 1,* 175–191.

Biklen, D. (1993). *Communication unbound.* New York: Teachers College Press.

Binder, C. (1996). Behavioral fluency: Evolution of a new paradigm. *The Behavior Analyst, 19,* 163–197.

Bogdashina, O. (2001). *A reconstruction of the sensory world of autism.* Sheffield, England: Sheffield Hallam University Press.

Bolte, E.R. (1998). Autism and *Clostridium tetani. Medical Hypotheses, 51,* 133–144.

Bondy, A.S., & Frost, L.A. (1994). The Picture Exchange Communication System. *Focus on Autistic Behavior, 9,* 1–19.

Bredekamp, S., & Copple, C. (Eds.). (1997). *Developmentally appropriate practice in early childhood programs* (Rev. ed.). Washington, DC: National Association for the Education of Young Children.

Brown, L., Nietupski, J., & Hamre-Nietupski, S. (1976). Criterion of ultimate functioning. In M.A. Thomas (Ed.), *Hey, don't forget about me!: Education's investment in the severely, profoundly, and multiply handicapped* (pp. 2–15). Reston, VA: Council for Exceptional Children.

Brown, R. (1973). *A first language: The early stages.* Cambridge, MA: Harvard University Press.

Bryson, S.E. (1997). Epidemiology of autism: Overview and issues outstanding. In D.J. Cohen & F.R. Volkmar (Eds.), *Handbook of autism and pervasive developmental disorders* (2nd ed., pp. 41–46). New York: John Wiley & Sons.

Buggey, T. (1995). An examination of the effectiveness of videotaped self-modeling in training specific linguistic structures to preschoolers. *Topics in Early Childhood Special Education, 15,* 434–458.

Buitelaar, J.K., van der Gaag, R.J., & van der Hoeven, J. (1998). Buspirone in the management of anxiety and irritability in children with pervasive developmental disorders: Results of an open-label study. *The Journal of Clinical Psychiatry, 59,* 56–59.

Camarata, S. (in press). *The assessment and treatment of speech intelligibility disorders in children.* Nashville: Bill Wilkerson Press.

Carpenter, M., Nagell, K., & Tomasello, M. (1998). Social cognition, joint attention, and communicative competence from 9 to 15 months of age. *Monographs of the Society for Research in Child Development, 63*(4, Serial No. 255), 1–142.

Carr, E., & Durand, V. (1985). Reducing behavior problems through functional communication training. *Journal of Applied Behavior Analysis, 18,* 111–126.

Carr, E.G., Levin, L., McConnachie, G., Carlson, J.I., Kemp, D.C., & Smith, C.E. (1994). *Communication-based intervention for problem behavior: A user's guide for producing positive change.* Baltimore: Paul H. Brookes Publishing Co.

Carter, A.S., Volkmar, F.R., Sparrow, S.S., Wang, J.J., Lord, C., Dawson, G., et al. (1998). The Vineland Adaptive Behavior Scales: Supplementary norms for individuals with autism. *Journal of Autism and Developmental Disorders, 28,* 287–302.

Casaccia-Bonnefil, P., Tikoo, R., Kiyokawa, H., Friedrich, V., Jr., Chao, M.V., & Koff, A. (1997). Oligodendrocyte precursor differentiation is perturbed in the absence of the cyclin-dependent kinase inhibitor p27Kip1. *Genes and Development, 11,* 2335–2346.

Cassano, G.B., McElroy, S.L., Brady, K., Nolen, W.A., & Placidi, G.F. (2000). Current issues in the identification and management of bipolar spectrum disorders in 'special populations.' *Journal of Affective Disorders, 59,* S69–S79.

Chadsey-Rusch, J. (1992). Toward defining and measuring social skills in employment settings. *American Journal on Mental Retardation, 96,* 405–418.

Charlop, M.H., & Trasowech, J.E. (1991). Increasing autistic children's daily spontaneous speech. *Journal of Applied Behavior Analysis, 24,* 747–761.

Charlop-Christy, M.H., Carpenter, M., Le, L., LeBlanc, L.A., & Kellet, K. (2002). Using the Picture Exchange Communication System (PECS) with children with autism: Assessment of PECS acquisition, speech, social-communicative behavior, and problem behavior. *Journal of Applied Behavior Analysis, 35,* 213–231.

Charman, T. (2002). The prevalence of autism spectrum disorders. Recent evidence and future challenges. *European Child & Adolescent Psychiatry, 11,* 249–256.

Chisolm, J.J., Jr. (2000). Safety and efficacy of meso-2,3-dimercaptosuccinic acid (DMSA) in children with elevated blood lead concentrations. *Journal of Toxicology—Clinical Toxicology, 38,* 365–375.

Cloninger, C.J. Designing collaborative educational services. In F.P. Orelove, D. Sobsey, & R.K. Silberman (Eds.), *Educating children with multiple disabilities: A collaborative approach* (4th ed., pp. 1–29). Baltimore: Paul H. Brookes Publishing Co.

Cody, H., Pelphrey, K., & Piven, J. (2002). Structural and functional magnetic resonance imaging of autism. *International Journal of Developmental Neuroscience, 20,* 421–438.

Cohen, M.J., Hall, J., & Riccio, C.A. (1997). Neuropsychological profiles of children diagnosed as specific language impaired with and without hyperlexia. *Archives of Clinical Neuropsychology, 12,* 223–229.

Coleman, J.G. (1999). *The early intervention dictionary: A multidisciplinary guide to terminology* (2nd ed.). Bethesda, MD: Woodbine House.

Connecticut Birth to Three Natural Environments Task Force. (1999). *Natural environments service guideline 2: Natural environments. Intervention guidelines for service providers and families.* Hartford: Connecticut Birth to Three System.

Cooper, J.O., Heron, T.E., & Heward, W.L. (1987). *Applied behavior analysis.* Columbus, OH: Merrill.

Courchesne, E., Carper, R., & Akshoomoff, N. (2003). Evidence of brain overgrowth in the first year of life in autism. *Journal of the American Medical Association, 290,* 337–344.

Creaghead, N.A. (1999). Evaluating language intervention approaches: Contrasting perspectives. *Language, Speech, and Hearing Services in Schools, 30,* 335–338.

Cuvo, A.J., & Davis, P.K. (1998). Establishing and transferring stimulus control: Teaching people with developmental disabilities. In J.K. Luiselli & M.J. Cameron (Eds.), *Antecedent control: Innovative approaches to behavioral support* (pp. 347–369). Baltimore: Paul H. Brookes Publishing Co.

Curatolo, P., Arpino, C., Stazi, M.A., & Medda, E. (1995). Risk factors for the co-occurrence of partial epilepsy, cerebral palsy and mental retardation. *Developmental Medicine and Child Neurology, 37,* 776–782.

Dawson, G., Klinger, L.G., Panagiotides, H., Lewy, A., & Castelloe, P. (1995). Subgroups of autistic children based on social behavior display distinct patterns of brain activity. *Journal of Abnormal Psychology, 23,* 569–584.

Delacato, C.H. (1966). Neurological organization and reading. Springfield, IL: Charles C Thomas.

DelGiudice-Asch, G., Simon, L., Schmeidler, J., Cunningham-Rundles, C., & Hollander, E. (1999). Brief report: A pilot open clinical trial of intravenous immunoglobulin in childhood autism. *Journal of Autism and Developmental Disorders, 29,* 157–160.

DeLong, G.R., Teague, L.A., & Kamran, M.M. (1998). Effects of fluoxetine treatment in young children with idiopathic autism. *Developmental Medicine and Child Neurology, 40,* 551–562.

Dempster, F.N. (1989). Spacing effects and their implications for theory and practice. *Educational Psychology Review, 1,* 309–330.

Deutsch, C.K., & Farkas, L.G. (1994). Quantitative diagnosis of craniofacial dysmorphology. In L.G. Farkas (Ed.), *Anthropometry of the head and face* (pp. 151–158). New York: Raven.

Dewey, D., Lord, C., & Magill, J. (1988). Qualitative assessment of the effect of play materials in dyadic peer interactions of children with autism. *Canadian Journal of Psychology, 42,* 242–260.

Division for Early Childhood. (2001). *DEC concept paper on developmental delay as an eligibility category.* Retrieved May 28, 2004, from http://www.dec-sped.org/pdf/positionpapers/Concept%20DevDelay.pdf

Doman, G. (1974). *What to do about your brain-injured child.* Garden City, NJ: Doubleday.

Drash, P.W., & Leibowitz, J.M. (1973). Operant conditioning of speech and language in the non-verbal retarded child. *Pediatric Clinics of North America, 20,* 233–243.

Drash, P., & Tudor, R. (1989). Cognitive development therapy: A new model for treatment of an overlooked population, developmentally delayed preschool children. *Psychotherapy in Private Practice, 7,* 19–41.

Drash, P.W., & Tudor, R.M. (2004). An analysis of autism as a contingency-shaped disorder of verbal behavior. *The Analysis of Verbal Behavior.*

DuBard, N.E., & Martin, M.K. (1994). *Teaching language-deficient children: Theory and application of the association method for multisensory teaching.* Cambridge, MA: Educators Publishing Service.

Dube, W.V., & McIlvane, W.J. (1999). Reduction of stimulus overselectivity with nonverbal differential observing responses. *Journal of Applied Behavior Analysis, 32,* 25–33.

Dunn, W. (1997a). The impact of sensory processing abilities on the daily lives of young children and their families: A conceptual model. *Infants and Young Children, 9*(4), 23–35.

Dunn, W. (1997b). Implementing neuroscience principles to support habilitation and recovery. In C. Christiansen & C. Baum (Eds.), *Occupational therapy: Enabling function and well-being* (pp. 182–232). Thorofare, NJ: Slack.

Dunn, W. (2001). The sensations of everyday life: Theoretical, conceptual and pragmatic considerations. *American Journal of Occupational Therapy, 55,* 608–620.

Dunn, W., Brown, T., & Youngstrom, M. (2003). Ecological model of occupation. In P. Kramer, J. Hinojosa, & C. Royeen (Eds.), *Perspectives in human occupation: Participation in life* (pp. 222–263). Philadelphia: Lippincott Williams & Wilkins.

Dunn, W., & Westman, K. (1997). The Sensory Profile: The performance of a national sample without disabilities. *American Journal of Occupational Therapy, 51,* 25–34.

Durand, V.M. (1990). *Severe behavior problems: A functional communication training approach.* New York: Guilford Press.

Durand, V.M. (1999). Functional communication training using assistive devices: Recruiting natural communities of reinforcement. *Journal of Applied Behavior Analysis, 32,* 247–267.

Durand, V.M., & Carr, E.G. (1992). An analysis of maintenance following functional communication training. *Journal of Applied Behavior Analysis, 25,* 777–794.

Durand, V.M., & Crimmins, D.B. (1992). *The Motivation Assessment Scale (MAS) administration guide.* Topeka, KS: Monaco.

Early Intervention Program for Infants and Toddlers with Disabilities, 34 C.F.R. § 303 (2003).

Eddy, D.M., & Hasselblad, V. (1994). Analyzing evidence by the confidence and profile method. In K.A. McCormick, S.R. Moore, & R.A. Siegel (Eds.), *Clinical practice guideline development: Methodology perspectives* (AHCPR Publication No. 95-0009). Rockville, MD: U.S. Department of Health and Human Services, Agency for Health Care Policy and Research.

Education for All Handicapped Children Act of 1975, 20 U.S.C. §§ 1400 *et seq.*

Education of the Handicapped Act (EHA) Amendments of 1986, PL 99-457, 20 U.S.C. §§ 1400 *et seq.*

Education of the Handicapped Act (EHA) of 1970, PL 91-230 § 601–662, 84 Stat. 175.

Feinberg, E., & Beyer, J. (1998). Creating public policy in a climate of clinical indeterminacy: Lovaas as the case example du jour. *Infants and Young Children, 10*(3), 51–66.

Feingold, B.F. (1973). *Introduction to clinical allergy.* Springfield, IL: Charles C Thomas.

Fenske, E.C., Krantz, P.J., & McClannahan, L.E. (2001). Incidental teaching: A non-discrete-trial teaching approach. In C. Maurice, G. Green, & R.M. Foxx (Eds.), *Making a difference: Behavioral intervention for autism* (pp. 75–82). Austin, TX: PRO-ED.

Ferrari, M., & Sternberg, R.J. (1998). The development of mental abilities and styles. In W. Damon (Series Ed.) & D. Kuhn, & R.S. Siegler (Vol. Eds.), *Handbook of child psychology: Vol. 2. Cognition, perception and language* (5th ed., pp. 899–946). New York: John Wiley & Sons.

Ferster, C.B. (1965). Arbitrary and natural reinforcement. *Psychological Record, 17*, 341–347.

Field, T., Lasko, D., Mundy, P., Henteleff, T., Kabat, S., Talpins, S., et al. (1997). Brief report: Autistic children's attentiveness and responsivity improve after touch therapy. *Journal of Autism and Developmental Disorders, 27*, 333–338.

Finegold, S.M., Molitoris, D., Song, Y., Liu, C., Vaisanen, M.L., & Bolte, E. (2002). Gastrointestinal microflora studies in late-onset autism. *Clinical Infectious Diseases, 35*(Suppl. 1), S6–S16.

Fombonne, E. (1999). The epidemiology of autism: A review. *Psychological Medicine, 29*, 769–786.

Forest, M., & Lusthaus, E. (1989). Promoting educational equality for all students: Circles and maps. In S. Stainback, W. Stainback, & M. Forest (Eds.), *Educating all students in the mainstream of regular education* (pp. 43–57). Baltimore: Paul H. Brookes Publishing Co.

Foxx, R.M. (1982). *Decreasing behaviors of persons with severe retardation and autism.* Champaign, IL: Research Press.

Foxx, R.M., & Azrin, N.H. (1973). The elimination of autistic self-stimulatory behavior by overcorrection. *Journal of Applied Behavior Analysis, 6*, 1–14.

Foxx, R.M., & Bechtel, D.R. (1983). Overcorrection: A review and analysis. In S. Axelrod & J. Apsche (Eds.), *The effects of punishment on human behavior* (pp. 133–220). New York: Academic Press.

Freeman, S.W. (1979). *The epileptic in home, school, and society.* Springfield, IL: Charles C Thomas.

Frith, U. (1989). *Autism: Explaining the enigma.* Oxford, England: Basil Blackwell.

Frith, U. (1992). Cognitive development and cognitive deficit. *The Psychologist, 5*, 13–19.

Frith, U., Morton, J., & Leslie, A.M. (1991). The cognitive basis of a biological disorder: Autism. *Trends in Neurosciences, 14*, 433–438.

Frost, L.A., & Bondy, A.S. (1994). *The Picture Exchange Communication System: Training manual.* Cherry Hill, NJ: Pyramid Educational Consultants.

Gall, M.D., Borg, W.R., & Gall, J.P. (1996). *Educational research: An introduction* (6th ed.). White Plains, NY: Longman.

Garvey, C. (1977). *Play.* Cambridge, MA: Harvard University Press.

Geroski, A.M., & Rodgers, K.A. (1998). Collaborative assessment and treatment of children with enuresis and encopresis. *Professional School Counseling, 2,* 128–134.

Ghaziuddin, M., Ghaziuddin, N., & Greden, J. (2002). Depression in persons with autism: Implications for research and clinical care. *Journal of Autism and Developmental Disorders, 32,* 299–306.

Ghaziuddin, M., Tsai, L., & Ghaziuddin, N. (1992). Comorbidity of autistic disorder in children and adolescents. *European Child and Adolescent Psychiatry, 1,* 209–213.

Giangreco, M.F., Cloninger, C.J., Dennis, R.E., & Edelman, S.W. (2000). Problem-solving methods to facilitate inclusive education. In R.A. Villa & J.S. Thousand (Eds.), *Restructuring for caring and effective education: Piecing the puzzle together* (2nd ed., pp. 293–359). Baltimore: Paul H. Brookes Publishing Co.

Gillberg, C. (1991). The treatment of epilepsy in autism. *Journal of Autism and Developmental Disorders, 21,* 61–77.

Giovanardi Rossi, P., Posar, A., & Parmeggiani, A. (2000). Epilepsy in adolescents and young adults with autistic disorder. *Brain and Development, 22,* 102–106.

Goldstein, E.B. (2001). *Blackwell handbook of perception.* Oxford, England: Blackwell.

Grayson, C.E. (Ed.). (2004, February). *Living with a wheat allergy.* Retrieved March 3, 2004, from WebMD, http://my.webmd.com/content/article/61/67464.htm?lastselectedguid={5FE84E90-BC77-4056-A91C-9531713CA348}

Green, J., Gilchrist, A., Burton, D., & Cox, A. (2000). Social and psychiatric functioning in adolescents with Asperger syndrome compared with conduct disorder. *Journal of Autism and Developmental Disorders, 30,* 279–293.

Greenberg, D.A., Hodge, S.E., Sowinski, J., & Nicoll, D. (2001). Excess of twins among affected sibling pairs with autism: Implications for the etiology of autism. *American Journal of Human Genetics, 69,* 1062–1067.

Greenspan, S.I. (1992a). *Infancy and early childhood: The practice of clinical assessment and intervention with emotional and developmental challenges.* Madison, CT: International Universities Press.

Greenspan, S.I. (1992b). Reconsidering the diagnosis and treatment of very young children with autistic spectrum or pervasive developmental disorder. *ZERO TO THREE Bulletin, 13,* 1–9.

Greenspan, S.I., & Weider, S. (1997). Developmental patterns and outcomes in infants and children with disorders in relating and communicating: A chart review of 200 cases of children with autism spectrum diagnoses. *Journal of Developmental and Learning Disorders, 1*(1), 87–141.

Gresham, F.M., & MacMillan, D.L. (1997). Autistic recovery: An analysis and critique of the empirical evidence on the Early Intervention Project. *Behavioral Disorders, 22,* 185–201.

Gresham, F.M., Sugai, G., & Horner, R.H. (2001). Interpreting outcomes of social skills training for students with high-incidence disabilities. *Exceptional Children, 67,* 331–344.

Grigorenko, E.L., Klin, A., Pauls, D.L., Senft, R., Hooper, C., & Volkmar, F. (2002). A descriptive study of hyperlexia in a clinically referred sample of children with developmental delays. *Journal of Autism and Developmental Disorders, 32,* 3–12.

Grimaldi, B.L. (2002). The central role of magnesium deficiency in Tourette's syndrome: Causal relationships between magnesium deficiency, altered biochemical pathways and symptoms relating to Tourette's syndrome and several reported comorbid conditions. *Medical Hypotheses, 58,* 47–60.

Guess, D., & Carr, E. (1991). Emergence and maintenance of stereotypy and self-injury. *American Journal on Mental Retardation, 96,* 299–319.

Gupta, S. (2000). Immunological treatments for autism. *Journal of Autism and Developmental Disorders, 30,* 475–479.

Gupta, S., Aggarwal, S., & Heads, C. (1996). Brief report: Dysregulated immune system in children with autism: Beneficial effects of intravenous immune globulin on autistic characteristics. *Journal of Autism and Developmental Disorders, 26,* 439–452.

H. Res. 1350, 108th Cong., 150 Cong. Rec. S5394–S5451 (2004) (enacted).

Halgin, R.P., & Whitbourne, S.K. (2003). *Abnormal psychology: Clinical perspectives on psychological disorders* (4th ed.). New York: McGraw-Hill.

Hancock, T.B., & Kaiser, A.P. (2002). The effects of trainer-implemented enhanced milieu teaching on the social communication of children with autism. *Topics in Early Childhood Special Education, 22,* 39–56.

Handen, B.L., Johnson, C.R., & Lubetsky, M. (2000). Efficacy of methylphenidate among children with autism and symptoms of attention-deficit hyperactivity disorder. *Journal of Autism and Developmental Disorders, 30,* 245–255.

Handen, B.L., Parrish, J.M., McClung, T.J., Kerwin, M.E., & Evans, L.D. (1992). Using guided compliance versus time out to promote child compliance: A preliminary comparative analysis in analogue context. *Research in Developmental Disabilities, 13,* 157–170.

Hardan, A., & Sahl, R. (1997). Psychopathology in children and adolescents with developmental disorders. *Research in Developmental Disabilities, 18,* 369–382.

Haring, T., & Breen, C. (1992). A peer-mediated social network intervention to enhance the social integration of persons with moderate and severe disabilities. *Journal of Applied Behavior Analysis, 25,* 319–333.

Harris, P.L. (2000a). Role play. In P.L. Harris (Ed.), *The work of the imagination* (pp. 29–57). Oxford, England: Blackwell.

Harris, P.L. (Ed.). (2000b). *The work of the imagination.* Oxford, England: Blackwell.

Harris, P.L., & Leevers, H.J. (2000). Pretending, imagery and self-awareness in autism. In S. Baron-Cohen, H. Tager-Flusberg, & D.J. Cohen (Eds.), *Understanding other minds: Perspectives from autism and cognitive neuroscience* (2nd ed., pp. 182–202). Oxford, England: Oxford University Press.

Harrower, J.K., & Dunlap, G. (2001). Including children with autism in general education classrooms: A review of effective strategies. *Behavior Modification, 25,* 762–784.

Hart, B.M., & Risley, T.R. (1982). *How to use incidental teaching for elaborating language.* Austin, TX: PRO-ED.

Heller, K., Mönks, F.J., Sternberg, R.J., & Subotnik, R.F. (Eds.). (2000). *The international handbook of giftedness and talent* (2nd ed.). Oxford, England: Elsevier.

Heller, T. (1908). Über Dementia infantilis. *Zeitschrift für die Erforschung und Behandlung des Jugendlichen Schwachsinns auf Wissenschaftlicher Grundlage, 2,* 17–28.

Herbert, M.R., Ziegler, D.A., Deutsch, C.K., O'Brien, L.M., Lange, N., Bakardjiev, A., et al. (2003). Dissociations of cerebral cortex, subcortical and cerebral white matter volumes in autistic boys. *Brain, 126,* 1182–1192.

Hermelin, B. (2001). *Bright splinters of the mind.* London: Jessica Kingsley Publishers.

Hiroto, D.S., & Seligman, M.E. (1975). Generality of learned helplessness in man. *Journal of Personality and Social Psychology, 31,* 311–327.

Holland, J.P. (1995). Development of a clinical practice guideline for acute low back pain. *Current Opinion in Orthopedics, 6,* 63–69.

Homme, L., Csanyi, A.P., Gonzales, M.S., & Rechs, J.R. (1969). *How to use contingency management in the classroom.* Champaign, IL: Research Press.

Horvath, K., Stefanatos, G., Sokolski, K.N., Wachtel, R., Nabors L., & Tildon, J.T. (1998). Improved social and language skills after secretin administration in patients with autistic spectrum disorders. *Journal of the Association for Academic Minority Physicians, 9,* 9–15.

Hosford, R.E. (1981). Self-as-models: A cognitive social-learning technique. *The Counseling Psychologist, 9,* 45–62.

Hosford, R., & Johnson, M. (1983). A comparison of self-observation, self-modeling, and practice without video feedback for improving counselor interviewing behaviors. *Counselor Education & Supervision, 23,* 62–70.

Howlin, P. (1986). An overview of social behavior in autism. In E. Schopler & G.B. Mesibov (Eds.), *Social behavior in autism* (pp. 103–132). New York: Kluwer Academic/Plenum.

Howlin, P., Baron-Cohen, S., & Hadwin, J. (1999). *Teaching children with autism to mind-read: A practical guide.* New York: John Wiley & Sons.

Hughes, C. (2001). Executive dysfunction in autism: Its nature and implications for everyday problems experienced by individuals with autism. In J.A. Burack & T. Chairman (Eds.), *The development of autism: Perspectives from theory and research* (pp. 255–275). Mahwah, NJ: Lawrence Erlbaum Associates.

IDEAdata.org. (2002). *Table AA7: Number of children served under IDEA Part B, by disability and age, during the 2002-03 school year.* Retrieved August 3, 2004, from http://www.IDEAdata.org/tables26th%5Car_aa7.htm

Individuals with Disabilities Education Act Amendments of 1997, PL 105-17, 20 U.S.C. 1400 *et seq.*

Individuals with Disabilities Education Act of 1990, PL 101-476, 20 U.S.C. §§ 1400 *et seq.*

Institute on Medicine, Board on Health Promotion and Disease Prevention, Immunization Safety Review Committee. (2004). *Immunization safety review: Vaccines and autism. Report of the Institute of Medicine.* Washington, DC: National Academies Press. Also available on-line: http://www.nap.edu/catalog/10997.htm

Israngkun, P.P., Newman, H.A., Patel, S.T., Duruibe, V.A., & Abou-Issa, H. (1986). Potential biochemical markers for infantile autism. *Neurochemical Pathology, 5,* 51–70.

Iwata, B.A., Kahng, S.W., Wallace, M.D., & Lindberg, J.S. (2000). The functional analysis model of behavioral assessment. In J. Austin & J.W. Carr (Eds.), *Handbook of applied behavior analysis* (pp. 61–90). Reno, NV: Context Press.

Iwata, B.A., Zarcone, J.R., Vollmer, T.R., & Smith, R.G. (1994). Assessment and treatment of self-injurious behavior. In E. Schopler & G.B. Mesibov (Eds.), *Behavioral issues in autism* (pp. 129–157). New York: Kluwer Academic/Plenum.

Johnston, J.M., & Pennypacker, H.S. (1980). *Strategies and tactics for human behavioral research.* Mahwah, NJ: Lawrence Erlbaum Associates.

Kalesnik, J. (1999). Developmental history. In E. Vazquez Nuttall, I. Romero, & J. Kalesnik (Eds.), *Assessing and screening preschoolers: Psychological and educational dimensions* (2nd ed., pp. 94–111). Boston: Allyn & Bacon.

Kamps, D.M., Leonard, B., Potucek, J., & Garrison-Harrell, L. (1995). Cooperative learning groups in reading: An integration strategy for students with autism and general classroom peers. *Behavioral Disorders, 21,* 89–109.

Kanner, L. (1943). Autistic disturbances of affective contact. *The Nervous Child, 2,* 217–250.

Kaplan, H.I., & Sadock, B.J. (1998). *Kaplan and Sadock's synopsis of psychiatry: Behavioral sciences, clinical psychiatry* (8th ed., pp. 1188–1189). Philadelphia: Lippincott Williams & Wilkins.

Kazdin, A.E. (2001). *Behavior modification in applied settings* (6th ed.). Belmont, CA: Wadsworth Thomson Learning.

Kenyon, P. (1999). *What would you do?: An ethical case workbook for human service professionals.* Belmont, CA: Brooks/Cole Thomson Learning.

Kidd, P.M. (2002). Autism, an extreme challenge to integrative medicine. Part 1: The knowledge base. *Alternative Medicine Review, 7,* 292–318.

King, N.J., & Gullone, E. (1990). Acceptability of fear reduction procedures with children. *Journal of Behavior Therapy and Experimental Psychiatry, 21,* 1–8.

Kinsbourne, M. (1991). Overfocusing: An apparent subtype of attention deficit-hyperactivity disorder. In N. Amir, I. Rapin, & D. Branski (Eds.), *Pediatric neurology: Behavior and cognition of the child with brain dysfunction* (Vol. 1., pp. 18–35). Basel, Switzerland: Karger.

Klein, N.J. (2001). Management of primary nocturnal enuresis. *Urologic Nursing, 21,* 71–76.

Knivsberg, A.M., Reichelt, K.L., Hoien, T., & Nodland, M. (2002). A randomised, controlled study of dietary intervention in autistic syndromes. *Nutritional Neuroscience, 5,* 251–261.

Kolb, B., & Whishaw, I.Q. (1996). *Fundamentals of human neuropsychology.* New York: W.H. Freeman & Co.

Koegel, R.L., Koegel, L.K., & Parks, D.R. (1995). "Teach the individual" model of generalization: Autonomy through self-management. In R.L. Koegel & L.K.

Koegel (Eds.), *Teaching children with autism: Strategies for initiating positive interactions and improving learning opportunities* (pp. 67–77). Baltimore: Paul H. Brookes Publishing Co.

Koegel, R., O'Dell, M., & Dunlap, G. (1988). Producing speech use in nonverbal autistic behavior by reinforcing attempts. *Journal of Autism and Developmental Disorders, 18,* 525–538.

Koegel, R.L., O'Dell, M.C., & Koegel, L.K. (1987). A natural language paradigm for teaching non-verbal autistic children. *Journal of Autism and Developmental Disorders, 17,* 187–199.

Krantz, P., MacDuff, G., Wadstrom, O., & McClannahan, L. (1991). Using video with developmentally disabled learners. In P. Dowrick (Ed.), *Practical guide to using video in the behavioral sciences* (pp. 256–266). New York: John Wiley & Sons.

Lattal, K.A. (1995). Contingency and behavior analysis. *The Behavior Analyst, 18,* 209–224.

Leckman, J.F. (2002). Tourette's syndrome. *Lancet, 360,* 1577–1586.

Leekam, S.R., Baron-Cohen, S., Perrett, D., Milders, M., & Brown, S. (1997). Eye-direction detection: A disassociation between geometric and joint attention skills in autism. *British Journal of Developmental Psychology, 15,* 77–95.

Lindsley, O.R. (1971). An interview. *Teaching Exceptional Children, 3,* 114–119.

Lindsley, O.R. (1990). Precision teaching: By teachers for children. *Teaching Exceptional Children, 22*(3), 10–15.

Lloyd, J.W. (2002). *Autism and secretin.* Retrieved March 22, 2004, from http://curry.edschool.virginia.edu/sped/projects/ose/information/secretin.html

Losardo, A., & Bricker, D. (1994). Activity-based intervention and direct-instruction: A comparison study. *American Journal on Mental Retardation, 98,* 744–765.

Lovaas, O.I. (1987). Behavioral treatment and normal education and intellectual functioning in young autistic children. *Journal of Consulting and Clinical Psychology, 55,* 3–9.

Lovaas, O.I., Ackerman, A., Alexander, D., Firestone, P., Perkins, M., Young, D.B., et al. (1981). *Teaching developmentally disabled children: The ME book.* Austin, TX: PRO-ED.

Lovaas, O.I., Koegel, R.L., & Schreibman, L. (1979). Stimulus overselectivity in autism: A review of research. *Psychological Bulletin, 86,* 1236–1254.

Lowe, T.L., Tanaka, K., Seashore, M.R., Young, J.G., & Cohen, D.J. (1980). Detection of phenylketonuria in autistic and psychotic children. *Journal of the American Medical Association, 243,* 126–128.

Lucarelli, S., Frediani, T., Zingoni, A.M., Ferruzzi, F., Giardini, O., Quintieri, F., et al. (1995). Food allergy and infantile autism. *Panminerva Medica, 37,* 137–141.

Luiselli, J.K., & Cameron, M.L. (Eds.). (1998). *Antecedent control: Innovative approaches to behavioral support.* Baltimore: Paul H. Brookes Publishing Co.

Madsen, K.M., Hviid, A., Vestergaard, M., Schendel, D., Wohlfahrt, J., Thorsen, P., et al. (2002). A population-based study of measles, mumps and rubella vaccination and autism. *New England Journal of Medicine, 347,* 1477–1482.

Malkoff-Schwartz, S., Frank, E., Anderson, B., Sherrill, J.T., Siegel, L., Patterson, D., et al. (1998). Stressful life events and social rhythm disruption in the onset of manic and depressive bipolar episodes: A preliminary investigation. *Archives of General Psychiatry, 55,* 702–707.

March, J.S., Leonard, H.L., & Swedo, S.E. (1995). Obsessive-compulsive disorders. In J.S. March (Ed.), *Anxiety in children and adolescents* (pp. 251–275). New York: Guilford Press.

Marcus, L., Garfinkle, A., & Wolery, M. (2001). Issues in early diagnosis and intervention with young children with autism. In E. Schopler, N. Yirmiya, C. Shulman, & L. Marcus (Eds.), *The research basis for autism intervention* (pp. 171–183). New York: Kluwer Academic/Plenum.

Mash, E.J., & Wolfe, D.A. (1999). *Abnormal child psychology.* Belmont, CA: Wadsworth Thomson Learning.

Masi, G., Cosenza, A., Mucci, M., & De Vito, G. (2001). Risperidone monotherapy in preschool children with pervasive developmental disorders. *Journal of Child Neurology, 16,* 395–400.

Masterton, B.A., & Biederman, G.B. (1983). Proprioceptive versus visual control in autistic children. *Journal of Autism and Developmental Disorders, 13,* 141–152.

Maurice, C. (1996). *Behavioral intervention for young children with autism: A manual for parents and professionals.* Austin, TX: PRO-ED.

McCall, R.B. (2001). *Fundamental statistics for behavioral sciences* (8th ed.). Belmont, CA: Wadsworth Thomson Learning.

McConnell, K. (1998). Developmental delays vs. developmental disorder in young children: Understanding the difference. *A Pediatric Perspective, 8*(4).

McDougle, C.J., Naylor, S.T., Cohen, D.J., Aghajanian, G.K., Heninger, G.R., Price, L.H. (1996). Effects of tryptophan depletion in drug-free adults with autistic disorder. *Archives of General Psychiatry, 53,* 993–1000.

McGee, G.G., Krantz, P.J., & McClannahan, L.E. (1985). The facilitative effects of incidental teaching on preposition use by autistic children. *Journal of Applied Behavior Analysis, 18,* 17–31.

McGinnis, M. (1963). *Aphasic children, identification by the association method.* Washington, DC: Alexander Graham Bell Association of the Deaf, The Volta Bureau.

McLean, M., Bailey, D.B., & Wolery, M. (1996). *Assessing infants and preschoolers with special needs* (2nd ed.). Columbus, OH: Merrill.

Mesibov, G.B. (1997). What is -NOS and how is it diagnosed? *Journal of Autism and Developmental Disorders, 27,* 497–498.

Mesibov, G.B., & Shea, V. (1996). Full inclusion and students with autism. *Journal of Autism and Developmental Disorders, 26,* 337–346.

Meyer, D.J., & Vadasy, P.F. (1994). *Sibshops: Workshops for siblings of children with special needs.* Baltimore: Paul H. Brookes Publishing Co.

Meyer, G.A., & Batshaw, M.L. (2002). Fragile X syndrome. In M.L. Batshaw (Ed.), *Children with disabilities* (5th ed., pp. 321–331). Baltimore: Paul H. Brookes Publishing Co.

Meyer, J.P., & Minshew, N. (2002). An update on neurocognitive profiles in Asperger syndrome and high-functioning autism. *Focus on Autism and Other Developmental Disabilities, 17,* 152–160.

Meyer, L.H., & Evans, I.M. (1989). *Nonaversive intervention for behavior problems: A manual for home and community.* Baltimore: Paul H. Brookes Publishing Co.

Miller-Kuhaneck, H. (2001). *Autism: A comprehensive occupational therapy approach.* Bethesda, MD: The American Occupational Therapy Association.

Miltenberger, R. (1997). *Behavior modification: Principles and procedures.* Pacific Grove, CA: Brooks/Cole Thomson Learning.

Miltenberger, R., Fuqua, R.W., & Woods, D.W. (1998). Applying behavior analysis to clinical problems: Review and analysis of habit reversal. *Journal of Applied Behavior Analysis, 31,* 447–469.

Miltenberger, R.G., & Lumley, V.A. (1997). Evaluating the influence of problem function on treatment acceptability. *Behavioral Interventions, 12,* 105–119.

Mirenda, P. (1997). Functional communication training and augmentative communication: A research review. *Augmentative and Alternative Communication, 13,* 207–225.

Mirenda, P. (2001). Autism, augmentative communication, and assistive technology: What do we really know? *Focus on Autism and Other Developmental Disabilities, 16,* 141–151.

Mitchell, P.B., & Malhi, G.S. (2002). The expanding pharmacopoeia for bipolar disorder. *Annual Review of Medicine, 53,* 173–188.

Moreno-Fuenmayor, H., Borjas, L., Arrieta, A., Valera, V., & Socorro-Candanoza, L. (1996). Plasma excitatory amino acids in autism. *Investigación Clínica, 37,* 113–128.

Mostert, M.P. (2001). Facilitated communication since 1995: A review of published studies. *Journal of Autism and Developmental Disorders, 31,* 287–313.

Mundy, P., Sigman, M., Ungerer, J., & Sherman, T. (1986). Defining the social deficits of autism: The contribution of nonverbal communication measures. *Journal of Child Psychology and Psychiatry and Allied Disciplines, 27,* 657–659.

Mundy, P., & Stella, J. (2000). Joint attention, social orienting, and nonverbal communication in autism. In S.F. Warren & J. Reichle (Vol. Eds.) & A.M. Wetherby & B.M. Prizant (Series Eds.), *Communication and language intervention series: Vol. 9. Autism spectrum disorders* (pp. 55–77). Baltimore: Paul H. Brookes Publishing Co.

Murphy, K.R., & Davidshofer, C.O. (1991). *Psychological testing: Principles and applications* (2nd ed.). Upper Saddle River, NJ: Pearson Prentice Hall.

Mustonen, T., Locke, P., Reichle, J., Solbrack, M., & Lindgren, A. (1991). An overview of augmentative and alternative communication systems. In J. Reichle, J. York, & J. Sigafoos (Ed.), *Implementing augmentative and alternative communication: Strategies for learners with severe disabilities* (pp. 1–37). Baltimore: Paul H. Brookes Publishing Co.

Myles, B.S., Cook, K.T., Miller, N.E., Rinner, L., & Robbins, L.A. (2000). *Asperger syndrome and sensory issues: Practical solutions for making sense of the world.* Shawnee Mission, KS: Autism Asperger Publishing.

Namerow, L.B., Thomas, P., Bostic, J.Q., Prince, J., & Mounteaux, M.C. (2003). Use of citalopram in pervasive developmental disorders. *Journal of Developmental and Behavioral Pediatrics, 24,* 104–108.

National Information Center for Children and Youth with Disabilities. (1997, November). *Office of Special Education Programs' IDEA Amendments of 1997 curriculum: Module 5. Free appropriate public education background text.* Retrieved May 28, 2003, from http://www.nichcy.org/Trainpkg/traintxt/5txt.htm

National Institute of Mental Health. (2003). *Childhood-onset schizophrenia: An update from the NIMH.* Retrieved May 28, 2004, from http://www.nimh.nih.gov /publicat/schizkids.cfm

National Institutes of Health. (2001, November 27). Study confirms secretin no more effective than placebo in treating autism symptoms. *NIH News Release.* Retrieved May 28, 2004, from http://www.nichd.nih.gov/new/releases/aut_sec.cfm

National Research Council, Division of Behavioral and Social Sciences and Education, Committee on Educational Interventions for Children with Autism. (2001). *Educating children with autism.* Washington, DC: National Academies Press.

Nelson, R., Roberts, M.L., & Smith, D.J. (1998). *Conducting functional behavioral assessments: A practical guide.* Longmont, CO: Sopris West.

New York State Department of Health, Early Intervention Program. (1999a). *Clinical practice guideline: Report of the recommendations. Autism/pervasive developmental disorders: Assessment and intervention for young children (age 0–3 years)* (Publication No. 4215). Albany: Author.

New York State Department of Health, Early Intervention Program. (1999b). *Clinical practice guideline: The guideline technical report. Autism/pervasive developmental disorders: Assessment and intervention for young children (age 0–3 years)* (Publication No. 4217). Albany: Author.

Newell, K.M., Incledon, T., Bodfish, J.W., & Sprague, R.L. (1999). Variability of stereotypic body-rocking in adults with mental retardation. *American Journal on Mental Retardation, 104,* 279–288.

Nijre, B. (1969). The normalization principle and its human management implications. In R.B. Koegel & W. Wolfensberger (Eds.), *Changing patterns in residential services for the mentally retarded.* Washington, DC: President's Committee on Mental Retardation.

No Child Left Behind Act of 2001, PL 107-110, 115 Stat. 1425, 20 U.S.C. §§ 6301 *et seq.*

Odom, S.L., & Strain, P.S. (1984). Peer-mediated approaches to promoting children's social interaction: A review. *American Journal of Orthopsychiatry, 54,* 544–557.

Odom, S.L., & Strain, P.S. (2002). Evidence-based practice in early intervention/ early childhood special education: Single subject design research. *Journal of Early Intervention, 25,* 151–160.

O'Neill, R.E., Horner, R.H., Albin, R.W., Sprague, J.R., Storey, K., & Newton, J.S. (1997). *Functional assessment and program development for problem behavior: A practical handbook* (2nd ed.). Pacific Grove, CA: Brooks/Cole Thomson Learning.

Owens, R.E. (1992). *Language development: An introduction.* New York: Macmillan.

Owley, T., McMahon, W., Cook, E.H., Laulhere, T., South, M., Mays, L.Z., et al. (2001). Multisite, double-blind, placebo-controlled trial of porcine secretin in autism. *Journal of the American Academy of Child and Adolescent Psychiatry, 40,* 1293–1299.

Ozonoff, S., South, M., & Miller, J.N. (2000). DSM-IV defined Asperger syndrome: Cognitive, behavioral, and early history differentiation from high functioning autism. *Autism, 4,* 29–46.

Page, T. (2000). Metabolic approaches to the treatment of autism spectrum disorders. *Journal of Autism and Developmental Disorders, 30,* 463–469.

Panskepp, J. (1979). A neurochemical theory of autism. *Trends in Neuroscience, 2,* 174–177.

Parette, H.P. (1997). Assistive technology devices and services. *Education and Training in Mental Retardation and Developmental Disabilities, 32,* 267–280.

Parette, P., & McMahan, G.A. (2002). Team sensitivity to family goals for and expectations of assistive technology. *Teaching Exceptional Children, 35*(1), 56–61.

Parker, R.M., & Szymanski, E.M. (1998). *Rehabilitation counseling: Basics and beyond* (3rd ed). Austin, TX: PRO-ED.

Pavlov, I. (1927). *Conditioned reflexes: An investigation of the physiological activity of the cerebral cortex* (W.H. Grant, Trans.). London: Oxford University Press.

Peterson, L., Reach, K., & Grabe, S. (2003). Health-related disorders. In E.J. Mash & R.A. Barkley (Eds.), *Child psychopathology* (2nd ed., pp. 716–750). New York: Guilford Press.

Pfeiffer, S., Norton, J., Nelson, L., & Shott, S. (1995). Efficacy of vitamin B6 and magnesium in the treatment of autism: A methodology review and summary of outcomes. *Journal of Autism and Developmental Disorders, 25,* 467–478.

Piven, J., & Palmer, P. (1999). Psychiatric disorder and the broad autism phenotype: Evidence from a family study of multiple-incidence autism families. *American Journal of Psychiatry, 156,* 557–563.

Piven, J., Palmer, P., Jacobi, D., Childress, D., & Arndt, S. (1997). Autism phenotype: Evidence from a family history study of multiple-incidence autism families. *American Journal of Psychiatry, 154,* 185–190.

Premack, D. (1965). Reinforcement theory. In D. LeVine (Ed.), *Nebraska Symposium on Motivation.* Lincoln: University of Nebraska Press.

Pretti-Frontczak, K., & Bricker, D. (2004). *An activity-based approach to early intervention* (3rd ed.). Baltimore: Paul H. Brookes Publishing Co.

Prizant, B.M., Wetherby, A.M., Rubin, E., & Laurent, A.C. (2003). The SCERTS Model: A transactional, family-centered approach to enhancing communication and socioemotional abilities of children with autism spectrum disorder. *Infants and Young Children, 16,* 296–316.

Prizant, B.M., Wetherby, A.M., Rubin, E., Laurent, A.C., & Rydell, P.J. (in press). *The SCERTS™ Model manual: A comprehensive educational approach for children with autism spectrum disorders* (Vols. I & II). Baltimore: Paul H. Brookes Publishing Co.

Puce, A., Allison, T., Gore, J., & McCarthy, G. (1995). Face-sensitive regions in human extrastriate cortex studied by functional MRI. *Journal of Neurophysiology,* 74, 1192–1199.

Quintana, H., Birmaher, B., Stedge, D., Lennon, S., Freed, J., Bride, J., et al. (1995). Use of methylphenidate in the treatment of children with autistic disorder. *Journal of Autism and Developmental Disorders, 25,* 283–294.

Rainforth, B., Giangreco, M., Smith, P.E., & York, J. (1995). Collaborative teamwork in training and technical assistance: Enhancing community supports for persons with developmental disabilities. In O. Karan & S. Greenspan (Eds.), *Community rehabilitation services for people with disabilities* (pp. 134–168). Newton, MA: Butterworth-Heinemann.

Rapee, R.M. (1995). Descriptive psychopathology of social phobia. In R.G. Heimberg, M.R. Liebowitz, D.A. Hope, & F.R. Schneier (Eds.), *Social phobia: Diagnosis, assessment, and treatment.* New York: Guilford Press.

Reamer, R., Brady, M., & Hawkins, J. (1998). The effects of video self-modeling on parents' interactions with children with developmental disabilities. *Education and Training in Mental Retardation and Developmental Disabilities, 33,* 121–143.

Rehabilitation Act Amendments of 1998, PL 105-220, 29 U.S.C. §§ 701 *et seq.*

Rehabilitation Act of 1973, PL 93-112, 29 U.S.C. §§ 701 *et seq.*

Reichle, J., York, J., & Sigafoos, J. (1991). *Implementing augmentative and alternative communication: Strategies for learners with severe disabilities.* Baltimore: Paul H. Brookes Publishing Co.

Rimland, B. (1964). *Infantile autism: The syndrome and its implications for a neural theory of behavior.* Upper Saddle River, NJ: Pearson Prentice Hall.

Rimland, B. (1990). Dimethylglycine (DMG), a nontoxic metabolite, and autism. *Autism Research Review International, 4*(2), 3. Also available on-line: http://www. autism.com/ari/editorial/dmg1.html

Rimland, B. (1994). New hope for safe and effective treatments for autism. *Autism Research Review International, 8,* 3.

Rimland, B., & Edelson, S.M. (2003). *Parent ratings of behavior effects of biomedical interventions* (Pub. 34, Rev. ed.). San Diego: Autism Research Institute.

Rimland, B., & Fein, D. (1988). Special talents of autistic savants. In L.K. Obler & D. Fein (Eds.), *The exceptional brain: Neuropsychology of talent and special abilities* (pp. 474–492). New York: Guilford Press.

Rubin, S.E., & Roessler, R.T. (1995). *Foundations of the vocational rehabilitation process* (4th ed.). Austin, TX: PRO-ED.

Sacks, O.W. (1995). *An anthropologist on Mars: Seven paradoxical tales.* New York: Alfred A. Knopf.

Salvia, J., & Ysseldyke, J.E. (2001). *Assessment* (8th ed.). Boston: Houghton Mifflin.

Sandall, S., McLean, M.E., & Smith, B.J. (Eds.). (in press). *DEC recommended practices in early intervention/early childhood special education.* Longmont, CO: Sopris West.

Sattler, J.M. (2001). *Assessment of children: Cognitive applications* (4th ed.). San Diego: Author.

Schall, C. (2002). A consumer's guide to monitoring psychotropic medication for individuals with autism spectrum disorders. *Focus on Autism and Other Developmental Disabilities, 17,* 229–235.

Schatz, J., & Hamdan-Allen, G. (1995). Effects of age and IQ on adaptive behavior domains for children with autism. *Journal of Autism and Developmental Disorders, 25,* 51–60.

Schopler, E., Mesibov, G.B., & Hearsey, K. (1995). Structured Teaching in the TEACCH system. In E. Schopler & G.B. Mesibov (Eds.), *Learning and cognition in autism* (pp. 243–268). New York: Kluwer Academic/Plenum.

Schreibman, L., Kohlenberg, B.S., & Britten, K.R. (1986). Differential responding to content and intonation components of a complex auditory stimulus by nonverbal and echolalic autistic children. *Analysis and Intervention in Developmental Disabilities, 6,* 109–125.

Schriger, D.L. (1995). Training panels in methodology. In K.A. McCormick, S.R. Moore, & R.A. Siegel (Eds.), *Clinical practice guideline development: Methodology perspectives* (AHCPR Publication No. 95-0009). Rockville, MD: U.S. Department of Health and Human Services, Agency for Health Care Policy and Research.

Schroeder, S.R., Tessel, R.E., Loupe, P.S., & Stodgell, C.J. (1997). Severe behavior problems among people with developmental disabilities. In W.E. MacLean, Jr. (Ed.), *Ellis' handbook of mental deficiency, psychological theory, and research* (pp. 439–464). Mahwah, NJ: Lawrence Erlbaum Associates.

Schultz, R.T., Gauthier, I., Klin, A., Fulbright, R.K., Anderson, A.W., Volkmar, F., et al. (2000). Abnormal ventral temporal cortical activity during face discriminations among individuals with autism and Asperger syndrome. *Archives of General Psychiatry, 37,* 331–340.

Schwartz, I., Garfinkle, A., & Bauer, J. (1998). The Picture Exchange Communication System: Communicative outcomes for young children with disabilities. *Topics in Early Childhood Special Education, 18,* 144–159.

Scott, J., Clark, C., & Brady, M.P. (2000). *Students with autism: Characteristics and instructional programming for special educators.* San Diego: Singular Publishing Group.

Scotti, J.R., Ujcich, K.J., Weigle, K.L., Holland, C.M., & Kirk, K.S. (1996). Interventions with challenging behavior of persons with developmental disabilities: A review of current research practices. *Journal of The Association for Persons with Severe Handicaps, 21,* 123–134.

Shackelford, J. (2002). *Informed clinical opinion* (NECTAC Notes No. 10). Chapel Hill: The University of North Carolina, Frank Porter Graham Child Development Institute, National Early Childhood Technical Assistance Center. Also available on-line: http://www.nectac.org/~pdfs/pubs/nnotes10.pdf

Shattock, P., Kennedy, A., Roswell, F., & Berney, T. (1990). Role of neuropeptides in autism and their relationship with classical neurotransmitters. *Brain Dysfunction, 3,* 328–345.

Shattock, P., & Whiteley, P. (2002). Biochemical aspects in autism spectrum disorders: Updating the opioid-excess theory and presenting new opportunities for biomedical intervention. *Expert Opinion on Therapeutic Targets, 6,* 175–183.

Shaw, W. (1998). *Biological treatments for autism and PDD.* Kansas: Author.

Siegel, B. (1996). *The world of the autistic child: Understanding and treating autistic spectrum disorders.* New York: Oxford University Press.

Sigafoos, J., & Drasgow, E. (2001). Conditional use of aided and unaided AAC: A review and clinical case demonstration. *Focus on Autism and Other Developmental Disabilities, 16,* 152–161.

Sigman, M., & Ruskin, E. (1999). Continuity and change in the social competence of children with autism, Down syndrome, and developmental delays. *Monographs of the Society for Research in Child Development, 64,* 1–114.

Sigman, M., & Ungerer, J. (1981). Sensorimotor skills and language comprehension in autistic children. *Journal of Abnormal Child Psychology, 9,* 149–165.

Simeonsson, R.J., & Rosenthal, S.L. (2001). Clinical assessment of children: An overview. In R.J. Simeonsson & S.L. Rosenthal (Eds.), *Psychological and developmental assessment: Children with disabilities and chronic conditions* (pp. 1–14). New York: Guilford Press.

Singh, V.K., Fudenberg, H.H., Emerson, D., & Coleman, M. (1988). Immunodiagnosis and immunotherapy in autistic children. *Annals of the New York Academy of Sciences, 540,* 602–604.

Skinner, B.F. (1938). *The behavior of organisms: An experimental analysis.* New York: Appleton-Century-Crofts.

Skinner, B.F. (1957). *Verbal behavior.* New York: Appleton-Century-Crofts.

Smith, I., & Bryson, S.E. (1998). Gesture imitation in autism: I. Nonsymbolic postures and sequences. *Cognitive Neuropsychology, 15,* 747–770.

Smith, M.R., & Lerman, D.C. (1999). A preliminary comparison of guided compliance and high-probability instructional sequences as treatment for noncompliance in children with developmental disabilities. *Research in Developmental Disabilities, 20,* 183–195.

Smith, P.K., & Vollstedt, R. (1985). On defining play: An empirical study of the relationship between play, and various play criteria. *Child Development, 56,* 1042–1050.

Snow, J., & Forest, M. (1987). Circles. In M. Forest (Ed.), *More education integration.* Toronto: The Roeher Institute.

Snowling, M., & Frith, U. (1986). Comprehension in "hyperlexic" readers. *Journal of Experimental Child Psychology, 42,* 392–415.

Sparrow, S., Balla, D., & Cicchetti, D. (1984a). *Vineland Adaptive Behavior Scales: Interview Edition, Expanded Form manual.* Circle Pines, MN: American Guidance Service.

Sparrow, S., Balla, D., & Cicchetti, D. (1984b). *Vineland Adaptive Behavior Scales: Interview Edition, Survey Form manual.* Circle Pines, MN: American Guidance Service.

Sue, D., Sue, D.W., & Sue, S. (2000). *Understanding abnormal behavior* (6th ed.). Boston: Houghton Mifflin.

Szatmari, P. (1992). The validity of autistic spectrum disorders: A literature review. *Journal of Autism and Developmental Disabilities, 22,* 583–600.

Szatmari, P., Bartolucci, G., Bremner, R., Bond, S., & Rich, S. (1989). A follow-up study of high functioning autistic children. Journal of Autism and Developmental Disorders, 19, 213–225.

Tager-Flusberg, H. (1999). A psychological approach to understanding the social and language impairments in autism. *International Review of Psychiatry, 11,* 325–334.

Takeda, A. (2003). *Zinc and brain function.* Paper presented at the 18th Symposium on Trace Nutrients Research, Kyoto, Japan. Summary available on-line: http://www.japanclinic.co.jp/gakuju/biryo_01.htm (click "List of Symposium Proceedings on Trace Nutrients Research, then click "The 18th")

Technology-Related Assistance for Individuals with Disabilities Act Amendments of 1994, PL 103-218 (March 9, 1994), 29 U.S.C. §§ 2201 *et seq.*

Technology-Related Assistance for Individuals with Disabilities Act of 1988, PL 100-407, 29 U.S.C. §§ 2201 *et seq.*

Temple, C.N., & Carney, R. (1996). Reading skills in children with Turner's syndrome: An analysis of hyperlexia. *Cortex, 32,* 335–345.

Tharpe, A.M. (1999). Auditory integration therapy: The magical mystery cure. *Language, Speech, and Hearing Services in Schools, 30,* 378–381.

Thorndike, R.L., Hagen, E.P., & Sattler, J.M. (1986). *Stanford-Binet Intelligence Scale* (4th ed.). Chicago: Riverside.

Travis, L.L., & Sigman, M. (1998). Social deficits and interpersonal relationships in autism. *Mental Retardation and Developmental Disabilities Research Reviews, 4,* 65–72.

Tuchman, R.F. (1997). Acquired epileptiform aphasia. *Seminars in Pediatric Neurology, 4,* 93–101.

Tuchman, R. (2000). Medical aspects of autism. In J. Scott, C. Clark, & M. Brady (Eds.), *Students with autism: Characteristics and instructional programming for special educators* (pp. 69–102). San Diego: Singular Publishing Group.

Tuchman, R.F., & Rapin, I. (1999). Regression in pervasive developmental disorders: Seizures and epileptiform electroencephalogram correlates. *Pediatrics, 99,* 560–566.

Turnbull, R. (2002). *Free appropriate public education: The law and children with disabilities.* Denver, CO: Love.

Turnbull, R., Turnbull, A., Shank, M., & Smith, S.J. (2004). *Exceptional lives* (4th ed). Upper Saddle River, NJ: Pearson Prentice Hall.

U.S. Department of Education. (2001). *To assure the free appropriate public education of all children with disabilities: Twenty-third annual report to Congress on the implementation of the Individuals with Disabilities Education Act.* Washington, DC: Author. Also available on-line: http://www.ed.gov/about/reports/annual/osep/2001/index.html

Visconti, P., Piazzi, S., Posar, A., Santi, A., Pipitone, E., & Rossi, P.G. (1994). Amino acids and infantile autism. *Developmental Brain Dysfunction, 7,* 56–62.

Volkmar, F. (1996). Diagnostic issues in autism: Results of the DSM-IV field trial. *Journal of Autism and Developmental Disorders, 26,* 155–157.

Volkmar, F.R., & Nelson, D.S. (1990). Seizure disorders in autism. *Journal of the American Academy of Child and Adolescent Psychiatry, 29,* 127–129.

Wakefield, A.J., Anthony, A., Murch, S.H., Thomson, M., Montgomery, S.M., Davies, S., et al. (2000). Enterocolitis in children with developmental disorders. *American Journal of Gastroenterology, 95,* 2285–2295.

Warren, S.A., & Bambara, L.M. (1989). An experimental analysis of milieu language intervention: Teaching the action-object form. *Journal of Speech and Hearing Disorders, 54,* 448–461.

Wassink, T.H., Piven, J., & Patil, S.R. (2001). Chromosomal abnormalities in a clinic sample of individuals with autistic disorder. *Psychiatric Genetics, 11,* 57–63.

Wechsler, D. (1991). *Wechsler Intelligence Scale for Children* (3rd ed.). New York: Harcourt Assessment.

Welsh, M.C., Pennington, B.F., & Rogers, S. (1987). Word recognition and comprehension skills in hyperlexic children. *Brain and Language, 32,* 76–96.

Werner, E., Dawson, G., Osterling, J., & Dinno, N. (2000). Brief report: Recognition of autism spectrum disorder before one year of age. A retrospective study based on home videotapes. *Journal of Autism and Developmental Disorders, 30,* 157–162.

Werner, E.B., & Munson, J.A. (2001). *Regression in autism: A description and validation of the phenomenon using parent report and home video tapes.* Poster session presented at the biennial meeting of the Society for Research in Child Development, Minneapolis.

Werry, J.S., & Taylor, E. (1994). Schizophrenia and allied disorders. In M. Rutter, E. Taylor, & L. Hersov (Eds.), *Child and adolescent psychiatry: Modern approaches* (3rd ed., pp. 594–615). Oxford, England: Blackwell Scientific.

Wert, B.Y., & Neisworth, J.T. (2003). Effects of video self-modeling on spontaneous requesting in children with autism. *Journal of Positive Behavior Interventions, 5,* 30–34.

Wetherby, A., & Prizant, B. (1989). The expression of communicative intent: Assessment guidelines. *Seminars in Speech and Language, 10,* 77–91.

Whalen, C., & Schreibman, L. (2003). Joint attention training for children with autism using behavior modification procedures. *Journal of Child Psychology and Psychiatry and Allied Disciplines, 44,* 456–468.

Williamson, G.G., Anzalone, M.E., & Hanft, B.E. (2000). Assessment of sensory processing, praxis, and motor performance. In Interdisciplinary Council on Developmental and Learning Disorders (Ed.), *Clinical practice guidelines: Redefining the standards of care for infants, children, and families with special needs* (pp. 155–258). Bethesda, MD: ICDL Press.

Wing, L. (1993). The definition and prevalence of autism: A review. *European Child and Adolescent Psychiatry, 2,* 61–74.

Wing, L., & Attwood, A. (1987). Syndromes of autism and atypical development. In D. Cohen, A. Donnellan, & R. Paul (Eds.), *Handbook of autism and pervasive developmental disorders* (pp. 3–19). New York: John Wiley & Sons.

Wing, L., & Gould, J. (1979). Severe impairments of social interaction and associated abnormalities in children: Epidemiology and classification. *Journal of Autism and Developmental Disorders, 9,* 11–29.

Wolery, M., Bailey, D., Jr., & Sugai, G. (1988). *Effective teaching: Principles and procedures of applied behavior analysis with exceptional students.* Boston: Allyn & Bacon.

Wolfberg, P.J. (1999). *Play and imagination in children with autism.* New York: Teachers College Press.

Wolfberg, P.J. (2003). *Peer play and the autism spectrum: The art of guiding children's socialization and imagination.* Shawnee Mission, KS: Autism Asperger Publishing Company.

Wolfberg, P., & Schuler, A. (1993). Integrated Play Groups: A model for promoting the social and cognitive dimensions of play. *Journal of Autism and Developmental Disorders, 23,* 1–23.

Wolfensberger, W. (1972). *The principle of normalization in human services.* Toronto: National Institute on Mental Retardation.

Woolf, S.H. (1991). *AHCPR Interim manual for clinical practice guideline development* (AHCPR Publication No. 91-0018). Rockville, MD: U.S. Department of Health and Human Services, Agency for Health Care Policy and Research.

Woolf, S.H. (1994). An organized analytic framework for practice guideline development: Using the analytic logic as a guide for reviewing evidence, developing recommendations, and explaining the rationale. In K.A. McCormick, S.R. Moore, & R.A. Siegel (Eds.), *Clinical practice guideline development: Methodology perspectives* (AHCPR Publication No. 95-0009). Rockville, MD: U.S. Department of Health and Human Services, Agency for Health Care Policy and Research.

World Health Organization. (1992). *The international statistical classification of diseases and related health problems* (10th ed.). Geneva: Author.

ZERO TO THREE's Diagnostic Classification Task Force. (1994). *Diagnostic classification of mental health disorders of infancy and early childhood (DC: 0-3).* Arlington, VA: ZERO TO THREE: National Center for Infants, Toddlers, and Families.

Zuddas, A., Di Martino, A., Muglia, P., & Cianchetti, C. (2000). Long-term risperidone for pervasive developmental disorder: Efficacy, tolerability and discontinuation. *Journal of Child and Adolescent Psychopharmacology, 10,* 79–90.

Appendices

The listing of materials and organizations presented in the following appendices is by no means exhaustive. New screening and assessment materials, curricula, and organizations are continually becoming available to meet the increasing needs of professionals and parents. Our selection of screening and assessment tools, curricula, and organizations was guided by a focus group composed of parents and professionals from the several fields involved in autism service delivery and research. In Appendix A, we attempted to include materials that are in wide current use as well as those that are new but show strong promise. We included the nature of the tests or curricula and what they purport to do but did not include specific information concerning psychometric properties of the materials (e.g., validity, reliability). In Appendix B, although there are exceptions, most organizations included are national, hold an annual conference, and have a sizable membership.

Screening and Assessment Tools and Curricula

This appendix includes two types of materials: 1) screening and assessment tools and 2) curricula and curriculum development resources. Screening tools (also called *screeners*) are brief and take little time to use. They are not used for diagnosis or to establish eligibility; rather, they are used to identify individuals who should be observed or otherwise appraised in a more detailed way (i.e., individuals who should be assessed). Assessments provide a more thorough analysis of an individual's strengths and needs and are frequently used as part of a diagnostic process. Assessment materials may also refer to those that are used to determine an individual's curricular needs as well as monitor the individual's progress in a curriculum (curriculum-based assessment). For each instrument or curriculum, the author(s), publisher, date of publication, and other relevant publication information are listed, followed by the age range, if any, at which the material is used.

SCREENING AND ASSESSMENT TOOLS

AAPEP
See Adolescent and Adult Psychoeducational Profile.

ABC
Autism Behavior Checklist. *See* Autism Screening Instrument for Educational Planning–Second Edition (ASIEP-2).

ABLLS
See Assessment of Basic Language and Learning Skills.

ADI-R
See Autism Diagnostic Interview–Revised.

Adolescent and Adult Psychoeducational Profile (AAPEP)

E. Schopler • PRO-ED • 1998
Ages: Adolescent to adult

The AAPEP is similar to the Psychoeducational Profile–Third Edition (PEP-3) and aids in planning for vocational and community placement in transition to adulthood. The test was designed for individuals with autism spectrum disorders (ASDs) who are functioning within the range of mild to severe mental retardation; it is also appropriate for use with individuals with mild to severe mental retardation who do not have ASDs. The profile employs direct observation and interviews. The formal assessment offers the basis for planning vocational placements and living arrangements. The informal assessment forms a cumulative record of all school–community placements in specific job sites.
Eric Schopler

Adolescent/Adult Sensory Profile

C. Brown & W. Dunn • Harcourt Assessment • 2002
Ages: Adolescent to adult

Self-reporting questionnaire that measures responses to sensory events in everyday life. The 60-item profile employs a 5-point Likert scale (*almost never, seldom, occasionally, frequently, almost always*) related to four quadrants of sensory processing in Dunn's (2000) model of sensory processing (sensation seeking, sensation avoiding, sensory sensitivity, and low registration).
Winnie Dunn

ADOS

See Autism Diagnostic Observation Schedule.

Ages & Stages Questionnaires®: Social-Emotional (ASQ:SE): A Parent-Completed, Child-Monitoring System for Social-Emotional Behaviors

J. Squires, D. Bricker, & E. Twombly (with assistance from S. Yockelson, M.S. Davis, & Y. Kim) • Paul H. Brookes Publishing Co. • 2002
Ages: 6–60 months

The ASQ:SE consists of parent-completed questionnaires for use at 6, 12, 18, 24, 30, 36, 48, and 60 months. Areas screened are self-regulation, compliance, communication, adaptive functioning, autonomy, affect, and interaction with people. Available in English or Spanish, each questionnaire takes 10–15 minutes to complete and 1–3 minutes to score. *The ASQ:SE User's Guide* (Squires, Bricker, & Twombly, 2002) includes instructions on use, validity data, tips on cultural sensitivity, case studies, and activities. *John T. Neisworth & Pamela S. Wolfe*

Analysis of Sensory Behavior Inventory–Revised Edition (ASBI-R)

K. Morton & S. Wolford • Skills with Occupational Therapy (P.O. Box 1785, Arcadia, CA 91077) • 1994

Ages: Any

The ASBI-R collects information about an individual's behaviors as they are related to sensory stimuli. Six sensory modalities are assessed: vestibular, tactile, proprioceptive, auditory, visual, and gustatory-olfactory. Ratings can be made about both sensory-avoidant and sensory-seeking behaviors within each modality. Information obtained from this tool may be helpful in completing a functional analysis of behavior and in designing effective intervention strategies, including accommodations and reinforcers for the individual.

Sensory processing differences are frequently seen in individuals with severe disabilities and challenging behaviors. Analyzing these differences may assist in understanding puzzling behaviors that have proven difficult to change. Interventions that accommodate individual differences frequently result in improved adaptive functioning.
John T. Neisworth & Pamela S. Wolfe

ASDS

See Asperger Syndrome Diagnostic Scale.

ASIEP-2

See Autism Screening Instrument for Educational Planning–Second Edition.

Asperger Syndrome Diagnostic Scale (ASDS)

B. Myles, S. Bock, & R. Simpson• PRO-ED • 2001

Ages: 5–18 years

A norm-referenced rating scale to help determine whether an individual has Asperger syndrome (AS). The scale has 50 yes/no items and can be completed in 10–15 minutes by a person who knows the individual. The items were drawn from all empirical articles published on AS and from criteria in the *Diagnostic and Statistical Manual of Mental Disorders, Fourth Edition, Text Revision* (American Psychiatric Association, 2000). The scale items are organized into cognitive, maladaptive, language, social, and sensorimotor areas. Normed on individuals with AS throughout the United States, this screening device differentiates AS from learning disabilities, attention-deficit/hyperactivity disorder (ADHD), behavior disorders, and classical autism with 85% accuracy. By comparing an individual's score with the normative sample, an examiner can determine the likelihood that the individual has AS.

The ASDS can be useful to 1) identify individuals who have AS, 2) chart an individual's behavioral progress after intervention, 3) pinpoint goals for a student's individualized education program (IEP), and 4) conduct research on individuals with AS.
Brenda Smith Myles

ASQ:SE
See Ages & Stages Questionnaires®: Social-Emotional.

Assessment of Basic Language and Learning Skills (ABLLS)
J.W. Partington & M. Sundberg • Behavior Analysts Incorporated • 1998
Ages: Any

A criterion-referenced assessment, curriculum guide, and skills-tracking system for individuals with autism or other developmental disabilities. The ABLLS contains a task analysis of skills necessary to communicate and learn. The assessment includes 476 skills from 25 skill areas such as *visual performance, imitation, receptive and expressive language* (e.g., requesting, labeling, intraverbal skills), *social interaction,* and *classroom and daily living skills.* The language component is based on Skinner's (1957) book *Verbal Behavior.*
James W. Partington

Assessment of Social and Communication Skills of Children with Autism
See DO-WATCH-LISTEN-SAY: Social and Communication Intervention for Children with Autism, *in the CURRICULA section of this appendix.*

ASSQ
See Autism Spectrum Screening Questionnaire.

Autism Behavior Checklist (ABC)

See Autism Screening Instrument for Educational Planning–Second Edition (ASIEP-2).

Autism Diagnostic Interview–Revised (ADI-R)

M. Rutter, A. Le Couteur, & C. Lord • Western Psychological Services • 2003

Ages: Mental age over 18 months

A 1.5-hour, standardized, semistructured parent interview that can be used to assess a child or an adult. A diagnosis is made based on scoring an algorithm that is consistent with criteria in the *Diagnostic and Statistical Manual of Mental Disorders, Fourth Edition, Text Revision* (*DSM-IV-TR;* American Psychiatric Association, 2000). The ADI-R has good criterion validity (96% sensitivity). Also, 23 of 25 children with mental retardation but not autism were diagnosed accurately as not having autism by the ADI-R (92% specificity) and thus is useful in diagnosis to differentiate autism and mental retardation (Lord, Rutter, & Le Couteur, 1994).

Catherine Lord

Autism Diagnostic Observation Schedule (ADOS)

C. Lord, M. Rutter, P.C. DiLavore, & S. Risi • Western Psychological Services • 1999

Ages: 15 months–40 years

A 30-minute semistructured play assessment of communication, social interaction, and imaginative play skills. The ADOS was developed to diagnose autism across a wide range of chronological and mental ages and was normed on individuals ranging from 15 months of age through 40 years. Each of the four modules was developed for a different developmental stage and language level, ranging from no expressive or receptive language to verbal fluency. A component previously known as the Prelinguistic Autism Diagnostic Observation Schedule (PL-ADOS) is included in the ADOS materials; it provides an opportunity to observe specific aspects of the child's social behavior, such as joint attention, imitation, and sharing of affect with the examiner and parent.

Each module consists of planned social occasions that provide opportunities for a range of social initiations and responses. Behavior ratings are used to formulate a diagnosis through the use of a diagnostic algorithm for each module (Lord, Rutter, DiLavore, & Risi, 1999). People who administer the ADOS must first attend a 2-day clinical training workshop or use training videotapes and a guidebook that are equivalent to attending the

workshop. (People who wish to use the ADOS in research must attend the workshop.)
Catherine Lord

Autism Screening Instrument for Educational Planning–Second Edition (ASIEP-2)

D. Krug, J. Arick, & P. Almond • PRO-ED • 1993
Ages: 18 months to adult

The ASIEP-2 permits the examiner to gather information on behavior in sensory, relating, body concept, language, and social self-help domains; vocal behavior; interaction; communication; learning rate. The ASIEP-2 subtests provide a profile of abilities in spontaneous verbal behavior, social interaction, education level, and learning characteristics.

Empirical evidence demonstrates a strong intercorrelation among the ASIEP-2 subtests and the ability to distinguish among groups of individuals with a variety of disabilities. Percentiles and standard scores are provided for the five subtests. The Autism Behavior Checklist (ABC; Krug, Arick, & Almond, 1980), now part of the ASIEP-2, is parent completed and scored and interpreted by a professional. The ABC is of some value when used with school-age children and as a supplement with other instruments.
John T. Neisworth & Pamela S. Wolfe

Autism Screening Questionnaire

See Social Communication Questionnaire (SCQ).

Autism Spectrum Screening Questionnaire (ASSQ)

S. Ehlers & C. Gillberg • 1999 • A screening questionnaire for Asperger syndrome and other high-functioning autism spectrum disorders in school age children. *Journal of Autism and Developmental Disorders, 29*(2), 129–141.
Ages: 6–21 years

A 27-item checklist for completion by people other than professionals who know the child; used to assess symptoms and characteristics of Asperger syndrome (AS) and other high-functioning autism spectrum disorders (ASDs) in children and adolescents with typical intelligence or mild mental retardation. Data for parent and teacher ratings in a clinical sample are presented with various measures of reliability and validity. Findings have indicated that the ASSQ is a useful brief screening device for the identification of autism spectrum disorders (ASDs) in clinical settings.
John T. Neisworth & Pamela S. Wolfe

Behaviour Function Inventory (BFI)

J.L. Adrien, S. Roux, G. Couturier, J. Malvy, P. Guérin, S. Debuly, et al. • 2001 • Towards a new functional assessment of autistic dysfunction in children with developmental disorders: The Behaviour Function Inventory. *Autism, 5,* 249–264.

Ages: 3–15 years

A 55-item inventory to assess disorders of psychological functioning in children with developmental disorders. Items are rated on a 5-point scale and are based on 11 neurophysiological functions, disorders of which are considered to contribute to the core autism syndrome: attention, perception, association, intention, motricity (capacity for spontaneous movement), imitation, emotion, contact, communication, cognition, and regulation. Statistical analysis computed on the 55 items identified six main dimensions of dysfunction: interaction, praxis, auditory, attention, emotional, and islet of ability. The rating of the BFI must be done by a clinician who is experienced with autism and trained to evaluate behaviors under different conditions. Because the BFI involves a 2-day observation period, it is more suited to clinical research than to routine clinical use.

Catherine Barthélémy

BSE-R

See Revised Behavior Summarized Evaluation Scale.

Caregiver-Teacher Report Form for Ages 1½-5

See Child Behavior Checklist for Ages 1½-5 (CBCL/1½-5).

CARS

See Childhood Autism Rating Scale.

CBCL/1½-5

See Child Behavior Checklist for Ages 1½-5.

CBCL/6-18

See Child Behavior Checklist for Ages 6-18.

CELF Preschool–2

See Clinical Evaluation of Language Fundamentals–Preschool, Second Edition.

CELF-4

Clinical Evaluation of Language Fundamentals–Fourth Edition. *See* Clinical Evaluation of Language Fundamentals–Preschool, Second Edition (CELF Preschool–2).

Checklist for Autism in Toddlers (CHAT)

S. Baron-Cohen, J. Allen, & C. Gillberg • 1992 • Can autism be detected at 18 months?: The needle, the haystack, and the CHAT. *British Journal of Psychiatry, 161,* 839–843.
(Also appears, with changes, in Baron-Cohen, S., Cox, A., Baird, G., Swettenham, J., Nightingale, N., Morgan, K., Drew, A., & Charman T. [1996]. Psychological markers in the detection of autism in infancy in a large population. *British Journal of Psychiatry, 168,* 158–163.)
Ages: 1½–2 years

A screening instrument developed in Britain used to identify children at risk for autism and other pervasive developmental disorders (PDDs) at an early age. The CHAT is a short checklist that can be filled out in 10–15 minutes by the parent and health care provider at the 18-month checkup. Section A has nine yes/no questions for the parent, designed to assess a range of developmental areas. Section B has four yes/no questions for the health care provider to check the actual behavior of the child. More than two *no* responses to the checklist items mean that the child should be referred to a specialist for diagnosis. The 23-item Modified Checklist for Autism in Toddlers (M-CHAT; Robins, Fein, Barton, & Green, 2001), designed for use in the United States, is filled out by the parent only. The questions include the original nine parent questions from the CHAT as well as questions based on symptoms thought to be present in very young children with autism. The CHAT and M-CHAT, although not norm-referenced, meet criteria for an adequate pediatric screening device and may be used as such (Robins et al., 2001).
Leah Bucknavage

Child Behavior Checklist for Ages 1½-5 (CBCL/1½-5)

T.M. Achenbach & L. Rescorla • University of Vermont, Research Center for Children, Youth, & Families • 2000
Ages: 1½–5 years

The CBCL/1½-5 is designed to assess social competence and behavior problems in children. It is completed by an adult informant (usually a primary caregiver) and is composed of two major scales—externalizing and internalizing behaviors—each of which has four subscales. It has been used as a follow-up measure for children who have been screened for but not yet diagnosed with autism and to chart the progress of children who have been diagnosed with autism. A separate but similarly formatted version of this test has been developed for teachers: the Caregiver-Teacher Report Form for Ages $1\frac{1}{2}$-5 (C-TRF/$1\frac{1}{2}$-5; Achenbach & Rescorla, 2000).

The CBCL/$1\frac{1}{2}$-5 is a revision of the CBCL/2-3 (Achenbach, 1992). From a new national normative sample and larger clinical samples, the following cross-informant syndromes were derived: Emotionally Reactive, Anxious/Depressed, Somatic Complaints, Withdrawn, Attention Problems, and Aggressive Behavior. A Sleep Problems syndrome also was derived from the CBCL/$1\frac{1}{2}$-5). In addition, Internalizing, Externalizing, and Total Problems scales are scored from the CBCL/$1\frac{1}{2}$-5 and the C-TRF/$1\frac{1}{2}$-5. The new Assessment Data Manager (ADM) Ages $1\frac{1}{2}$-5 Module software systematically compares up to eight preschool forms. The similar layouts of the parent- and teacher-completed profiles permit comparison of multiple hand-scored profiles.

The CBCL/$1\frac{1}{2}$-5 uses scales oriented to the *Diagnostic and Statistical Manual of Mental Disorders, Fourth Edition* (*DSM-IV*; American Psychiatric Association, 1994): Affective Problems, Anxiety Problems, Pervasive Developmental Problems, Attention Deficit/Hyperactivity Problems, and Oppositional Defiant Problems. The Language Development Survey (LDS) is included in the CBCL/$1\frac{1}{2}$-5 to aid in identifying language delays. The survey obtains parents' ratings of problem items plus descriptions of problems, disabilities, what concerns parents most about their child, and the best things about their child. The LDS also obtains parents' reports of children's expressive vocabularies and word combinations, plus risk factors for language delays.

John T. Neisworth & Pamela S. Wolfe

Child Behavior Checklist for Ages 6-18 (CBCL/6-18)

T.M. Achenbach & L. Rescorla • University of Vermont, Research
Center for Children, Youth, & Families • 2001

Ages: 6–18 years

The CBCL/6-18 (a revision of the CBCL/4-18) incorporates new normative data, includes new scales oriented to the *Diagnostic and Statistical Manual of Mental Disorders, Fourth Edition* (*DSM-IV*; American Psychiatric

Association, 1994), and complements the new Teacher's Report Form for Ages 6-18 (TRF/6-18; Achenbach & Rescorla, 2001). The CBCL/6-18 obtains reports from a child's primary caregiver (usually a parent) regarding the child's competencies and behavioral and emotional problems. The parent provides information for 20 competence items covering the child's activities, social relations, and school performance. The CBCL/6-18 has 118 items regarding specific behavioral and emotional problems; two more open-ended items permit reporting of additional problems. The CBCL/6-18 scoring profiles consist of three competence scales (Activities, Social, and School); Total Competence; eight cross-informant syndromes; and Internalizing, Externalizing, and Total Problems. The cross-informant syndromes, which draw on information from the CBCL/6-18 and TRF/6-18, are Aggressive Behavior, Anxious/Depressed, Attention Problems, Rule-Breaking Behavior, Social Problems, Somatic Complaints, Thought Problems, and Withdrawn/Depressed. The six *DSM-IV*–oriented scales are Affective Problems, Anxiety Problems, Somatic Problems, Attention Deficit/Hyperactivity Problems, Oppositional Defiant Problems, and Conduct Problems.

John T. Neisworth & Pamela S. Wolfe

Childhood Autism Rating Scale (CARS)

E. Schopler, R. Reichler, & B. Renner • Western Psychological
  Services • 1998
Ages: 2 years and older

The CARS is a 15-scale rating instrument designed to replace subjective and contradictory diagnostic labeling with public, quantifiable ratings based on behavioral observations, and to screen for a distinction between children in the autism spectrum and those with mental retardation and other diagnostic categories. The CARS is standardized and is perhaps the most widely used scale in diagnosing autism. It is designed to rate both the intensity and the frequency of the behaviors associated with autism. Validity is reported from numerous sources, including parent reports, teacher observations, and diagnostic records. Despite the fact that the definition of autism has changed over time and varies according to which intervention system is used for a particular child, the CARS remains a testing instrument with robust psychometric reliability and validity properties. Two training videotapes are available for using and scoring the CARS.

Eric Schopler

Clinical Evaluation of Language Fundamentals–Preschool, Second Edition (CELF Preschool–2)

E. Semel, E.H. Wiig, & W.A. Secord • Harcourt Assessment • 2004
Ages: 3–6 years

The CELF Preschool–2 is a tool for identifying, diagnosing, and performing follow-up evaluations of language deficits. It assesses receptive and expressive language ability, including semantics, morphology, syntax, and auditory memory.

The related CELF-4 (Semel, Wiig, & Secord, 2003) is intended for individuals ages 5–21 and provides composite scores for language strengths and weaknesses; receptive and expressive language; language structure; language content; language content and memory; and working memory. Additional Observational Rating Scales and the Pragmatics Profile provide authentic measures of language in school and at home.
John T. Neisworth & Pamela S. Wolfe

Communication and Symbolic Behavior Scales™ (CSBS™), Normed Edition

A.M. Wetherby & B.M. Prizant • Paul H. Brookes Publishing Co. • 2003
Ages: Functional communication age of 6–24 months (chronological age 6 months to 6 years)

A norm-referenced assessment tool designed to assist professionals in naturalistic assessment of the communicative and symbolic behaviors of infants, toddlers, and preschoolers for intervention planning. The sampling procedures consist of structured and unstructured situations designed to encourage spontaneous communication and play; a caregiver questionnaire allows additional information to be gathered. The CSBS measures communicative functions, gestural behavior, vocal and verbal communicative means, reciprocity, social-affective signaling, and symbolic behavior. Precise scoring guidelines lead to a profile of strengths and weaknesses on 22 scales and seven cluster areas. Norm tables present standard scores and percentiles by chronological age from 8 to 24 months and by language stage from the prelinguistic to the multiword stage. Research with the CSBS has documented a profile that distinguishes children with autism spectrum disorders (ASDs) from children with developmental language disorders.
Amy M. Wetherby

Communication and Symbolic Behavior Scales Developmental Profile™ (CSBS DP™), First Normed Edition

A.M. Wetherby & B.M. Prizant • Paul H. Brookes Publishing Co. • 2002 • Paul H. Brookes Publishing Co.

Ages: Functional communication age of 6–24 months (chronological age 6 months to 6 years)

A norm-referenced screening and evaluation tool designed to determine the communicative competence of children for early identification and monitoring of progress. The CSBS DP consists of three components: 1) a 1-page Infant-Toddler Checklist based on parent report for screening; 2) a 4-page Caregiver Questionnaire based on parent report for follow-up evaluation; and 3) a 30-minute Behavior Sample for a face-to-face evaluation of the child interacting with the caregiver and clinician. The CSBS DP measures seven prelinguistic predictors for each of the three components: emotion and eye gaze, communication, gestures, sounds, words, understanding, and object use. Norm tables present standard scores and percentiles by chronological age from 6 to 24 months for seven clusters, three composites (Social, Speech, and Symbolic), and total score. Research has documented the effectiveness of the CSBS DP Infant-Toddler Checklist as a screening tool for children with autism spectrum disorders (ASDs) and children with other communication disorders. Research has also shown children with ASDs can be distinguished from children with other developmental delays and with typical development based on videotape analysis of the CSBS DP Behavior Sample, which systematically observes "red flags" of ASD.
Amy M. Wetherby

Conners' Rating Scales–Revised (CRS-R)

Conners' Parent Rating Scale–Revised (CPRS-R)

Conners' Teacher Rating Scale–Revised (CTRS-R)

Conners-Wells' Adolescent Self-Report of Symptoms (CASS)

C.K. Conners • Pearson Assessments • 1996

Ages: 3–17 years (CPRS-R & CTRS-R); 12–17 years (CASS)

The CRS-R consist of three research and clinical instruments that are designed to track childhood behavior problems more commonly associated with attention-deficit/hyperactivity disorder (ADHD) than with autism and other pervasive developmental disorders (PDDs). Sometimes ADHD symptoms are observed among individuals with autism, and rating scales such as

the CSR-R have been used with these individuals. The CSR-R include parent and teacher rating scales as well as an adolescent self-report scale, all of which are available in long and short forms. (For more information on these scales, see Conners, Sitarenios, Parker, & Epstein, 1998a, 1998b, and Conners et al., 1997, respectively.)
Curtis K. Deutsch

CSBS™, Normed Edition
See Communication and Symbolic Behavior Scales™, Normed Edition.

CSBS DP™, First Normed Edition
See Communication and Symbolic Behavior Scales Developmental Profile™, First Normed Edition.

C-TRF/1½-5
Caregiver-Teacher Report Form for Ages 1½-5. *See* Child Behavior Checklist (CBCL) for Ages 1½-5.

Developmental Play Assessment (DPA) Instrument
K. Lifter, B. Sulzer-Azaroff, S. Anderson, & G. Cowdery • 1993 • Teaching play activities to preschool children with disabilities: The importance of developmental considerations. *Journal of Early Intervention, 17,* 139–159.
Ages: Infant to preschool

The DPA Instrument is used to assess the play development of children with disabilities relative to the play of children without disabilities. The developmental quality of toy play is evaluated according to the level of pretend play and the frequency and variety of play activities within the level identified. (For more information, see Lifter, 2000, and Lifter, Sulzer-Azaroff, Anderson, & Cowdery, 1993.)
John T. Neisworth & Pamela S. Wolfe

Early Coping Inventory (ECI)
S. Zeitlin, G.G. Williamson, & M. Szczepanski • Scholastic Testing Service • 1988
Ages: Developmental age 4–36 months

An observational instrument to assess the coping behaviors that are used by infants and toddlers in everyday living. Analysis of a child's scores provides information about level of coping effectiveness and coping style, strengths, and weaknesses. The inventory has 48 items divided into three categories: sensorimotor organization, reactive behavior, and self-initiated behavior. It is designed to be used for children between 4 and 36 months chronological age or for older children who function within this developmental range. *John T. Neisworth & Pamela S. Wolfe*

EASIC-R
See Evaluating Acquired Skills in Communication–Revised.

ECI
See Early Coping Inventory.

Evaluating Acquired Skills in Communication–Revised (EASIC-R)
A.M. Riley • PRO-ED • 1994
Ages: 3 months to 8 years

An informal communication skills inventory of receptive and expressive language in children with autism. The EASIC-R assesses semantics, syntax, morphology, and pragmatics communication skills at five levels from prelanguage to more complex expressive skills. In the receptive portion of the inventory, the examinee responds by pointing or following a directive. The expressive inventory requires that the individual respond by using verbalization or sign or other forms of augmentative and alternative communication (AAC). Responses are coded as *spontaneous, cued, imitated, manipulated, no response,* or *wrong.* Each skill is determined to be either *accomplished, emerging,* or *not yet developed.* Age ranges for each skill are noted for a typically developing child. A skills profile (for monitoring progress) and 142 Goals and Objectives cards are also provided. Although developed for individuals with autism, the EASIC-R has also been used successfully with other children who have developmental language delays.
Monica D. Manning

Family Assessment Interview
R.W. Albin, J.M. Lucyshyn, R.H. Horner, & K.B. Flannery • Paul H. Brookes Publishing Co. • 1996 • Contextual fit for behavior support plans: A model for "goodness of fit." In R. Koegel, L. Koegel, & G. Dunlap (Eds.), *Positive behavioral support: Including People with difficult behavior in the community* (p. 92).
Ages: Any

The Family Assessment Interview is a simple protocol for collecting information from families in preparation for selecting and designing an intervention plan. Items in this brief instrument are designed to enable a good contextual fit for the intervention strategy. Family members' ideas and reactions to the function of problem behaviors, support strategies, and issues for implementation are actively solicited in the interview and throughout the assessment and support plan development process. The Family Assessment Interview focuses on the ways in which the family structures its daily tasks and routines. It helps family members envision successful strategies for addressing problem behaviors. Sources of stress and support for the family are identified and discussed. *John T. Neisworth & Pamela S. Wolfe*

Functional Emotional Assessment Scale for Infancy and Early Childhood (FEAS)
S.I. Greenspan, G. DeGangi, & S. Wieder • The Interdisciplinary Council on Developmental and Learning Disorders • 2001
Ages: Birth to 5 years

A systematic in-depth approach to assessing emotional functioning during infancy and early childhood. The FEAS enables clinicians, educators, and caregivers to assess and monitor the child's functional, emotional, and developmental levels and to create a treatment plan based on the child's individual profile. The scale uses a 5-point rating system (*capacity not present, capacity is fleeting, capacity intermittent, capacity present most of the time, capacity always present in all circumstances*). Seven areas are included for assessment: Self-Regulation (3 months); Intentional Two-Way Communication (9 months); Complex Sense of Self I (13 months); Complex Sense of Self II (18 months); Emotional Ideas (24 months); Emotional Capacity (30 months); and Emotional Thinking (36 months). A final set of items (unlabeled) covers 42–48 months. *Devender R. Banda*

GADS
See Gilliam Asperger Disorder Scale.

GARS
See Gilliam Autism Rating Scale.

Gilliam Asperger Disorder Scale (GADS)
J.E. Gilliam • PRO-ED • 2001
Ages: 3–21 years

A norm-referenced test for the evaluation of children with behavioral problems who may have Asperger disorder. The GADS is completed by a parent and professional who know the child. The test provides documentation about the essential behavior characteristics of Asperger disorder necessary for diagnosis. Four subscales containing a total of 32 items describe specific observable and measurable behaviors. Eight additional items are included for parents to contribute data about their child's development during the first 3 years of life.

The GADS can be used for assessment, for documentation of behavioral progress, for identification of goals for the child's individualized education program (IEP), and for research. The GADS is the only test that discriminates individuals with Asperger disorder from individuals with autism and other behavioral disorders.
John T. Neisworth & Pamela S. Wolfe

Gilliam Autism Rating Scale (GARS)
J.E. Gilliam • PRO-ED • 1995
Ages: 3–21 years

Designed for use by teachers, parents, and professionals, the GARS is a behavior checklist designed to identify and diagnose autism and estimate the intensity of the behaviors associated with autism. The 56 items on the GARS are based on the definitions of autism adopted by the *Diagnostic and Statistical Manual of Mental Disorders, Fourth Edition* (*DSM-IV*; American Psychiatric Association, 1994). The items are grouped into four subtests: stereotyped behaviors, communication, social interaction, and developmental disturbances. The items in the first three areas address specific current, measurable behaviors, whereas those in the last area focus on development during the first 3 years of life.

The scale takes approximately 5–10 minutes to complete and may be completed by anyone who has a thorough knowledge of the individual's behaviors or by someone who is able to directly observe the individual. Behaviors are assessed using objective, frequency-based ratings. The instrument yields an overall Autism Quotient and standard scores in each of the four areas. The Autism Quotient provides the probability of the child's being diagnosed with autism and the severity of autism. Information is provided about the differential diagnosis of autism in relation to other disorders, to help discriminate between individuals with autism and those with disorders such as emotional disturbance, mental retardation, and speech and language disorders.
Theresa Gibbons

Infant/Toddler Sensory Profile
W. Dunn • Harcourt Assessment • 2002
Ages: Birth to 3 years

A caregiver questionnaire, available in English or Spanish, designed to measure children's responses to sensory events in everyday life. There are 36 items in the profile for infants birth to 6 months of age and 48 items for children 7–36 months of age. Caregivers complete the questionnaire using a 5-point Likert scale (*almost always, frequently, occasionally, seldom, almost never*). The profile yields four quadrant scores: sensation seeking, sensation avoiding, sensory sensitivity, and low registration. Some researchers have suggested that children who have various disabilities (including developmental delay, autism, or health impairments) may have significantly different patterns of sensory processing from peers and children in other disability groups.
Winnie Dunn

Krug Asperger's Disorder Index (KADI)
D.A. Krug & J.R. Arick • PRO-ED • 2003
Ages: 6–21 years

A norm-referenced test to identify individuals with Asperger disorder. The 32-item scale accurately distinguishes individuals with Asperger disorder from individuals with other forms of high-functioning autism. The information gathered by the KADI can be useful in an assessment of a student's educational needs. The KADI also identifies individuals who do *not* have Asperger disorder.
John T. Neisworth & Pamela S. Wolfe

Language Development Survey (LDS)
See Child Behavior Checklist for Ages 1½-5 (CBCL/1½-5).

MAS
See Motivation Assessment Scale.

Modified Checklist for Autism in Toddlers (M-CHAT)
D.L. Robins, D. Fein, M.L. Barton, & J.A. Green • 2001
The Modified Checklist for Autism in Toddlers: An initial study investigating the early detection of autism and pervasive developmental disorders. *Journal of Autism and Developmental Disorders, 31,* 131–143.
Ages: 18 months to 2 years

The M-CHAT is an American adaptation of the Checklist for Autism in Toddlers (CHAT; Baron-Cohen, Allen, & Gillberg, 1992), which was developed in Britain. The M-CHAT is a parent-report checklist designed to detect autism spectrum disorders (ASDs) in young children. The instrument is designed for use during 18- and 24-month well-baby visits to a pediatrician's office; it is brief, easy to administer, and simple to score. Preliminary data (Robins et al., 2001) indicate that the M-CHAT has promising psychometric properties, particularly improved sensitivity as compared with the original CHAT. Longitudinal follow-up suggests that most diagnoses made at 18–30 months old were consistent with diagnoses made at 4–5 years old and that the M-CHAT is a valuable tool for the early detection of ASDs.

Diana L. Robins

Motivation Assessment Scale (MAS)
V.M. Durand & D. Crimmins • Monaco and Associates • 1992
Ages: Any

Used to help identify the function of challenging behaviors. The 16-item measure assesses motivation of behavior in four areas: social attention, tangible rewards, escape/avoidance, and sensory feedback. The MAS can be completed in 5–10 minutes by parents, teachers, and/or other people in close contact with the individual displaying the challenging behavior. Although the MAS is of some use to identify potential functions of challenging behavior, the interview information it yields is less reliable than direct observation and measurement.

Melissa L. Zona, Kristin V. Christodulu, & V. Mark Durand

PDDST-II
See Pervasive Developmental Disorder Screening Test–II.

PEP-3
See Psychoeducational Profile, Third Revision.

Pervasive Developmental Disorder Screening Test–II (PDDST-II)
B. Siegel • Harcourt Assessment • 2004
Ages: 18–36 months

The PDDST-II is designed to be administered when concerns about possible autism spectrum disorders (ASDs) arise. The PDDST-II is designed as a screening test and is a parent-report measure. As such, it does not constitute a full clinical description of early signs of autism but does reflect those early signs that have been found to be reportable by parents and correlated with later clinical diagnosis.

Different stages of the PDDST-II correspond to representative populations in various settings. Stage I is designed for use in primary care pediatric settings, where the vast majority of parents express initial complaints about symptoms that prove to be significant in diagnoses of ASDs. The reference population was patients who were clinically screened and then referred to an autism specialty clinic (and who eventually received diagnoses of Autistic Disorder, Pervasive Developmental Disorder-Not Otherwise Specified [PDD-NOS], or another developmental disorder, but who had at least a few symptoms of autism). The control population was high-risk preterm infants (at risk of mild to moderate neurological dysfunction.

Stage II is designed for use in developmental clinics, where children are often first assessed for possible developmental disorders. The reference population was patients with diagnoses of Autistic Disorder or PDD-NOS. The control population was patients clinically screened as appropriate for an autism evaluation but who eventually received diagnoses outside of the autism spectrum, such as mental retardation or developmental language disorders.

Stage III is designed for use in specialty clinics for children suspected of ASD. The reference population was patients with diagnoses of Autistic Disorder. The control population is patients with diagnoses of PDD-NOS. *John T. Neisworth & Pamela S. Wolfe*

PL-ADOS
Prelinguistic Autism Diagnostic Observation Schedule (PL-ADOS). *See* Autism Diagnostic Observation Schedule (ADOS).

PLS-4
See Preschool Language Scale, Fourth Edition.

Prelinguistic Autism Diagnostic Observation Schedule (PL-ADOS)
See Autism Diagnostic Observation Schedule (ADOS).

Preschool Language Scale, Fourth Edition (PLS-4)
I.L. Zimmerman, V.G. Steiner, & R.E. Pond • Harcourt Assessment • 2002
Ages: Birth through 6 years, 11 months

The PLS-4 has two standardized subscales, Auditory Comprehension and Expressive Communication, that allow evaluation of a child's relative ability in receptive and expressive language. When comparing scores, one can determine whether deficiencies are primarily receptive or expressive in nature or whether they reflect a delay or disorder in communication. Precursors of receptive skills (with a focus on attention abilities) and precursors to expressive skills (with a focus on social communication and vocal development) are also assessed. Included are the Caregiver Questionnaire and manipulatives for use during the assessment. Available in English or in Spanish.

John T. Neisworth & Pamela S. Wolfe

Psychoeducational Profile, Third Revision (PEP-3)
E. Schopler, R. Reichler, A. Bashford, M. Lansing, & L. Marcus •
PRO-ED • In press
Ages: Developmental age 1–7 years (chronological age 1–12 years)

An assessment instrument for children on the autism spectrum that provides a developmental assessment in four major domains: communication, motor skills, personal self-care, and maladaptive behaviors. The PEP-3 has nine subtests: cognitive verbal performance, receptive language, expressive language, fine motor, gross motor, visual-motor imitation, social reciprocity, emotional expression, and repetitive behaviors. Test item are scored as *pass, emerge,* or *fail.* Large comparison groups of children with autism ($n = 425$) and typical children ($n = 180$) enable comparisons of examinees with either the group with autism or the typical group. The PEP-3 also includes a Home Observation Form for parents' rating of their child's level of development and for ratings for the child's personal self-care and adaptive behaviors. The PEP-3 and its previous editions combine scores from direct observation at school or in a clinical setting with the reports from home observations to provide information from multiple sources and contexts (Schopler, Reichler, Bashford, Lansing, & Marcus, 1990).

Eric Schopler

Revised Behavior
Summarized Evaluation Scale (BSE-R)
C. Barthélémy, S. Roux, J.L. Adrien, L. Hameury, P. Guérin, B.
Garreau, et al. • 1997 • Validation of the Revised Behavior
Summarized Evaluation Scale. *Journal of Autism and
Developmental Disorders, 27,* 139–153.
Ages: 3–15 years

Developed for the assessment of behaviors associated with autism in children with developmental disorders, the BSE-R consists of 29 items each

rated 1–5. Statistical analysis of the 29 items identified 13 core disturbances of autism that differentiate it from other developmental disorders. These core disturbances relate not only to social interaction disorders, and attention and sensory disturbances, but also to imitation behavior, emotional reactions, and communication processes. Videotape recordings permit review of behavioral sequences by index raters. This scale was not developed for diagnostic assessment but rather for progressive recording of the evolution of patients both treated over long periods and included in short-term controlled therapeutic studies.
Catherine Barthélémy

SCQ
See Social Communication Questionnaire.

Screening Tool for Autism in Two-Year-Olds (STAT)
W.L. Stone, E.E. Coonrod, & O.Y. Ousley • 2000 • *Journal of Autism and Developmental Disorders, 30*(6), 607–612.
Ages: 2–3 years

A screening measure designed to distinguish children at risk for autism from those with other developmental disorders such as global developmental delay or language delay. The STAT consists of 12 items administered within a play context and takes about 20 minutes to complete. STAT items assess social-communicative behaviors, including imitating the actions of adults, directing attention to objects or activities of interest, coordinating eye contact and vocalizations to communicate, participating in back-and-forth play, and engaging in functional play. Scoring results in categorization as *at risk* or *not at risk* for autism.
Wendy L. Stone

SEEC
See Vineland Social-Emotional Childhood Scales.

Sensory Profile
W. Dunn • Harcourt Assessment • 1999
Ages: 3–10 years

A caregiver questionnaire that measures a child's responses to sensory events in everyday life. The profile has 125 items and a short screener of 38 items. Caregivers complete the questionnaire using a 5-point Likert scale (*almost always, frequently, occasionally, seldom, almost never*). The Sensory Profile con-

tains sections corresponding to each sensory system, including the modulation of sensory input across sensory systems and behavioral and emotional responses related to sensory processing. Children who have various disabilities, including autism, Asperger syndrome (AS), and attention-deficit/hyperactivity disorder (ADHD), have been shown to have significantly different patterns of sensory processing (Dunn, 1999).
Winnie Dunn

Social Communication Questionnaire (SCQ)
M. Rutter, A. Bailey, & C. Lord • Western Psychological Services •
2003
Ages: Toddler to adult

A 40-item screening instrument, previously known as the Autism Screening Questionnaire. The SCQ is based on the *Diagnostic and Statistical Manual of Mental Disorders, Fourth Edition, Text Revision* (American Psychiatric Association, 2000), criteria for autism and can be used with all age groups. The lifetime version focuses on the individual's entire developmental history, providing a total score that is interpreted in relation to specific cut-off points. The current behavior version looks at the individual's behavior over the most recent 3-month period.
Catherine Lord

STAT
See Screening Tool for Autism in Two-Year-Olds.

Teacher's Report Form for Ages 6-8 (TRF/6-8)
See Child Behavior Checklist for Ages 6-18.

Temperament and Atypical Behavior Scale (TABS): Early Childhood Indicators of Developmental Dysfunction
S.J. Bagnato, J.T. Neisworth, J.J., Salvia, & F.M. Hunt • Paul H.
Brookes Publishing Co. • 1999
Ages: 11–71 months

A norm-referenced scale to assess critical temperament and self-regulation problems. A 15-item screener can be completed by parents in 5 minutes. If the screener indicates a potential problem, the parents complete the full 55-item assessment, which requires about 15 minutes. Results provide eval-

uation of atypical behavior in four factor domains: detached, hypersensitive-active, underreactive, and dysregulated. The *TABS Manual* (Neisworth, Bagnato, Salvia, & Hunt, 1999) provides psychometric information and item-by-item research-based strategies for intervention and for minimizing problematic behaviors.
John T. Neisworth & Pamela S. Wolfe

Test of Pragmatic Language (TOPL)
D. Phelps-Terasaki & T. Phelps-Gunn • PRO-ED • 1992
Ages: 5–12 years

A 40-item standardized, norm-referenced test designed to assess a variety of pragmatics, such as requesting, informing, and regulating, in a variety of contexts. The TOPL measures a child's ability to use language in social situations. Professionals present pictures of dilemmas to the child. Six sub-components include physical setting, audience, topic, purpose, visual-gestural cues, and abstraction. The TOPL takes approximately 30–45 minutes to complete.
Monica D. Manning

Test of Problem Solving–Elementary, Revised (TOPS–Elementary, Revised)
L. Bowers, R. Huisingh, M. Barrett, J. Orman, & C. LoGiudice • LinguiSystems • 1994
Ages: 6–11 years

A diagnostic test of problem solving and critical thinking for elementary school–age children. It can be used to assess a student's language-based critical thinking skills based on the student's language strategies using logic and experience. The questions focus on a broad range of critical thinking skills, including clarifying, analyzing, generating solutions, evaluating, and using affective thinking.
Monica D. Manning

TOPL
See Test of Pragmatic Language.

TOPS–Elementary, Revised
See Test of Problem Solving–Elementary, Revised.

TRF/6-18

Teacher's Report Form for Ages 6-18. *See* Child Behavior Checklist for Ages 6-18 (CBCL/6-18).

Vineland Adaptive Behavior Scales (VABS)

Interview Edition–Survey Form

Interview Edition–Expanded Form

S. Sparrow, D. Balla, & D. Cicchetti • American Guidance Service • 1984

Ages: Birth to 18 years, 11 months

Classroom Edition

P. Harrison • 1985

Ages: 3 years to 12 years, 11 months

A measure of adaptive and maladaptive behavior used to diagnose mental retardation, assess the adaptive behavior program plan, and conduct research. The VABS is useful in assessing adaptive and maladaptive behavior of children regardless of their primary diagnoses, and it is employed in appraising the adaptive behavior of children with autism and other pervasive developmental disorders (PDDs). The Survey Form has 297 items, and administration time is 20–60 minutes. The Expanded Form contains 577 items, can be used in educational planning, and takes 60–90 minutes. It takes approximately 20 minutes to complete the Classroom Edition, which contains 244 items and relies on classroom observations. There is also an optional Maladaptive Behavior domain on both Interview Editions that assesses lesser and more serious maladaptive behaviors.

Ellen R. Borsuk

Vineland Social-Emotional Childhood Scales (SEEC)

S.S. Sparrow, D.A. Balla, & D.V. Cicchetti • American Guidance Service • 1998

Ages: Birth to 5 years, 11 months

A parent report that yields a measure of social-emotional skills in early childhood, based on the Vineland Adaptive Behavior Scales (VABS; Sparrow, Balla, & Cicchetti, 1984a, 1984b). SEEC is an early childhood measure to evaluate levels of social-emotional behavior in individuals with disabilities and to gauge how the disabilities affect daily functioning. The items iden-

tify strengths and weaknesses in specific areas in interpersonal relationships, play and leisure time, coping skills, and a composite. SEEC is useful for program planning, selecting activities, and monitoring progress.
John T. Neisworth & Pamela S. Wolfe

CURRICULA AND CURRICULUM DEVELOPMENT RESOURCES

The ABA Program Companion: Organizing Quality Programs for Children with Autism and PDD
J.T. Fovel • DRL Books, Inc. • 2002

This manual is designed for professionals establishing applied behavior analysis (ABA) programs for young children with autism. Chapters address using consequences, describing behavior, using antecedents, teaching formats and settings, using discrete trials, importance of task analysis, using language training, using incidental teaching, promoting social integration, providing group instruction, and planning and organizing an individualized curriculum. A section of the book contains information on organizing an individualized curriculum and includes sample skill programs (e.g., matching, motor imitation, receptive labeling, expressive labeling, receptive instructions). A CD-ROM is included.

Competent Learner Model (CLM)
Tucci Learning Solutions (http://www.tuccionline.com/CLM.html) • n.d.

CLM integrates applied behavior analysis (ABA), direct instruction, and precision teaching (PT) practices (Tucci, 2004; Tucci, Hursh, & Laitinen, 2004). It offers five learning solutions to help learners become successful in everyday environments: Course of Study, Performance Assessments, Coaching, Curriculum, and Collaborative Consultations. The learning solutions support educators and parents to arrange instructional conditions for learners to develop the seven Competent Learner Repertoires (CLRs): Observer, Listener, Talker, Reader, Writer, Problem Solver, and Participator.
1. The Course of Study uses programmed instruction with video examples within a personalized system of instruction to promote mastery of competencies through performance checkouts by trained CLM Coaches.
2. The Performance Assessments (i.e., Competent Learner Repertoire Assessments [CLRAs] and Performance Reviews for Educators and

Parents) assist educators to appropriately place their learners in validated curricula by providing a profile of their learners' strengths and
weaknesses across all seven of the CLRs.

3. The Curriculum provides detailed instructional formats designed to
   strengthen all seven CLRs. It consists of two levels that take the new
   learner from CLRs that are not established to established and maintained of all seven CLRs. Completion of the second level of the CLM
   Curriculum prepares learners in validated curricula at the kindergarten
   or beginning first-grade level.

4. The Coaching promotes mastery of the educators' and parents' Course
   of Study units and the eventual oversight of the arranging and rearranging of the instructional conditions. The trained CLM Coaches are
   governed by Personalized System of Instruction guidelines.

5. In the Collaborative Consultation, behavior analysts provide assistance
   to educators and parents regarding the contingencies operating in a
   given situation.

Vicci Tucci & Daniel E. Hursh

DO-WATCH-LISTEN-SAY: Social and Communication Intervention for Children with Autism
K.A. Quill • Paul H. Brookes Publishing Co. • 2000

This manual provides an assessment tool (Assessment of Social and
Communication Skills of Children with Autism) and intervention guidelines for teachers, parents, and other educators. Five major areas are addressed in the manual: perspectives on autism (cause, prevalence, and so
forth), assessment of communication and social skills, intervention methods, guidelines for curriculum, and resources. The manual also contains a
glossary of terms and sample target goals and objectives and describes the
use of methods such as visual cues, prompting, social supports, social scripts,
and augmentative and alternative communication (AAC). Three curricula
focusing on core skills, social skills, and communication form the latter part
of the manual. Each curriculum includes objectives, activities, strategies,
vignettes, and progress monitoring forms.

John T. Neisworth & Pamela S. Wolfe

GRIP
Growth, Relationships, Independence, and Participation. *See* Individualized
Goal Selection (IGS) Curriculum.

Individualized Goal Selection (IGS) Curriculum

R.G. Romanczyk, S. Lockshin, & M. Matey • Clinical Behavior Therapy Associates (Suite 5, 3 Tioga Boulevard, Apalachin, NY 13732) • 1998

The IGS Curriculum is designed for use in goal selection for young students with autism spectrum disorders (ASD). It presents more than 2,000 specific goals. The organization of the IGS Curriculum allows for developing an individualized curriculum plan to address a student's skill needs and weaknesses. Student strengths are used to provide a foundation for the acquisition of new skills.

The IGS Curriculum provides a reference for behavioral targets for applied behavior analysis (ABA) intervention, although the curriculum is not based on intervention methodology. The IGS Curriculum provides a standard language to enhance communication among service providers, educators, and parents. In addition, the IGS Curriculum provides a structure for goal selection that is developmentally sequenced; skills are arranged from simple to more complex developmental skills.

Growth, Relationships, Independence, and Participation (GRIP) is a model presented in the IGS Curriculum. It provides a process for establishing communication, shared goals, and child expectations between service providers and parents. Service providers and parents use the GRIP model to refine goals for each child in order to achieve consensus as to the goals selected, priorities, implementation strategies, and how closely the goals match the needs of the child. The GRIP model focuses attention on

- Providing continuing and expanding positive physical, intellectual, emotional, and behavioral growth
- Developing and maintain positive and sustained social and work relationships
- Developing the skills necessary to enable personal independence
- Developing the skills, motivation, and knowledge to permit active participation in the life of family and community

GRIP is utilized at many stages throughout a child's intervention program because parent and child priorities and goals change over time.
John T. Neisworth & Pamela S. Wolfe

More Than Words: The Hanen Program® for Parents of Children with Autism Spectrum Disorder

F. Sussman • The Hanen Centre • 1999

A guidebook for parents of children with autism spectrum disorders (ASDs) that addresses communication and social skills. It includes descriptions of

strategies that draw on current research. Contents include checklists for recognizing a child's sensory preferences regarding movement, touch, sound, sight, smell, and taste; learning more about the child's communication (e.g., communication stages); setting goals; following the child's lead; using music to teach; using books; and teaching turn taking, social games, receptive language, use of visual strategies, proper use of toys, and general play strategies. The final section of the book includes strategies for making friends.
John T. Neisworth & Pamela S. Wolfe

The Reading and Writing Program: An Alternative Form of Communication
N. Watthen-Lovaas & E. Lovaas • PRO-ED • 1999

A program for teaching children with autism and other children who have difficulty acquiring spoken language. The program is designed to teach reading and writing through the use of visual stimuli only. Methods include matching printed letters, matching printed words, relating printed words with objects and vice versa, using a communication board to facilitate beginning reading and writing skills, and using letters to spell words and words to write sentences. The program parallels the spoken language programs detailed in *Teaching Individuals with Developmental Delays: Basic Intervention Techniques* by O.I. Lovaas (2003).
John T. Neisworth & Pamela S. Wolfe

Social Skills Training for Children and Adolescents with Asperger Syndrome and Social-Communications Problems
J.E. Baker • Autism Asperger Publishing Co. • 2003

Includes chapters on instructional strategies, behavior management, and generalization. This curriculum identifies 70 skills commonly difficult for individuals with Asperger syndrome (AS) and other autism spectrum disorders (ASDs). Material related to each skill includes activity sheets describing ways teachers and caregivers can model and provide practice and reinforce skills at home and elsewhere.
John T. Neisworth & Pamela S. Wolfe

Solving Behavior Problems in Autism: Improving Communication with Visual Strategies
L. Hodgdon • QuirkRoberts Publishing • 1999

This manual focuses on use of visual strategies for managing behavior problems. It is a practical guide for teachers. Topics include behavior manage-

ment (e.g., what behavior is, what behavior problems are, what common causes of behavior problems are), understanding communication (e.g., how communication develops, communication problems and how they affect behavior), assessment, improving communication, visual strategies (e.g., schedules, calendars), self-management, and use of visual tools to regulate behavior (e.g., communicating "no," establishing rules) and to improve language skills.
John T. Neisworth & Pamela S. Wolfe

Teach Me Language: A Language Manual for Children with Autism, Asperger's Syndrome, and Related Developmental Disorders
S. Freeman & L. Dake • SKF Books • 1997

This manual for explicit teaching of communication skills contains highly specific lessons as well as methods for achieving objectives. Several conditions of the learner are required. The child must be a visual learner (which is almost always the case with individuals with autism and other pervasive developmental disorders [PDDs]), must be able to sit at a table for instruction, must be relatively compliant and able to follow simple directions, and must be able to communicate in some way (verbal or nonverbal). Topics include social language (e.g., topical conversations, finding out about someone, reciprocal commenting, daily language, emotions), general knowledge (e.g., occupations and community helpers, places in the community, sports, geography), grammar and syntax (e.g., pronoun referents, verbs, nouns, questions), advanced language (e.g., story writing, topic sentences, paragraphs, finding the main idea), and academic concepts (e.g., categorization, brainstorming, comprehension, math concepts, calendars). The lessons are scripted and include exercises for individuals to complete. Methods are based on principles of applied behavior analysis (ABA) such as reinforcement, prompting, and fading.
John T. Neisworth & Pamela S. Wolfe

Teaching Individuals with Developmental Delays: Basic Intervention Techniques
O.I. Lovaas • PRO-ED • 2003

Based on the work of O.I. Lovaas and includes programs by other prominent autism specialists. Topics include what to teach and how to teach, discrimination learning, receptive identification of objects and of behaviors, early play skills, self-help, verbal imitation, expressive labeling of objects and of behaviors, early abstract language and grammar, prepositions, and

emotions. Strategies are included for visual learning, reading and writing, communication, involving parents in treatment, and data collection; considerations for home-based programs are also discussed. This book also addresses issues related to behavior delays and excesses (e.g., evaluation of behavioral treatments, excessive tantrums and self-injurious behavior (SIB), and attention problems. This is a sequel to *Teaching Developmentally Disabled Children: The ME Book* (Lovaas, 1981) and parallels the written language programs detailed in *The Reading and Writing Program: An Alternative Form of Communication* (Watthen-Lovaas & Lovaas, 1999).
John T. Neisworth & Pamela S. Wolfe

Teaching Social Skills to Youth: A Curriculum for Child Care Providers
T. Dowd & J. Tierney • Boys Town Press • 1992

Although not specifically designed for children with autism, this manual is used by many behaviorally oriented specialists. The content and methods are based on a program that has been in place at Boys Town. The manual discusses individual teaching techniques, including specifying behaviors, planned teaching formats, promoting generalization during training, and corrective teaching. A major section presents social skills training in group settings and a social skills curriculum. The book details task analyses for basic social skills (e.g., showing sensitivity, accepting decisions of authority, controlling anger, being on time, apologizing, coping with change, delaying gratification).
John T. Neisworth & Pamela S. Wolfe

A Work in Progress
R. Leaf & J. McEachin • DRL Books • 1999

This manual provides information on behavior management strategies and a curriculum for intensive behavioral treatment. The book is a user-friendly guide for professionals and parents who are planning intensive behavioral instruction. The content is based on validated behavior analysis strategies. Twelve chapters cover topics including therapy format, number of hours suggested for therapy, evaluation, reinforcement, and behavior programs. Problem areas detailed include sleeping, toileting, eating, playing, and social behavior. Following the 12 chapters is a detailed curriculum based on the use of discrete trial training. More than 50 curricular objectives are specified, and sample lessons are given (e.g., compliance, nonverbal imitation,

pronoun usage, asking questions, social awareness). The manual concludes with assessment forms for planning and monitoring progress.
John T. Neisworth & Pamela S. Wolfe

REFERENCES

Achenbach, T.M. (1992). *Manual for the Child Behavior Checklist/2-3 and 1992 profile.* Burlington: University of Vermont, Department of Psychiatry.

Achenbach, T.M., & Rescorla, L.A. (2000). *Manual for ASEBA preschool forms & profiles.* Burlington: University of Vermont, Research Center for Children, Youth, & Families.

Achenbach, T. M., & Rescorla, L.A. (2001). *Manual for ASEBA school-age forms & profiles.* Burlington, VT: University of Vermont, Research Center for Children, Youth, & Families.

American Psychiatric Association (APA). (1994). *Diagnostic and statistical manual of mental disorders* (4th ed.). Washington, DC: Author.

American Psychiatric Association (APA). (2000). *Diagnostic and statistical manual of mental disorders* (4th ed., Text rev.). Washington, DC: Author.

Baron-Cohen, S., Allen, J., & Gillberg, C. (1992). Can autism be detected at 18 months?: The needle, the haystack, and the CHAT. *British Journal of Psychiatry, 161,* 839–843.

Conners, C.K., Sitarenios, G., Parker, J.D., & Epstein, J.N. (1998a). The revised Conners' Parent Rating Scale (CPRS-R): Factor structure, reliability, and criterion validity. *Journal of Abnormal Child Psychology, 26,* 257–268.

Conners, C.K., Sitarenios, G., Parker, J.D.A., & Epstein, J.N. (1998b). Revision and restandardization of the Conners' Teacher Rating Scale (CTRS-R): Factor structure, reliability, and criterion validity. *Journal of Abnormal Child Psychology, 26,* 279–291.

Conners, C.K., Wells, K.C., Parker, J.D., Sitarenios, G., Diamond, J.M., & Powell, J.W. (1997). A new self-report scale for assessment of adolescent psychopathology: Factor structure, reliability, validity, and diagnostic sensitivity. *Journal of Abnormal Child Psychology, 25,* 487–497.

Dunn, W. (1999). *The Sensory Profile manual.* San Antonio, TX: Harcourt Assessment.

Dunn, W. (2000). Habit: What's the brain got to do with it? *The Occupational Therapy Journal of Research, 20,* 6–20.

Krug, D.A., Arick, J., & Almond, P. (1980). Behavior checklist for identifying severely handicapped individuals with high levels of autistic behavior. *Journal of Child Psychology and Psychiatry and Allied Disciplines, 21,* 221–229.

Lifter, K. (2000). Linking assessment to intervention: The Developmental Play Assessment (DPA) Tool. In K. Gitlin-Weiner, A. Sandgrund, & C.E. Schaefer (Eds.), Play diagnosis and assessment (2nd ed., pp. 228–261). New York: John Wiley & Sons.

Lifter, K., Sulzer-Azaroff, B., Anderson, S., & Cowdery, G. (1993). Teaching play activities to preschool children with disabilities: The importance of developmental considerations. *Journal of Early Intervention, 17*, 139–159.

Lord, C., Rutter, M., & Le Couteur, A. (1994). Autism Diagnostic Interview-Revised: A revised version of a diagnostic interview for caregivers of individuals with possible pervasive developmental disorders. *Journal of Autism and Developmental Disorders, 24*, 659–685.

Lord, C., Rutter, M., DiLavore, P.C., & Risi, S. (1999). *Autism Diagnostic Observation Schedule*. Los Angeles: Western Psychological Services.

Lovaas, O.I. (1981). *Teaching developmentally disabled children: The ME book*. Baltimore: University Park Press.

Lovaas, O.I. (2003). *Teaching individuals with developmental delays: Basic intervention techniques*. Austin, TX: PRO-ED.

Neisworth, J.T., Bagnato, S.J., Salvia, J., & Hunt, F.M. (1999). *TABS manual for the Temperament and Atypical Behavior Scale: Early Childhood Indicators of Developmental Dysfunction*. Baltimore: Paul H. Brookes Publishing Co.

Robins, D.L., Fein, D., Barton, M.L., & Green, J.A. (2001). The Modified Checklist for Autism in Toddlers: An initial study investigating the early detection of autism and pervasive developmental disorders. *Journal of Autism and Developmental Disorders, 31*, 131–143.

Schopler, E., Reichler, R.J., Bashford A., Lansing M.D., & Marcus L.M. (1990). *Individualized Assessment and Treatment for Autistic and Developmentally Disabled Children: Vol. 1. Psychoeducational Profile Revised (PEP-R)*. Austin, TX: PRO-ED.

Semel, E., Wiig, E.H., & Secord, W.A. (2003). *Clinical Evaluation of Language Fundamentals–Fourth Edition (CELF-4)*. San Antonio, TX: Harcourt Assessment.

Skinner, B.F. (1957). *Verbal behavior*. New York: Appleton-Century-Crofts.

Sparrow, S., Balla, D., & Cicchetti, D. (1984a). *Vineland Adaptive Behavior Scales: Interview Edition, Expanded Form manual*. Circle Pines, MN: American Guidance Service.

Sparrow, S., Balla, D., & Cicchetti, D. (1984b). *Vineland Adaptive Behavior Scales: Interview Edition, Survey Form manual*. Circle Pines, MN: American Guidance Service.

Squires, J., Bricker, D., & Twombly, E. (2002). *The ASQ:SE User's Guide for the Ages & Stages Questionnaires®: Social-Emotional: A Parent-Completed, Child-Monitoring System for Social-Emotional Behaviors*. Baltimore: Paul H. Brookes Publishing Co.

Tucci, V. (2004). *The Competent Learner Model: An introduction*. Aptos, CA: Tucci Learning Solutions.

Tucci, V., Hursh, D.E., & Laitinen, R.E. (2004). The Competent Learner Model (CLM): A merging of applied behavior analysis, direct instruction, and precision teaching. In D.J. Moran & R. Mallot (Eds.), *Evidence-based educational methods* (pp. 109–123). San Diego: Elsevier.

Watthen-Lovaas, N., & Lovaas, E. (1999). *The reading and writing program: An alternative form of communication*. Austin, TX: PRO-ED.

Organizations

GOVERNMENT AGENCIES

U.S. Department of Education, Office of Special Education and Rehabilitative Services (OSERS)
400 Maryland Avenue SW
Washington, D.C. 20202
202-205-5465
http://www.ed.gov/about/offices/list/osers/index.html

OSERS provides support to parents and individuals, school districts, states, and university professional preparation programs in three areas: special education, vocational rehabilitation, and research. OSERS provides funding for research and for programs that serve individuals with disabilities from infancy through adulthood. The office also provides information and technical assistance to parents and community members. In addition, OSERS develops and implements policy and legislation that fund a number of support programs, including the National Institute on Disability and Research Rehabilitation (NIDRR), Office of Special Education Programs (OSEP), and Rehabilitation Services Administration (RSA).

U.S. Department of Health and Human Services, National Institutes of Health (NIH)
9000 Rockville Pike
Bethesda, MD 20892
301-496-4000
E-mail: nihinfo@od.nih.gov
http://www.nih.gov/

Several institutes within NIH address autism spectrum disorders (ASDs), including the Collaborative Programs of Excellence in Autism (CPEAs) and

Unless otherwise noted, the authors of the entries in Appendix B are John T. Neisworth and Pamela S. Wolfe.

Studies to Advance Autism Research and Treatment Network (STAART), both of which study the possible causes of and treatments for autism.

Collaborative Programs of Excellence in Autism

Boston University CPEA
Research focuses: Language and social communication in autism
Principal Investigator: Helen Tager-Flusberg
Laboratory of Developmental Cognitive Neuroscience
Department of Anatomy and Neurobiology
Boston University School of Medicine
715 Albany Street
L-814
Boston, MA 02118-2526
E-mail: htagerf@bu.edu

University of California, Davis, CPEA
Research focuses: Movement, regression, and developmental course
   in autism
Principal Investigator: Sally Rogers
UC Davis M.I.N.D. Institute
2825 50th Street
Sacramento, CA 95817
888-883-0961; 916-703-0268
E-mail: sjrogers@ucdavis.edu

University of California, Irvine, CPEA
Research focuses: Genetics, brain structure, and regression in autism
Principal Investigator: M. Anne Spence
Department of Pediatrics
UC Irvine Medical Center
101 City Drive
Orange, CA 92868
714-456-8848
E-mail: maspence@uci.edu

University of California, Los Angeles, CPEA
Research focuses: Language, communication, and genetics in autism
Principal Investigator: Marian Sigman
UCLA Center for Autism Research and Treatment (CART)

760 Westwood Plaza
Los Angeles, CA 92868
310-825-0180
E-mail: info@autism.ucla.edu
http://www.autism.ucla.edu/index2.html

University of Pittsburgh CPEA

Research focuses: Information processing, visual processing, motor
  function, and language in high-functioning autism and Asperger
  syndrome (AS)
Principal Investigator: Nancy Minshew
Autism Research Program
Webster Hall
Suite 300
3811 O'Hara Street
Pittsburgh, PA 15213
866-647-3436; 412-246-0818
E-mail: autismrecruiter@msx.upmc.edu
http://www.pitt.edu/~nminshew/

University of Rochester CPEA

Research focuses: Genetic and teratologic studies of autism in
  humans and animal models
Principal Investigator: Patricia Rodier
University of Rochester Medical Center
601 Elmwood Avenue
Box 603
Rochester, NY 19642
716-275-2582
E-mail: Patricia_Rodier@urmc.rochester.edu

University of Texas Health Science Center at Houston CPEA

Research focuses: Communication and social behavior in autism and
  brain structure in autism (including animal models)
Principal Investigator: Katherine Loveland
The Autism Research Laboratory
Center for Human Development Research
University of Texas Mental Sciences Institute
1300 Moursund Street
Houston, TX 77030

713-500-2580
http://www.uth.tmc.edu/chdr/autism_lab.htm

University of Utah CPEA
Research focuses: Genetics, brain development, and serotonin and
   immune system function in autism
Principal Investigator: William McMahon
Utah Autism Research Project
421 Wakara Way
Suite 143
Salt Lake City, UT 84108
801-585-9098
http://utahautismresearchprogram.genetics.utah.edu

University of Washington CPEA
Research focuses: Genome studies, early diagnosis, language and
   cognition, and neuroimaging
Principal Investigator: Geraldine Dawson
Contact: Cathy Brock
Autism Research Program Project
Autism Center
Center for Human Development and Disability
Box 357920
University of Washington
Seattle, WA 98195
800-994-9701
E-mail: cbrock@u.washington.edu
http://depts.washington.edu/uwautism/research/participation.html

Yale University CPEA (in collaboration with University of Michigan, University of Chicago, and Harvard University)
Research focuses: Genetics in autism, Asperger syndrome, and
   related disorders; nervous system changes in autism; and behavior
   and puberty in autism
Principal Investigator: Fred Volkmar
Yale Child Study Center
230 South Frontage Road
New Haven, CT 06520-7900
203-785-5930

STAART Network Projects

Autism Research Center of Excellence
(Multisite center involving Boston University School of Medicine;
   Dartmouth Medical School; Tufts/New England Medical Center;
   and The Waisman Center at the University of Wisconsin, Madison)
Research focuses: Social and affective processes in autism
   and co-occurring emotional and behavior problems in autism
Directors: Helen Tager-Flusberg and Susan Folstein
Lab of Developmental Cognitive Neuroscience
Contact: Gretchen Shuman
617-414-2358
E-mail: gshuman@bu.edu
http://www.bu.edu/anatneuro/dcn/autism/staart.htm

Baltimore–Washington STAART Center
(Multisite center involving Kennedy Krieger Institute,
   Children's National Medical Center, The Johns Hopkins
   University, Morgan State University, and Georgetown University)
Research focus: Neurobiological origins of motor planning and
   communication impairments in autism
Directors: Rebecca Landa and Mark L. Batshaw
Contact: Terrylynn Tyrell
443-923-7559
E-mail: tyrell@kennedykrieger.org

Greater New York Autism Research Center of Excellence
(Multisite center involving Mount Sinai School of Medicine, New
   York State Psychiatric Institute/Research Foundation for Mental
   Hygiene, University of Toronto, State University of New York at
   Stony Brook, and North Shore–Long Island Jewish Health System)
Research focus: Functions of the serotonin system in
   autism, especially those related to repetitive behaviors
Director: Eric Hollander
Contact: Kate Esposito
212-241-2993
E-mail: katherine.esposito@mssm.edu

North Carolina STAART Center for Autism Research
Research focuses: Gene, brain, and behavior relationships in autism

Director: Joseph Piven
Contact: Kathy Ellis
E-mail: Kathy_Ellis@unc.edu

UCLA Center for Autism Research and Treatment (CART)
Research focuses: Developmental and biological
   bases of autism and experimental interventions
Director: Sigman
E-mail: info@autism.ucla.edu
http://www.autism.ucla.edu/index2.html

University of Rochester STAART Center
Research focuses: Individual differences in response to treatments;
   early intensive behavioral intervention and gluten-free, casein-free
   diet
Director: Patricia Rodier
Contact: Jane Halpin
E-mail: jane_halpin@URMC.rochester.edu

University of Washington STAART Center for Excellence in Autism
Research focuses: Early recognition of autism with a focus on
   social; linguistic; neuropsychological; and electrophysiological,
   structural, and chemical brain characteristics; and efficacy of early
   intensive behavioral intervention related to neurocognitive factors
Director: Geraldine Dawson
Contact: Cathy Brock
206-543-5153
E-mail: cbrock@u.washington.edu
http://depts.washington.edu/uwautism/research/current.html#staart

Yale Child Study Center STAART
Research focuses: Neurodevelopmental process and risk
   factors, visual scanning of social stimuli, listening preferences,
   face training, and psychopharmacological treatment of autism
Director: Fred Volkmar
Contact: Kathleen Koenig
203-785-2510
E-mail: kathy.koenig@yale.edu

NATIONAL PROFESSIONAL ORGANIZATIONS ON AUTISM AND OTHER PERVASIVE DEVELOPMENTAL DISORDERS

American Academy of Child and Adolescent Psychiatry (AACAP)

3615 Wisconsin Avenue NW
Washington, DC 20016-3007
202-966-7300
Fax: 202-966-2891
http://www.aacap.org

A professional medical organization of psychiatrists focused on the diagnosis and treatment of children and adolescents who evidence cognitive, affective, and behavior disorders. AACAP's overall mission is to advocate and promote the mental and public health needs of children. AACAP also promotes research and continuing and distance education.

American Medical Association (AMA)

515 N. State Street
Chicago, IL 60610
800-621-8335
http://www.ama-assn.org/

A national professional organization for physicians and their patients. The AMA establishes and maintains standards for professional ethics and holds annual conferences. Practicing physicians are required to obtain continuing professional development.

The American Occupational Therapy Association (AOTA)

4720 Montgomery Lane
Post Office Box 31220
Bethesda, MD 20824-1220
Voice: 301-652-2682
TDD: 800-377-8555
Fax: 301-652-7711
http://www.aota.org/index.asp

A national professional association for occupational therapists, occupational therapy assistants, and students of occupational therapy.

American Physical Therapy Association (APTA)
1111 North Fairfax Street
Alexandria, VA 22314-1488
800-999-APTA (800-999-2782); 703-684-APTA (703-684-2782)
http://www.apta.org/

A national professional organization related to physical therapy practice, research, and education.

American Psychiatric Association (APA)*
1000 Wilson Boulevard
Suite 1825
Arlington, VA 22209-3901
703-907-7300
http://www.psych.org/

A medical specialty society with more than 37,000 members that focuses on the treatment of individuals with mental disorder, including mental retardation and substance-related disorders. Its goal is to ensure humane care for all individuals with mental disorders. The American Psychiatric Association publishes scholarly journals and books, including the *Diagnostic and Statistical Manual of Mental Disorders (DSM)*, which currently is in its fourth edition, text revision (*DSM-IV-TR;* 2000).
Marley W. Watkins

American Psychological Association (APA)*
750 First Street NE
Washington, DC 20002-4242
800-374-2721; 202-336-5500
http://www.apa.org/

The American Psychological Association represents more than 155,000 members, making it the largest national association of psychologists. This scientific and professional organization establishes and maintains ethical guidelines; holds annual conferences; publishes books and scholarly journals; promotes and advocates for psychological science and practice; accredits doctoral programs and internships in clinical, counseling, and school psychology; and provides continuing professional development.
Marley W. Watkins

---

*The American Psychiatric Association and the American Psychological Association are both referred to as APA but are separate organizations.

American Speech-Language-Hearing Association (ASHA)

10801 Rockville Pike
Rockville, MD 20852
Voice or TTY (professionals/students): 800-498-2071
Voice or TTY (public): 800-638-8255
http://www.asha.org/

A professional organization for speech-language pathologists (SLPs), audiologists, and speech and hearing scientists. Certificates of Clinical Competence are awarded to audiologists and SLPs who meet ASHA guidelines. ASHA provides graduate school accreditation as well as code of ethics with guidelines and position statements for SLPs and audiologists. The organization also provides a variety of activities designed to support professionals and the public as well as to enhance research in the area of communication.
Nancy Kneff

Association for Behavior Analysis (ABA)

219 South Park Street
Kalamazoo, MI 49001
269-492-9310
Fax: 269-492-9316
E-mail: mail@abainternational.org
http://www.abainternational.org/

An international professional organization of behavior analysts. The organization establishes and maintains ethical guidelines, holds annual conferences, and provides continuing professional development.

Association for the Advancement of Behavior Therapy (AABT)

305 Seventh Avenue
16th Floor
New York, NY 10001-6008
212-647-1890
Fax: 212-647-1865
http://www.aabt.org/

A national organization of mental health professionals and students who practice or conduct research in empirically based or cognitive behavior therapy.

Council for Exceptional Children (CEC)
1110 North Glebe Road
Suite 300
Arlington, VA 22201
Voice: 703-620-3660
TTY: 703-264-9446
Fax: 703-264-9494
E-mail: service@cec.sped.org
http://www.cec.sped.org/

An international professional association whose mission is to support special educators and other professionals who work with individuals who have special needs.

The Division for Early Childhood (DEC)
634 Eddy Avenue
Missoula, MT 59812
406-243-5898
Fax: 406-243-4730
E-mail: dec@dec-sped.org
http://www.dec-sped.org/index.html

A division of the Council for Exceptional Children (CEC), DEC is a national organization of individuals who work with children (birth through 8 years) with special needs and their families.

National Organization for Rare Disorders (NORD)
55 Kenosia Avenue
P.O. Box 1968
Danbury, CT 06813-1968
Voice: 203-744-0100
Toll-free voice-mail: 800-999-6673
TTY: 203-797-9590
Fax: 203-798-2291
E-mail: orphan@rarediseases.org
http://www.rarediseases.org

Founded in 1983, NORD provides information and resource links related to rare disorders, including autism (even though many professionals no longer consider autism a rare disorder). Information regarding caring for a person with a rare disease and genetic counseling are available. The organization sponsors symposia and maintains a web site listing announcements, meetings, and publications (e.g., *NORD Resource Guide*, with information on more than 1,200 disease-specific organizations and support groups). NORD awards grants that provide seed money for research regarding diagnosis and treatment of rare disorders, including autism and related disorders. NORD maintains a rare disease database that is made available through subscription to more than 100 teaching hospitals, libraries, schools, and universities. The NORD web site lists approximately 20 organizations related to autism.

ZERO TO THREE: National Center for Infants, Toddlers and Families

ZERO TO THREE is a national nonprofit organization that was established in 1977 by a multidisciplinary group of researchers, clinicians, and community leaders. ZERO TO THREE's mission is to promote the healthy development of infants and toddlers in the United States by supporting and strengthening families, communities, and those who work on their behalf. ZERO TO THREE is dedicated to advancing current knowledge; promoting beneficial policies and practices; communicating research and recommended practices to a wide variety of audiences; and providing training, technical assistance, and leadership development.

- ZERO TO THREE's Leadership Development Initiative offers leadership training and opportunities for ongoing multidisciplinary collaboration to outstanding individuals at the beginning of their careers or at mid-career.
- ZERO TO THREE's National Training Institute brings together approximately 1,500 participants each December for a multidisciplinary exchange of new knowledge from research and practice.
- The ZERO TO THREE Policy Institute is a research-based, nonpartisan effort that brings the voice of infants and toddlers to public policy, especially with respect to Early Head Start, child care, early intervention (EI), welfare, child welfare, and infant mental health.
- The ZERO TO THREE Press publishes the bimonthly *Zero To Three* journal, *Diagnostic Classification of Mental Health Disorders of Infancy and Early Childhood (DC: 0-3),* books, curricula, and other materials for parents, students, and professionals who work with infants, young children, and their families.

Emily Fenichel

NATIONAL AUTISM ADVOCACY ORGANIZATIONS

Association for Science in Autism Treatment (ASAT)
Post Office Box 7468
Portland, ME 04112-7468
207-253-6008
E-mail: info@asatonline.org
http://www.asatonline.org/

A national organization formed by parents and professionals dedicated to disseminating scientifically valid information about autism and its treatment.

Autism Network International (ANI)
Autism Network International
Post Office Box 35448
Syracuse, NY 13235-5448
http://ani.autistics.org/

A self-advocacy organization relevant to individuals with autism that is operated by individuals with autism. ANI is based on the following principles:
1. The best advocates are self-advocates.
2. The lives of individuals with autism are meaningful and worthwhile.
3. Supports should optimize functioning in the world.
4. All are entitled to appropriate support services.
5. The social styles of individuals with autism should be respected and valued, rather than requiring people to "fit in."
     ANI also provides advocacy for individuals with autism. ANI is a forum for individuals with autism to receive peer support and share information and social experiences.

Autism Society of America (ASA)
7910 Woodmont Avenue
Suite 300
Bethesda, MD 20814-3067
800-3AUTISM (800-328-8476); 301-657-0881
http://www.autism-society.org/

The largest national organization founded by parents of children with autism. Its membership includes parents, family members, special education teachers, administrators, medical doctors, therapists, nurses, and aides. ASA does not advocate a particular theory or philosophy but instead promotes parent choice.

International Rett Syndrome Association (IRSA)
9121 Piscataway Road
Clinton, MD 20735
800-818-RETT (800-818-7388); 301-856-3334
Fax: 301-856-3336
E-mail: irsa@rettsyndrome.org
http://www.rettsyndrome.org/

A partnership of parents and professionals committed to sharing information related to Rett syndrome. Membership includes parents and professionals.

MAAP Services for Autism and Asperger Syndrome
Post Office Box 524
Crown Point, IN 46307
219-662-1311
Fax: 219-662-0638
E-mail: chart@netnitco.net
http://www.maapservices.org/

An organization (for families of *m*ore advanced individuals with *a*utism, *A*sperger syndrome [AS], and *p*ervasive developmental disorders [PDDs]) that shares information through conferences, workshops, a newsletter, and technical assistance.

National Alliance for Autism Research (NAAR)
99 Wall Street
Research Park
Princeton, NJ 08540
888-777-NAAR
Fax: 609-430-9163
http://www.naar.org/

NAAR promotes biomedical research on and science-based approaches for autism. NAAR provides grants to researchers for innovative studies and for postdoctoral fellowships to recruit new researchers to focus on autism and funds collaborative research programs to yield scientific advances in autism research.

Organization for Autism Research (OAR)
2111 Wilson Boulevard
Suite 600
Arlington, VA 22201
703-351-5031
E-mail: OAR@researchautism.org
http://www.researchautism.org/

An organization committed to biomedical and applied autism research. OAR focuses on five principal areas: diagnosis, treatment, education, vocation, and housing.

TASH (formerly The Association for Persons with Severe Handicaps)
29 W. Susquehanna Avenue
Suite 210
Baltimore, MD 21204
410-828-8274
Fax: 410-828-6706
http://www.tash.org/index.htm

An international association of individuals with disabilities, family members, advocates, and professionals seeking to foster inclusion of individuals with disabilities in society.

TASH serves as a clearinghouse for information and links individuals with resources, expert assistance toward fighting inequities, legal expertise, and targeted advocacy.